T H E
DUEL

THE
DUEL

10 MAY–31 JULY 1940

The Eighty-Day Struggle Between

CHURCHILL AND HITLER

JOHN LUKACS

TICKNOR
& FIELDS
NEW YORK

For information about permission to reproduce selections from this book,
write to Permissions, Ticknor & Fields, Houghton Mifflin Company,
2 Park Street, Boston, Massachusetts 02108.

Library of Congress Cataloging-in-Publication Data

Lukacs, John, date.
The duel / John Lukacs.
p.   cm.
Includes bibliographical references (p.   ) and index.
ISBN 0-89919-967-4   ISBN 0-395-61863-0 (pbk.)
1. World War, 1939–1945—Campaigns—Western.   2. World War,
1939–1945—Great Britain.   3. World War, 1939–1945—Germany.
4. Churchill, Winston Leonard Spencer, Sir, 1874–1965.   5. Hitler,
Adolf, 1889–1945.   I. Title.
D759.L84   1991
90-11263   940.54′21—dc20
CIP

Map by Charles P. Segal

Printed in the United States of America

BTA   10   9   8   7   6   5   4   3   2

To the memory of
BRIGADIER CLAUDE NICHOLSON,
defender of British honor at Calais
and
ADAM VON TROTT ZU SOLZ,
defender of German honor in Berlin

The sociologist, etc., deals with his material as if the outcome were given in the known facts: he simply searches for the way in which the result was already determined in the facts. The historian, on the other hand, must always maintain towards his subject an indeterminist point of view. He must constantly put himself at a point in the past at which the known factors still seem to permit different outcomes. If he speaks of Salamis, then it must be as if the Persians might still win. . . .

— Johan Huizinga,
The Idea of History

CONTENTS

T H E
DUEL

I

THE EIGHTY DAYS' DUEL

IN THE YEAR 1940 Easter fell very early. This meant that Pentecost would come early too, Whitsunday on the twelfth of May. In England and Europe this was a two-day holiday.

On the tenth of May, a Friday, all over Western Europe the night was clear and starry, presaging a beautiful spring day. In the first hour of that day an unusual train, pulled by two great steam engines, consisting of ten exceptionally long dark green coaches, slid to a halt at a switch near Hagenow station, on the long straight track between Hannover and Hamburg. This was the special train with the special carriages built for Adolf Hitler and his entourage, massive, dark and sleek, one of the impressive instruments of the Third Reich, made of the best German steel. Its code name was "Amerika."

A few minutes after midnight, Western European time, this train changed course, so efficiently and silently that hardly any of its occupants woke to notice that it began to move again, and in a direction different from its earlier one. It had been going northward. Its occupants had not been told where to; the destination seemed to be Hamburg. Most of them thought that the Führer was off to Norway, most of which country had been conquered by his forces during the previous three weeks. He himself had made an oblique remark to that effect to one of his female secretaries. Now, at one in the morning, Berlin time (German clocks had been set forward an hour when the war had begun), the great train started steaming to the west.

Four hours later it hissed to a stop. The insides of those amply armored and paneled carriages were awake with the muffled stirring that is the matutinal sound in all sleeping cars. Their inhabitants pulled up their shades; they glimpsed a station building that had no nameplate. All nameplates had been removed. What they could see all around were the yellow signs and markers of the German Wehrmacht. Presently they learned that they were in Euskirchen, a small German town between Bonn and Aachen, close to the Belgian frontier. Then they were driven to a group of barracks up the hill from the village of Rodert in the Münstereifel. That would be their spartan headquarters for the next twenty-three days, in a forest clearing that many of them would recall with pleasure because of the many trees and the endless variety of birds chirping and twittering. Its code name was "Felsennest," the Rock Eyrie.

The "Chef" (this was how his staff referred to Hitler) was fresh, determined, nervous. His appearance at that hour was quite unusual for him. His habit was to stay up late. Customarily he would not rise and make his toilet until after eleven. He made a gesture to his staff, who quickly gathered around him, eager to hear what the Führer was about to say. "Gentlemen," he said, "the offensive against the Western Powers has begun." Immediately they could hear from the distance the damp thudding of artillery. Forest, birdsong and gunfire: in that great German dawn hour it was bliss to be alive.

The greatest adventure in Adolf Hitler's career had now started. It would gather speed at a rate unimagined by anyone, including himself. In less than forty days he would be the master of Europe, perhaps of most of the world. His new German flag would fly from the North Cape to the Pyrenees. His armies would conquer Western Europe at a cost of men and equipment that was less than what the German imperial army had spent at a comparable time for the sake of a few miles across the trenches in World War I.

Much of this would be the result of military decisions that he, Hitler, had made. Twenty years before, after he had decided to become a politician, people dismissed him: how could this untutored outsider be the leader of a German political party of importance? He fooled them; he proved that he was a master at German national politics; he won. He became the German chancellor, and people again underestimated him: what could this demagogue, with his provincial mind, know about diplomacy and Europe? He fooled them; he proved to be a formidable statesman; in six years he made Germany greater than Bismarck had ever done, and he achieved all of that without war. People now said: A war? What kind of a war? With a Germany bereft of the kind of navy, colonies, materials and the assets that Imperial Germany had had in 1914? He fooled them again. In May 1940 the strategy of the Western European campaign had been selected by Hitler — the plan to strike through the Ardennes, to fool the Allies, to make straight for the English Channel. It was a plan of genius.

Napoleon once said that in war, as in prostitution, amateurs are often better than professionals. Hitler may have been an amateur at generalship, but he possessed the great professional talent applicable to all human affairs: an understanding of human nature and the understanding of the weaknesses of his opponents. That was enough to carry him very far.

Very far. He would sweep away the French and force the British out of Europe. Then he would lay down his terms of peace to the British that they would have to accept.

He was almost sure of these matters on that sunlit, bird-twittering day of the tenth of May. Almost, but not quite. He was nervous, too: anxious whether the plans for the main army group would work; anxious about the weather; aware that the decisive news about his plan, "Sichelschnitt," the sickle-cut slice leftward across northernmost France, trapping the French and British armies in Belgium, would not be at hand for a few days yet. However, all seemed to go well that day. When the late May evening fell, he and his staff already felt at home, unpacked and ensconced in the Rock Eyrie. He had a short meeting in the small map room before retiring unusually early (but then he had been up unusually early). Before that he read, among the various news dispatches from the outside world, brought and arranged for him by Walther Hewel, his Foreign Minister Joachim von Ribbentrop's liaison man in his headquarters, that across the Channel Winston Churchill had become the prime minister of England.

That happened sometime in the early evening. We do not have any record of Hitler's words reacting to the news. He knew that a political crisis had been churning in London for some days. We can be reasonably sure that Hitler was not surprised. He had once before remarked that one day Chamberlain might be gone and the British then would give Churchill a try. A try, but not much more. He knew that Churchill was one of the bitterest, perhaps *the* bitterest, of his enemies. For this, but also for other reasons, Hitler despised him.

He was wrong to do so. It is dangerous for a man to underestimate a determined opponent. In any event, we do not know what Hitler thought of the news from London when he retired for the night on the tenth of May. It seems that he did not yet wholly comprehend how, beneath and beyond the great war of armies and navies and entire peoples that he had now started in Western Europe, he would be involved in something like a hand-to-hand duel with Churchill.

CHURCHILL COULD hardly have been more different from Adolf Hitler; as different as were their days on that tenth of May.

Their physical appearance could not have been more different. Stepping into his barracks that morning Hitler wore his simple uniform. Churchill wore silk pajamas, a multicolored dressing gown that was indifferently tied around his girth and carpet slippers on his naked feet. He padded around in them, breathing heavily. Hitler ate a sparse breakfast. Soon Churchill would sit down to a large platter of bacon and fried eggs and light his first cigar.

In the same hour, perhaps at the same moment when Hitler made his announcement to his personal staff, at five-thirty in the morning at that forest clearing, Churchill had woken up as the telephone rang on the night table of his apartment atop Admiralty House in London. The Germans were invading Holland. For a moment the portent of the news was not clear: only Holland? or was this the beginning of the great German attack across Western Europe? Less than an hour later it was all too clear. They were invading Belgium as well as Holland; they were bombing airfields in France. By this time the brightness of the May morning had absorbed the dawn. The enormous smoky swelling of London was washed clear by the pale blue light.

London was then, in 1940, still the largest city in the world, with more people even than New York, Moscow, Berlin, Tokyo. Most of its people were not yet stirred by the war. The people of Britain were not, of course, mere spectators of the duel that was about to begin. Nor were the German people. Both Hitler and Churchill depended on their peoples. But there was a difference. Hitler was in the saddle, Churchill was not — or at least not yet. And those saddles were not at all alike, nor were their mounts. The German people were strong, disciplined, obedient, many of them unwilling to exercise their minds beyond the obviously efficient constraints of that obedience. The character and the experiences of the British people were different. Their political, if not altogether social, democracy, with its parliamentary government, had made their leaders dependent on their moods. The very conditions and processes whereby those moods were registered by their political leadership were complicated and indirect.

The English people are not intellectual. They, too, are often unwilling to think about certain things — but that unwillingness was different from its German variety. They are unwilling to make up or to change their minds until the strong impression of unavoidably visible evidence compels them to do so. "We'll cross that bridge when we get to it" — few English expressions are more typical than that one. On the tenth of May in 1940 many of them, including their elected representatives in Parliament, thought they had reached one of those bridges. Oddly enough, that had nothing to do with the tremendous news of that day, that with the German invasion of Western Europe the Second World War had indeed begun. What was happening was the crystallization of a national feeling: to replace Chamberlain at the head of their government.

Otherwise their morning progressed as usual. The brown and yellow brick houses of the suburbs, the glistening brass on the doors in Mayfair, the lumbering red buses, the coal-and-plush smell of the Underground, the gardening and the games planned for the two Whitsun days were solid, familiar, seemingly unalterable. The war had begun in earnest, but not a single German bomber appeared over England.

That day in Westminster a bridge was crossed. The story of that day, its unfolding hour by hour, has been told often by historians and participants and biographers and memoirists, including Churchill himself (who, surely unwittingly and to no advantage to his account, mistook the date of a crucial meeting that had actually taken place the day before). It was an extraordinary day for Churchill, as it was for his enemy two hundred miles to the east. Churchill, like Hitler, was customarily a late getter-upper. (While Hitler was not to be disturbed until eleven, Churchill would on occasion work with his papers and give orders from his bed and bathtub.) Now he breakfasted well before seven. The news of the war was coming in. He was ready to set out on that clear, cool morning from Admiralty House to the emergency meeting of the War Cabinet.

Since the previous afternoon he knew that the bridge would be crossed, that he would become prime minister. He had said that in so many words to his son the night before, on the telephone. Now, as he was ready to go, his private secretary rushed up: his son was calling him again. His father was brief. "Oh, I don't know about that. Nothing matters now except beating the enemy." This was not for public consumption. There is every reason to believe that he meant it. One of the striking things about Churchill during that day is the absence of any sense of triumph now that the bridge was to be opened for him.

Then there came a hitch. Chamberlain had changed his mind. The day before, he told Churchill and Halifax that he had to resign. Now he was clinging to power again. As the Cabinet sat, with the war news pouring in, Chamberlain said that he thought he should stay on until the outcome of the great battle in Belgium that was beginning. Churchill said nothing. Later that morning some of Chamberlain's former minions were deserting him. There was unanimous agreement about one thing: a national government must be formed, with Labour ministers participating in it. The National Executive Committee of the Labour Party had its annual conference in the rooms and basement of a middle-class hotel in Bournemouth. They had said that they would not serve under Chamberlain, but their final statement had not yet been made. At half past eleven there was another War Cabinet. German parachutists had taken the airfield at Rotterdam. The Dutch court and cabinet were fleeing their country. Churchill brought up a few technical items; the impression he made was indifferent. At four-thirty the War Cabinet met again. The dramatic scenes across the Channel were flaring from afar; the meeting droned on, as cabinet or committee meetings often do. However, everyone knew that what mattered now was what the politicians of the Labour Party — numerically speaking, very much a minority in the House of Commons — were to say about a national government. Around five they telephoned their answer. They would not serve with Chamberlain as premier. Churchill was still silent. Chamberlain still kept from mentioning Churchill's name. Finally, and wearily, at the end of that last Cabinet of the day Chamberlain said that he had to resign.

Then he drove to Buckingham Palace to inform the king. It was after the latter's teatime. George VI was saddened; he trusted Chamberlain; he was not sure about Churchill; he had hoped it would be Halifax. An hour later Churchill was driven to the palace. The king received him "most graciously." There was a moment of English understatement, devoid of all pomp, the king teasing Churchill, to which the latter responded with ease. The king laughed and said, "I want you to form a Government." Churchill said that he would do so. He went on to explain some of the details.

London was now bathed in a light blue twilight. The distance from Buckingham Palace to Admiralty House is short and straight. Behind the driver Churchill was accompanied only by Inspector W. H. Thompson, his bodyguard. For a long minute Churchill was silent. Then he said that Thompson must have known why he had been called to the palace. Thompson said that he knew; he congratulated Churchill and said, "I only wish the position had come your way in better times, for you have an enormous task." Churchill, unlike Hitler, was a man of unrepressed feelings. Tears, on some occasions, would come into his eyes. This was one of them. He said to Thompson, "God alone knows how great it is. I hope that it is not too late. I am very much afraid it is. We can only do our best." Then he bit his lips and clambered out of the car, walking up the Admiralty House steps with a grim and determined face.

The bridge was now behind him. After a very long day (and bereft of his customary refreshing afternoon nap) he threw himself with a surge of energy into details. He wrote many letters, including a generous one to Chamberlain. When, after the war and many years later, he described the events of that day he may have been inaccurate in a detail or two. But there is a revealing passage at the end. "As I went to bed at about 3 A.M., I was conscious of a profound sense of relief. At last I had the authority to give directions over the whole scene. I felt as if I were walking with Destiny, and that all my past life had been but a preparation for this hour and for this trial." He concluded this passage with a strangely dull thud of a phrase: "Facts are better than dreams." Perhaps he meant to tell his readers that he then fell into a blessedly calm and dreamless sleep.

This was at three in the morning of the eleventh of May, Saturday. Hitler was fast asleep. He had begun his day earlier than had Churchill, but Churchill outlasted him that day. There may have been a portent in this. But portents, as such, are matters that we can see only in retrospect.

SO WE arrive at the history of the duel between Adolf Hitler and Winston Churchill during the eighty days from 10 May to 1 August in the year 1940. On that duel in May, June and July depended the

Second World War and the fate of the world thereafter. During those eighty days Churchill alone stood in Hitler's path, to prevent his winning the war. After those eighty days other important presences cast their shadows on the world scene. The situations of the duelists changed. Hitler began to consider an invasion of Russia that might precede, or even eliminate the necessity of, an invasion of England. This consideration in Hitler's mind began to crystallize at the very same moment when Franklin Roosevelt's sympathy for Churchill's Britain and his antipathy to Hitler's Germany finally crystallized into his determination to proceed from unneutral expressions to unneutral acts. After August 1940 Churchill was no longer alone. Another five hundred days later Roosevelt's America and Stalin's Russia came into the war. But while Churchillian Britain could have lost the Battle of Britain in August and September 1940; while Churchill and the Allies could have lost the war even in 1941 and perhaps even in 1942; while even after that it became more and more evident that Britain could not defeat Germany even with the full participation of the United States in the war — we must contemplate two matters that are recognized insufficiently, if at all. One is that during those eighty days in May, June and July 1940 Hitler came closer to winning the war than we have been accustomed to think. The other is that Churchill's position was not as strong as we have been accustomed to think. Both Hitler and Churchill knew this. They also knew each other rather well, though they had not met. Hence the fascination of this duel, which was, of course, a duel of minds.

We must not overdramatize that figure of speech. The historian, while aware of the sickly peril of self-deception latent in his avowal of belief in some kind of "scientific" objectivity, must be aware, too, of the temptations of excessive dramatization that inevitably involve the misuse of words. A duel, by its very nature, is physical. It has the marks of something feudal or medieval: a tournament. Well, Churchill may have been a knight of sorts but not one clothed in shining armor. (Oddly, it was the plebeian Hitler whom a German artist once portrayed wearing a glistening suit of armor and holding a proud spear: the painting was printed on a German postage stamp.) In a duel each of the two foes has the chance to slay or at least overthrow the other. In 1940 all Churchill could do was to parry Hitler's thrusts and perhaps wound him, here and there, on occasion; but he could neither kill nor overthrow nor mortally wound him. Yet, in a way, he defeated — or, rather, outlasted — his opponent, once the latter had begun to change his mind.

All of this gives the lie to the determinist and social-scientific (and, at least in one sense, democratic) philosophy of the modern world, according to which history is "made" by material conditions and institutions and their organization, and no longer formed by the thoughts, words and acts (in sum, by the character: in itself an old-fashioned word, eschewed by political scientists and sociologists) of outstanding men. There can be no question that in 1940 the fate of much of the world — and the subsequent destiny of much of the twentieth century — depended on these two men, Hitler and Churchill (and later on Roosevelt, Stalin and de Gaulle, without whom the course of the Second World War would have been very different).

What matters is the mental, even more than the material, character of a man. Hitler and Churchill were powerful thinkers. Everything depended on how and what they really thought, including the principal element of their duel: how their minds perceived and projected each other. Neither Hitler nor Churchill had a wholly original idea, because there is no such thing as a wholly original idea. But each single thought in this world is perceived (and expressed) by each human being in a different way. What matters in this world is what people, including Hitler and Churchill in 1940, think and believe; but their beliefs, ideas and thoughts exist no more independently of them than they themselves exist independently of the rest of the world. Ideas matter only when men incarnate them. In this respect not only materialists such as Marx but idealists such as Dostoevsky were wrong. In sum, mind is not only more important and anterior to matter; but what men do to ideas is both more important and more real than what ideas do to men.

There are ideas that may be immortal; but their conception is almost always historical — that is, they are not immaculate. In 1940 Hitler and Churchill were the chief antagonists of a tremendous struggle, not only of different nations, with their different armies, products, habits, customs, laws. They also represented two of the three enormous historical movements whose struggles, having emerged after the First World War and now coming to a climax in 1940, governed the history of almost every nation.

AT THE time of this writing — fifty years after 1940 — at least one, perhaps two generations have grown up who see the history of this century being marked by the global conflict of Capitalism versus

Communism, or call it Democracy versus Communism. This perspective is false.

The main feature of the historical landscape of the twentieth century is that of the two world wars. They are the two great mountain ranges in the shadows of which we even now live. They changed the world more than any of the world wars and revolutions of the centuries that had preceded them. They separate us from the world before 1914, which not only to us but already to the generation immediately following the First World War seems, and seemed, extremely remote. The Bolshevik Revolution in Russia, the ascent of the United States to the superpower of the world, the end of the colonial empires, the division of Europe, the atom bomb, etc., etc., were the consequences of these wars, not their causes. (

It is senseless to consider ideas as if they were independent of human beings. This is true about every one of the forces and movements of history, which ultimately are the results of ideas rather than of material elements, since the latter are but the outcomes of ideas. The incarnations of the main historical factors are now, as they have been for several centuries, the nations of the world. This was not always so in the past, and it will not always be so in the future. The modern nation — as distinct from the state — is a relatively recent development. Marx and Lenin and much of democratic social science notwithstanding, the great wars and struggles of the twentieth century were, and still are, those of the nations rather than of the classes of the world. Thus the two world wars were to a large extent, though not entirely or exclusively, the results of Germany's struggle against other nations, of the German nation's ascent to world power, of its potentiality to dominate Europe — in retrospect, the last of the military and political attempts of a great European nation and state to do so. But there was more to it than that.

The principal force of the twentieth century is nationalism. It has been the fatal, or near fatal, error of Communism as well as Democracy to ignore that until it is — almost — too late. The greatest and most powerful apostle of modern nationalism was Adolf Hitler. But he, too, was not alone. He was a superlative — I am employing this word not in its commendatory sense — incarnation of a historical movement that, at least for twenty or twenty-five years, in novel forms seemed to overrun the world. From about 1920 to 1945, the quarter century that corresponds to the span of the political career of Hitler (though not of Churchill), the history of the world (and not only of Europe) was marked by a triangular struggle. There was Communism, incarnated and represented then by the Soviet Union. There was Democracy — parliamentary and, by and large, liberal democracy — incarnated and represented by the English-speaking nations and by most of the nations of Western and northern Europe. And there was a new historical force, inadequately called "Fascism," the first national appearance of which was Mussolini's dictatorship in Italy, but the power of attraction of which later became eclipsed by Hitler's Third Reich in Germany, a National Socialist state that remained its principal incarnation until Germany's defeat in 1945.

In that crucial year of 1940 — and for many years before and for some years thereafter — National Socialism was the strongest of these three. We know, and we often forget, that eventually it took the combined forces of the, in many ways unusual and short-lived, alliance of Britain, the United States and Soviet Russia to defeat Germany. None of them — not even the alliance of any two of them, not even the tremendous material weight of the British and the American empires — could accomplish that. This was not merely the result of the fighting qualities, the organization and the discipline of the German armed forces, though it had much to do with that. It had much, perhaps even more, to do with the fact that the idea Hitler incarnated and represented was a very powerful one. This is why it is not only historically wrong but dangerous to see Hitler and Hitlerism as no more than a strange parenthesis in the history of the twentieth century, the transitory rise and fall of a madman.

In spite of its international pretensions and propaganda Communism did not go very far outside the Soviet Union. Lenin was convinced that the Communist assumption of power in Russia in 1917 was only a fortunate accident, that what happened there would soon repeat itself in many other states in Europe and Asia (in Lenin's view, first of all in Germany). But this did not happen. Alone among the great revolutions of the world — consider only how the American and French revolutions had soon been emulated by a host of other peoples, in Latin America and in Western Europe, often without the support of American or French armies — Communism was unable to achieve power anywhere outside the Soviet Union until after the Second World War. Indeed, within the Russian empire itself the price that Lenin had to pay for the survival of his Communist regime was a shrinking of that empire, an eastward retreat from Russia's domains. By 1924 he was succeeded by Stalin, who unlike Lenin was a statesman rather than a revolutionary, a nationalist and not an internationalist, and an isolationist for many years to come.

But during the twenties and especially the thirties not only Communism but Democracy, too, was in retreat. For a short time after 1918 it seemed that the victory of the Western democracies in the First World War naturally led to the prevalence of liberal parliamentary democracy in most nations of the world, especially in Europe. That did not last. During the twenty years before 1940 liberal parliamentary democracy failed and was abandoned by the peoples of Italy, Turkey, Portugal, Spain, Bulgaria, Greece, Rumania, Yugoslavia, Hungary, Albania, Poland, Estonia, Latvia, Lithuania, Austria, Germany — not to speak of Japan, China and many Central and South American countries. These changes were not the results of external pressure. They were the results of spontaneous developments. As early as 1930 it seemed (and this was three years before Hitler's coming to power in Germany) that the rise of authoritarian dictatorships in the wake of the failure of parliamentary and capitalist democracy was a natural and worldwide phenomenon. We shall see that Churchill himself was inclined to see things that way. The character of these dictatorships varied from country to country. Most of them were not "totalitarian," in the later accepted sense of that term. Some of these national dictatorships resisted Hitler. But, by and large, Democracy was in retreat. It gave the impression of institutions and ideas that were tired and outworn. The very political map of Europe reflected this. In Western and northern Europe parliamentary democracy still prevailed. In central, southern and Eastern Europe it had given way to nationalist dictatorships. In the far eastern reaches of the Continent, isolated from the rest of Europe by its own iron curtain, moldered the dark, muddy, solitary giant state of Communist Russia.

There was another, more profound mutation. At the time of the First World War it was reasonable and proper to think and speak of a war involving "Germany," "France," "Britain." The fact that these nations had different constitutions and governmental systems was a secondary factor. When in 1939 the Second World War broke out it was again a war of nations, involving Germany, Poland, France, Britain; but everyone knew that there was more to it than that. The Germany of 1939 was not the Germany of 1914, and not only because Adolf Hitler was a different man from William II. There was now a National Socialist Germany, a Third Reich, an incarnation of a philosophy and an ideology that was an essential, perhaps *the* essential, element in its character and behavior. And there was yet another, no less important mutation. During every war in the history of mankind there have been people in every tribe or state or empire or nation who opposed that war and, consequently, their government that was waging it. But in 1914 there were few people who wished for and who actually worked for the victory of an enemy. Even Lenin, wishing for the collapse of the Tsarist Russian government, did not want to see the victory of Germany; he would accept German funds and German help but he was not a German agent. By 1940 much of this had changed. There were people, in many cases a considerable minority, who opposed their government and its waging war not for pacifist but for political and ideological reasons; and these included their sympathies for the political and ideological systems of their own nation's enemies. Within Germany there was a small but historically memorable minority of decent men and women who wished for Hitler's downfall — if necessary, through a military defeat of their nation accomplished by its opponents. Within nearly every nation of the world there were conventicles of Communists who, without the slightest scruple of loyalty to their country and government, were wishing and willing to enhance the power of Soviet Russia. Within every nation, including the Western democracies, there were people who not only opposed the war — this war, against the German Third Reich — but whose opposition was inseparable from (indeed, often it was motivated by) their contempt for the democratic politics and government of their own nation, and from their consequent respect for what Hitler and his order seemed to represent. In the countries conquered by Hitler, Czechoslovakia, Denmark, Norway, Holland and Belgium, the purposes of "collaborationists" — that is, people who wished to exercise influence and power through their acceptance of German supremacy — were seldom separable from their respect for Hitler's Germany, which they believed was not only winning the war but which deserved to win it, as indeed their former liberal and democratic systems had deserved to disappear. Within France convinced Nazi sympathizers were few; but there were many men and women whose contempt for their seemingly corrupt and ineffectual governmental and social system debouched naturally into their dislike for France's waging war in alliance with Britain. Even in the United States, where "isolationism" was widespread and politically strong, consistent isolationists were few and far between. Most isolationists, bitter opponents of Roosevelt and his administration, were not opposed to armaments and the military. What they opposed was *this* war, the war waged by the aged and corrupt British and French empires against Germany, and the inclinations of Roosevelt and others to side with the former.

A very frequent element in this kind of thinking was anti-Communism. The psychology of anti-Communism is a complex matter that has not yet received the attention it deserves. Most people who opposed the struggle against Hitler were not necessarily his sympathizers. But they were convinced — or, more precisely, they had convinced themselves — that the great danger to their nation and to the world was Communism (and thus Soviet Russia rather than National Socialist Germany); and Hitler was an anti-Communist, after all. That there were influential people with such inclinations in Britain, too, was something that Churchill and his friends had to consider. Their presence was a worrisome and by no means unimportant element.

Still, the personality of Hitler, outside Germany, was such that whatever respect he inspired — and some respect was, after all, almost naturally due him because of the unbroken record of his astounding successes — he inspired little affection, let alone love. Even men and women who resolutely chose to commit themselves to his side sensed the cold clarity of his ruthlessness. There was not much emanation of warmth from this man. There was something non-human in his coldness, different from the Machiavellian — that is, rational and Latin — coldness of Napoleon's mind. Notwithstanding the adulation with which the many millions of German-speaking peoples surrounded him, Hitler was a very lonely man.

On the other side stood Churchill. We have been accustomed to seeing him as a quintessential incarnation of John Bull, the British bulldog (as some of his photographs show). But now, as the great duel begins, we must make another observation. Altogether — and, oddly, not always out of harmony with that bulldog impression — there was a rotundity to Churchill, encompassing not only hardness but also softness, a human quality that was somehow grandfatherly and old-fashioned. I am writing this because on that night of the tenth of May in the 1,940th year of Our Lord, Churchill stood for more than England. Millions of people, especially across Europe, recognized him now as the champion of their hopes. (In faraway Bengal India there was at least one man, that admirably independent writer and thinker Nirad Chaudhuri, who fastened Churchill's picture to the wall of his room the next day.) Churchill was *the* opponent of Hitler, the incarnation of the reaction to Hitler, the incarnation of the resistance of an old world, of old freedoms, of old standards against a man incarnating a force that was frighteningly efficient, brutal and new. Few things are as wrong as the tendency to see Hitler as a reactionary. He was the very antithesis of that. The true reactionary was Churchill. At that moment in the history of mankind what Hitler represented was the brutal, and by no means illogical, efficiency of popularly supported and mechanically organized force. What Churchill represented was the reaction to that. The great question then was: would that be enough?

AFTER THE war had come in September 1939 Simone Weil wrote on a fragment of paper: ". . . we need first of all to have a clear conscience. Let us not think that because we are less brutal, less violent, less inhuman than our opponents we will carry the day. Brutality, violence, and inhumanity have an immense prestige that schoolbooks hide from children, that grown men do not admit, but that everyone bows before. For the opposite virtues to have as much prestige, they must be actively and constantly put into practice. Anyone who is merely incapable of being as brutal, as violent, and as inhuman as someone else, but who does not practice the opposite virtues, is inferior to that person in both inner strength and prestige, and he will not hold out in such a confrontation."

II

THE FIRST
COINCIDENCE

The 10th of May

IN MAY 1940 Hitler was fifty-one years old. Churchill was sixty-five. There was a unity in Churchill's life. From his early youth he strove for a public career. Hitler's life was divided in half. He was a wounded soldier, alone in a hospital, when in November 1918 he learned the news of the defeat and collapse of the Second German Reich. Then: "I decided to become a politician." Thus he ended the first, the autobiographical, portion of *Mein Kampf.* He stated that again, including it in his relatively unknown but very telling long speech to German officers in May 1944: "When, in the year 1918, I decided to become a politician, this meant the whole transformation of my entire life." This was true. That decisive turning point (coming relatively late, in the thirtieth year of his life) came through a sudden and drastic illumination. There have been few such experiences in the lives of statesmen and politicians. It was, rather, something that happens to visionaries and saints, as to Paul on the road to Damascus or to Joan of Arc. In Hitler's case that was his reaction to his nation's humiliation and defeat. On the sixteenth of May in 1940 such a reaction struck Charles de Gaulle like an arrow in the heart. He described it in his incomparable war memoirs. It came suddenly when he saw, for the first time, the shamefulness of the French rout. "If I live, I will fight, wherever I must, as long as I must, until the enemy is defeated and the national stain washed clean." In that moment de Gaulle's political career began. But there the similarity ceases. In de Gaulle's prose there is the essence of a bitter love of his nation, a love that was stronger than his hate of its enemies. With Hitler the opposite was true. No one can gainsay Hitler's love for Germany; but that love was only implicit, subordinated as it was to his hatreds of what he saw as his enemies, external and internal ones.*

Hitler rose from soldier to politician and then to national leader and statesman; and, on the first of September 1939, to be a soldier again. These were the chapters of his life, chronologically definable but not altogether separable. Nor are the public and the private inclinations of a man separable altogether. In November 1937 he told his generals to prepare for war. Then he convinced himself that time was working against Germany, and against himself. Against Germany: because the rearming of the Western democracies had begun, and because, as he once or twice told his confidants, the military advantage that Germany then had would erode after a few years, by 1942 or 1943. (Mussolini, rightly, tried to convince him of the contrary. In the absence of war the Western democracies would not sustain a hard, strenuous effort to prepare for it. But he could not influence Hitler.) Against himself: because sometime during the winter of 1937–38 he began to think that he was not well, that he would not live for long. (He said this to very few people, but his circle witnessed a change in his private habits, in his diet, his withdrawing from the convivialities of his cohorts and his increasing dependence on medicaments, ingesting more and more pills.) In the first hours of the war, on the morning of 1 September 1939, he appeared in the Reichstag in a simple gray uniform, wearing the single decoration of the Iron Cross (first class) that he had earned during the First World War. He announced that he would not shed this uniform for the duration of the war, and he did not.

That was the moment when Hitler's guiding star became Frederick the Great rather than Bismarck: the soldier-king rather than the architect of a united Germany. But, for all of his respect for Bismarck, the latter was never his real guiding star. It was not only that he made few references to Bismarck during his political career and in his long speeches and private monologues; it was not only that his political

---

* There exists an early evidence of this in Goebbels's diary in 1926, shortly after he had met Hitler: "His most beautiful phrase [*sein schönstes Wort*] yesterday: 'God had graced our struggle abundantly. God's most beautiful gift bestowed on us is the hate of our enemies, whom we in turn hate from the bottom of our hearts.' "

methods were devoid of the occasional moderation of Old Otto; it was not only that Hitler's folkish populism, with its concomitant aim to unite most, if not all, of the German-speaking peoples of Europe into a Greater Germany and to dominate the entire Continent would have been alien to Bismarck. The fact was that in less than two years he, Hitler, achieved a German Reich that was greater and more powerful than the Germany created by Bismarck. He, Hitler, incorporated Austria, Bohemia and Moravia into Germany, and all that without blood and iron, without war. But now war had come; and, as in the career of the Great Frederick, the soldier was now annealed to the statesman; indeed, the aims of the latter now depended on the resolute achievements of the former. In that first war speech Hitler referred to Frederick. He would refer to him again and again until the very last days of the war, drawing inspiration from the historical memory of how Frederick the Great, besieged by enemies from every side, eventually triumphed because of his single-minded resolution and fortitude, whereby he split his enemies as their coalition fell apart. That was Hitler's conviction, too, surely and especially by December 1941, when he saw that he had to face the coalition of Britain, America and Russia. He would weld the German people even closer together; he and they would be indefatigable, unconquerable, rising to the necessities of a total war until that unnatural coalition of their enemies would break apart. But that was still in the future: we are running ahead of our story.

Hitler came close to splitting the alliance of his opponents a few days before that fateful first of September in 1939. He had just achieved a stunning political triumph, an unexpected diplomatic revolution unequaled in modern history. Britain and France had been counting on an alliance with Soviet Russia — the Soviet Russia that was the avowed enemy of Hitler, the reduction and destruction of which Hitler had proposed in *Mein Kampf*. But that Western-Russian alliance did not come about. Instead it was he, Hitler, who made a pact with Stalin, eliminating Russia from all of the military calculations and hopes of the Western democracies. That was a super-Bismarckian feat. Hitler hoped against hope that this new and great event alone would dissuade the British from honoring their guarantee to Poland. This did not happen. Then — during the six days from 25 to 31 August (his plan had been to begin the war against Poland on the twenty-sixth) he tried to drive a wedge (those were his words) between Britain and Poland. He nearly succeeded. There was a welter of confused negotiations, messages, intermediaries, intrigues. On 27

August Hitler, among other things, spoke to Sir Nevile Henderson, the British ambassador, about not only a settlement but an alliance with Great Britain. Let us pause here for a moment. Had such an arrangement come about, Hitler would have achieved another super-Bismarck: he would have an alliance with both Russia and Britain, with the effect of dominating Europe in between those two. But no matter how hesitant, Chamberlain's government did not respond to such an offer. It was too late, and the wedge did not go deep enough. No matter how reluctantly, Britain and France declared war on Germany fifty-six hours after Hitler invaded Poland. The Reluctant War had begun. It would end eight months later, on 10 May 1940.

There is no question that Hitler wished for an alliance with Britain, or at least for the neutrality of the latter. From his youth he disliked France and the French. But he respected the British. From the earliest speeches in his political career, and later in *Mein Kampf,* he gave vent to his conviction that the grave mistake of William II and his government had been to war against Britain; the German effort of expansion in the First World War should have been directed eastward. After he had become the master of Germany in 1933 he made several efforts — and, at times, unusually voluble public and private, spoken and written expressions of his conviction — to impress upon Englishmen and Englishwomen that his new Germany had no quarrel with the British Empire; indeed, that he admired the British Empire. In this respect it behooves us to make an important observation. It is wrong to believe that, as late as 1940, Hitler wanted "world domination." He wanted to rule Europe. In this he was more akin to Napoleon than to William II. He did not understand for a long time that the British — or at least some of the British — would be, at best, uncomfortable and, at worst, opposed to such a bargain. If, as the saying goes, the British Empire grew up in a fit of thoughtlessness, the same kind of thoughtlessness kept the British people from thinking much about divisions of the world. In any event, Hitler in 1935 offered, and the British accepted, an Anglo-German naval agreement that kept German naval rearmament limited, with a total tonnage not more than 35 percent of that of the British. He would not repeat William's mistake of entering into a naval race with the British, threatening their empire.

But sometime in 1937 Hitler began to see a duality in the British attitude. On the one hand he saw the reluctance of Chamberlain and the Chamberlainites and of many influential and reputable Englishmen and Englishwomen to range England among Germany's enemies.

He saw how they tolerated his conquest of Austria and Czechoslovakia. He saw their relative indifference to the aggressive symptoms of his regime. On the other hand — and not only because of the increasing evidence of British rearmament — he had to consider the increasing possibility that Britain would at some point go to war with Germany, and he had to prepare for that. He was not happy with that prospect. But he thought he could deal with it. He knew that such a British decision would come reluctantly. So, he thought — and he was again correct in thinking that — they would wage war against him reluctantly, too. The time would then come when he would convince them to make peace with him — at a time when they would be militarily incapable of staying their ground anywhere on the Continent, perhaps after their small expeditionary force would have been forced out of Europe.

In any event, on 1 September 1939 Hitler assumed a new role: the Führer not only of the German state and people but of their armed forces as well. During the Polish campaign he was full of energy. He visited the front lines often, peering across the fields at burning Warsaw through a large military periscope. (This was the only time during six years of war that he went up to the front; thereafter he would conduct the war from his headquarters.) His generals and military planners had done well in Poland, where Hitler interfered little with the general strategy. A few days after the Polish campaign had ended he offered his peace to Britain and France in a speech. He knew that there were people in Britain who were willing to consider a peace under certain terms. Yet he did not exaggerate his hopes in that regard. As early as 12 September, when the Polish campaign was still in full swing, he spoke to a few generals of the necessity to prepare a swift campaign in the west. He was not surprised at the unwillingness of the French (and the British) to attack his few divisions in the west while the bulk of his army was involved in Poland. The reluctance of the Western democracies to declare war against him was followed by their reluctance to wage war in earnest. What Hitler now wanted to do was push that reluctance further: to make the British realize that their war against him made no sense. The instrument for this was a rapid campaign leading to the German conquest of Western Europe. He thought that time was of the essence. Now, for the first time, he actively intervened in the military planning. He pushed for this Western European invasion to begin around 12 November. For once his generals convinced him that it was impossible. Soon an unusually frozen winter descended on Europe. He had to wait until the late spring.

But now he had taken it upon himself to be at the helm of the war plans, and by no means only nominally so, or only in his capacity of giving their final fiat. A plan, prepared by General Erich von Manstein, attracted him. His mind jumped at it; he kept looking at it; he revised it; he chose it, to the extent that, if Manstein was its real draftsman, it would not be much of an exaggeration to say that Hitler was its architect. Among other things, the Manstein plan wonderfully complemented his political strategy. It was a reverse of the famous Schlieffen Plan of World War I, and not its extension, which was what the Western Allies foresaw. In their considered opinion, the Hitler version of a Schlieffen would simply extend the German invasion of Western Europe into Holland, beyond Belgium; and the Western response would be an advance into Belgium, meeting the Germans halfway across that country and in southwestern Holland. (Both Germans and Allies discounted serious operations along the Maginot Line, at least during the first decisive stage of a Western European campaign; both knew that a German frontal attack on the Maginot was not in the cards.) What Manstein and Hitler chose, their reverse Schlieffen, was a main German thrust not from the right to the left but from the left to the right: a rapid motorized advance across the wooded hills of the Ardennes and across the Meuse, making straight for the Channel ports, cutting off the French divisions and the small British Expeditionary Force in Belgium. Sickle-Cut, "Sichelschnitt," was the name of the plan, properly so; for that was what it was. At this stage of his life and career Hitler knew in his bones that he was both destined and able to command the military strategy of this war; that the destiny of a great statesman and of a great commander was one and the same, fed from the same kind of talent.

Then came a hitch — but a hitch that would eventually increase his military prestige further. The British and the French — we shall soon see how and why — were trying to open another front against Germany away from the west, in the north, probably in Norway. The previous autumn, after Poland, Admiral Raeder began to speak to Hitler about the necessity of occupying Norway. But Hitler said no. Only in March 1940 did he decide on a swift and daring plan, in order to preclude the British from getting a toehold in Norway, to beat them to it. On the first of April lunch in the Chancellery in Berlin was served a little later than usual. The generals gathered around Hitler. His words were recorded in the War Diary of the Army High Command. They tell us much about his mind and his confidence at the time. The Führer

> describes this enterprise [code name "Weserübung"] not only as especially daring but as one of the "most impertinent operations" of modern military history. *Exactly therefore* [my italics] he sees in that one of the basic factors of its success. . . .
>
> . . . He, the Führer, is not a man who avoids necessary decisions and struggles, leaving them to his successors. . . . All of these circumstances show that Germany's situation is very favorable, it could not be improved in the coming years.
>
> He himself possesses the nerves that are required for such a struggle, he also knows nearly all of his enemies personally, and considers them unimpressive; he feels that his personality is far superior to theirs.

His main opponent in the Norwegian campaign was Churchill. Hitler surely bested him there. Thus he had reason to be as confident, if not more so, on the tenth of May as he was on the first of April. Probably that was the reason, too, why on that day he seems to have paid relatively little attention to the news that Churchill had become the British prime minister.

LET US now turn to Churchill's political progress — if progress that was — to the tenth of May.

A year before, Churchill held no political office at all. Two years before that he was, by and large, a discredited politician, shunned and distrusted by the majority of his own political party, the ruling party in Britain. The reasons for this were both general and particular. Generally speaking, people in Britain thought Churchill to be impulsive, erratic, wordy, unduly combative, a maverick, perhaps a publicity hound; in one word, unsteady. (This was the Churchill who had Charlie Chaplin and Albert Einstein visit him and let himself be photographed with them.) He had his admirers, who not only sympathized with his ideas but recognized his exceptional abilities, but few of them were influential in the politics of the 1930s. Particular events, from late 1936 to the spring of 1939, would confirm this unfavorable impression. In early December 1936 Churchill chose to be a vocal advocate of the hapless king, Edward VIII. Against the congealing respectable opinion opposing the royal consortship of the twice-divorced Mrs. Simpson, Churchill chose to champion that marriage and that monarch (as we shall later see, wrongly). But more important and more lasting than the memory of that episode was his vocal and increasingly relentless opposition to the inclinations and the decisions taken by the Chamberlain government. Churchill kept criticizing and attacking the great majority of the Conservative Party, of which he was a member, and at a time when the inclinations and choices of that party and government had the support of most of the people of Britain and of its Dominions.

The issue was Hitler. For many years Churchill saw him and the rise of his aggressive, armed Germany as a mortal danger. Until the late spring of 1939 Chamberlain and his people did not. There is no need in this book to present yet another analysis of the motives of "appeasement," a respectable word whose meaning would later become sullied because of its association with Chamberlain's inclination to extend his good will to Hitler. The main element in that "appeasement," however, was not cowardice but an insufficiency of vision. On the other side Churchill's vision amounted to more than bravado and it was not superficial. But that did nothing for his reputation then; as a matter of fact, it would reduce that reputation further, at least for a while.

Nineteen thirty-eight was Hitler's most successful year; and Churchill's worst. In that year Hitler's Third Reich became the greatest power in Europe and perhaps in the world. He joined Austria to the Reich. Then he took a large piece of Czechoslovakia; and all over Europe governments recognized that their existence depended on being on good terms with Germany. The key event in 1938 was Munich. Czechoslovakia had an alliance with France and with the Soviet Union. Yet the decision for war and peace hinged on London. The French would not stand by Czechoslovakia unless the British would do so; and the Russians, rather obliquely, made their eventual decision subsequent to that of the French, especially when they knew that the French would not march. So at Munich everyone gave in to Hitler; and many people welcomed what they saw as Chamberlain's act of wise statesmanship. Churchill did not. Before Munich he wrote to a friend: "we seem to be very near the bleak choice between War and Shame. My feeling is that we shall choose Shame, and then have War thrown in a little later on even more adverse terms than at present." After Munich came what may have been one of his finest hours: a great speech he delivered in the House of Commons. ("We are in the presence of a disaster of the first magnitude. . . . Do not let us blind ourselves to that. . . . And do not suppose that this is the end. This is only the beginning of the reckoning. This is only the first sip, the first foretaste of a bitter cup which will be proffered to us.") But he had not many supporters in 1938. He came close to being censured by his own constituents, the voters of Epping.

The moral purpose and tone of that speech was magnificent. Yet on another, practical level Churchill was wrong about Munich. We know, or ought to know, two essential matters about the Munich crisis that Churchill did not know, or indeed admit. One is that for Britain to go to war in October 1938 could have been a disaster. Its air force gained much in numbers and strength from October 1938 to September 1939. Many of the Dominions were unwilling to go to war at the time of Munich; in September 1939 they were not. Hitler was not bluffing in 1938. He would have smashed Czech resistance in a few days. After that accomplished fact he would have offered peace to Britain and France that public opinion in these countries may have been inclined to accept. For many years afterward Hitler said that he rued not having gone to war in 1938, dissuaded as he had been by Chamberlain then. The other essential matter involves Russia. Churchill was convinced — he repeated this as late as 1948, in the first volume of his war memoirs — that at the time of Munich Russia would have joined the Western democracies against Hitler, a combination that a year later would not occur. Churchill was wrong: all of the evidence that has come to the surface indicates that Stalin was no more inclined to defend Czechoslovakia and go to war with Hitler in 1938 than was Chamberlain.

Nineteen thirty-eight, in sum, was a very dark year in Churchill's life. Among his own people he was unpopular. He could rely on but small groups of political friends and journalists and Central European émigrés, with whom he would meet on occasion, gathering and sifting information. They listened to him with respect. Some of them sensed that he not only deserved but was destined for a great role. But how would that come about? And when? His personal life was affected by his isolation. There were somber nights in that year when he, an excellent sleeper, could not sleep. His finances were never a primary consideration in his life; but his income from his journalism was not sufficient; his personal debts were larger than usual. Late in March 1938 he was just about to advertise Chartwell, his beloved country house, for sale when one of his supporters, Sir Henry Strakosch, a London financier of Jewish ancestry, paid off his debts. In

London he lived in what for him was a relatively modest abode, 11 Morpeth Mansions, near Victoria Station, the occasional head-quarters of his conspiracies with his friends and supporters against the policy of Chamberlain. In turn Chamberlain's close friends (Sir Joseph Ball and Sir Samuel Hoare) were tapping Churchill's telephone.

In mid-March 1939 his prospects brightened. That was Hitler's doing, not his own. Taking advantage of a crisis between Slovaks and Czechs, Hitler decided to march into Prague and annex what remained of Czechia to the Reich. That was a mistake, because what had remained of Czechoslovakia was a virtual vassal state of his after Munich; because in doing what he did Hitler broke at least one of his promises at Munich; because all of this led to a belated but swift revolution of public opinion in Britain. During the last fortnight of March 1939 Chamberlain had to change his course. He now came to think that the only way to avoid war was to let the Germans know what a British government twenty-five years before had not done: to declare that the next German aggression would mean war with Great Britain. The British guarantee to Poland (the first and last time that Britain would commit itself to war in the defense of an Eastern European state) did not deter Hitler, who knew that Chamberlain's decision was a reluctant act taken by a reluctant government of a — perhaps — reluctant nation. But in March 1939 Churchill's stock among his own people began to rise. Consequently Chamberlain felt compelled to include Churchill in his government, indeed, in his War Cabinet. He was made First Lord of the Admiralty. On the first day of the war Churchill walked into the same Admiralty room he had occupied in August 1914, twenty-five years before.

Churchill, unlike Hitler, wore no uniform that day. He walked around in his dark vested suit, wearing one of his dotted bow ties, with a gold watch chain across his girth, the only oddity in his appearance being his high-crowned black hat — a portly figure with a physical aura that was old-fashioned, near-Edwardian but solid. Only later in the war, after 1940, would he sometimes wear uniforms and don naval or military caps of his choosing — his occasional indulgence for the British male's inclination to dress up.

FOR EIGHT months and ten days Churchill was a member of Neville Chamberlain's government. His position and his authority were important; indeed, they were increasing. But he was not in full charge. His character and his temperament were very different from Chamberlain's. So was his view of the war. To say that Chamberlain hated it and that Churchill welcomed it may be too much. But no matter how imprecise, such a statement contains an essential element of truth. There is much evidence of that. Ten days into the war Chamberlain wrote a letter to his sister Hilda, a confidante, about the difficulties he had when he had tried, wearily, to postpone the British declaration of war as long as he could. "The House of Commons was out of hand, torn with suspicions and ready . . . to believe the Government guilty of any cowardice and treachery." Six weeks into the war he wrote Hilda that the sinking of German submarines gave him "an uncomfortable feeling"; had they called at British ports in peacetime "we should probably say what good fellows the officers and men were." He had come around to loathing Hitler but not the Germans; his loathing of the war was inseparable from his willingness to think that the war might soon end, and that this war should consist mainly of putting economic pressure on Germany. On 5 November 1939 he wrote Franklin Roosevelt that the war might be over soon, not because the Germans would be defeated but by their realization that they cannot win "and that it isn't worth their while to go on getting thinner and poorer." Churchill's view of the war could not have been more different. But he was not always impressive. In March 1940 President Roosevelt sent Sumner Welles to visit the capitals of the warring nations. Welles thought that Churchill drank too much. At a dinner at Downing Street with Chamberlain, Churchill and other government figures on 12 March, Welles thought he saw Churchill drunk; he also heard Sir Samuel Hoare dismissing Churchill: "*He* would be willing to fight for a hundred years."

What is amazing is Churchill's loyalty to Chamberlain during this time. This was due not only to Churchill's political calculation. He was, of course, dependent on Chamberlain's keeping him in the War Cabinet; he also knew that any evidence of his disagreement with Chamberlain would be dangerous to him and to the unity of the British people and their war effort. Yet the absence of his criticism of Chamberlain was not only public, it was also private. Here we come to one of Churchill's endearing — surely, to this writer, his most endearing — qualities: his magnanimity. Generosity is a virtue: yet it often means not more than the willingness to give of one's possessions. Magnanimity is both rarer and greater: the capacity of giving of oneself. Magnanimity, too, is often the true source of loyalty. During the months of the Reluctant War Chamberlain himself grew to appreciate that. In many ways he and Churchill came closer together, and not merely because of the political necessity of national unity. At times, and at least in one part of his mind, Chamberlain began to think that perhaps he and Churchill were complementary in this war, that for some things Churchill was needed, while for others, including the leadership, he, Chamberlain, was the right man. That was a conversion of sorts: not from enmity to amity but of something less categorical but also deeper, from the inclinations of distrust to the increase of trust. It was not a total change: we have seen that as late as the tenth of May Chamberlain still did not want to hand the government over to Churchill; but it was there, and it was largely made by Churchill's largeness of mind.

The nature of the Reluctant War did nothing to stiffen the resolve of the people of Britain. It may not have weakened it (though there was a small, subdued groundswell in October for a compromise peace), but it did not nurture it either. Often it is not from the records of politicians and governments that we may glimpse the atmosphere of a certain time, the mental climate of people. E. M. Delafield (Elizabeth Monica Dashwood) was a lovely Englishwoman who made a small name for herself in the thirties by writing delightful, funny, self-deprecating books in the form of diaries, with the titles beginning *The Provincial Lady.* . . . Her last book (she would die relatively young) was *The Provincial Lady in Wartime,* about autumn in 1939. On 29 September, she wrote, "weather continues lovely, garden all Michaelmas daisies, dahlias and nasturtiums — autumn roses a failure, but cannot expect everything — and Aunt Blanche and I walk about under the apple-trees and round the tennis-court and ask one another who could ever believe that England is at war? Answer is, alas, only too evident — but neither of us makes it aloud." Her patriotism is unexceptionable; like many middle-class Englishwomen of her kind, she longs to do something for the war effort. But here is Lady Blowfield, one of her superiors. "Useful to put before public important points. Feel more hopeful about this, and ask what points? There is, replies Lady Blowfield, the question of Root Vegetables. English housewives do not make the best use of these, in cooking. An attractive pamphlet on the subject of Root Vegetables might do a lot just now." It is November, and an old lady "relates, in very aggrieved tones, that she was paying a visit in Scotland when National Registration took place and her host and hostess registered her without her knowledge or permission. This resulted in her being issued with a ration book. She does not wish for a ration book. She didn't ask for one, and won't have one." For late 1939 *The Provincial Lady in Wartime* is as good a guide to the atmosphere as Evelyn Waugh's *Put Out More Flags* and *Men at Arms*.

In October Churchill and his wife moved from their flat to an apartment in Admiralty House. During the first four months of the war the Admiralty results were a mixed bag; still, in the balance, good rather than bad, which contributed to the gradual increase in Churchill's reputation. (Among other events a German submarine penetrated the nets and defenses of Scapa Flow and sank the battleship *Royal Oak;* but then the German battleship *Graf Spee* was engaged, wounded and forced by three smaller British warships to repair to the neutral port of Montevideo, whereupon *Graf Spee* scuttled itself.) Then came one of the strangest chapters of the war. Stalin attacked Finland.* The Finns fought very well and drove the Russians back in several places. The British and French governments perked up. They had already allowed themselves to be convinced by experts that Hitler's Germany was desperately dependent on Swedish iron ore imports and that, especially for several months in the winter, this iron ore could not be shipped to Germany except southward along the coast of Norway.

The economic experts were woefully wrong, as usual; but there was more to that. The Finnish war against Soviet Russia was popular in Paris and London — and also in the United States, among anti-Communists, Republicans and isolationists. Moreover, neither the French nor the British government were averse to opening up a front against the Germans, preferably far away from Western Europe, at relatively limited risk and expense, in places where the Germans would be hampered by the limitations of their navy. Thus during the frozen January of 1940 the idea ripened in London and Paris of assisting the Finns, perhaps by sending a small expeditionary force to Finland through northern Norway and Sweden, on the way getting control of the Norwegian port of Narvik and the iron ore rail line heading there; in sum, killing two birds with one stone — if necessary, at the risk of engaging in a war with the Soviet Union. This was the most harebrained plan of the Second World War. By and large, Churchill was in favor of it. Eventually the imbecile scheme collapsed, as the Finns concluded a peace with the Russians a day or so

---

* Again an example of the unpredictability of history: three months after the Second World War had begun between Germany, Poland, France and Britain, the only land fighting was taking place between Finns and Russians.

before the first Anglo-French troops were to sail from Scotland,
without knowing exactly where. The peak of the idiocy was the underestimation of the Russians. (Only after the British archives were
opened in 1970 does one find that as late as March and April 1940
British reconnaissance planes flew over the Caucasus, photographing
Batum and Baku and drawing Russian antiaircraft fire — or that in
January 1940 the British chargé d'affaires in Moscow insouciantly
advised the Chamberlain government that "the effective and continuous bombardment of Baku should ... present no great difficulty to
us and it alone should be sufficient to bring Russia to her knees
within a very short time.")

But the Finnish war was not yet over when there came a first over-
ture of the Duel, an event whose concatenations were to lead to the
fateful tenth of May, when Hitler and Churchill's duel in full force
began. This flash involved not Finland but Norway; it involved not
iron ore shipments but a clash of ships. The *Altmark* was a German
supply ship, carrying in its hold British sailors, prisoners who had
been rescued and collected by the *Graf Spee* during its early forays in
the South Atlantic and then transferred to the *Altmark*. The *Altmark*
was now crawling southward in Norwegian territorial waters, making
for a German port. Churchill ordered a British destroyer to track it
down, attack it, board it. This happened on 16 February in the Jös-
singford. (Thereafter Vidkun Quisling and his pro-German followers
in Norway would call their pro-English countrymen "Jössingers.")
The boarding was swift and successful; the British prisoners in the
hold heard the shout of their rescuers: "The Navy's here!" That small
drama redounded to Churchill's benefit. But it made Hitler sit up and
change his plans. He was now convinced that Churchill wanted to lay
his hands on Norway. All right, then: he would beat him to it. Three
days after the *Altmark* episode he called in General Nikolaus von Falkenhorst. That general, in 1918, had commanded the landing of a
small German force in Finland. Hitler said to Falkenhorst: "Sit down
and tell me what you did." The general explained. Then Hitler, walking up and down, gave Falkenhorst a very impressive list of reasons
why it must be Norway. (The protection of the iron ore imports was
the last and least important item on his list.) On 1 March — the Finnish war was not yet over — Hitler gave orders that the invasion of
Denmark and Norway must now precede the Western European
campaign.

It is important to recognize that Churchill had drafted his first
minute (a short memorandum) about mining the Norwegian coastal

waters as early as 27 November 1939 — that is, before the Finnish war broke out. The Royal Navy would lay mines in Norwegian waters whether the Norwegian government wanted them or not. If the Germans came out to fight (and Churchill hoped that they would), the navy would be there, more than a match for them, and then the British would get hold of the principal ports of Norway. So the Reluctant War would evolve into something important and effective; the theater of war would extend into Norway, where the navy should have the upper hand.

It was not until after complicated and wearisome negotiations that in early April the British and French cabinets made their decision in accord with Churchill's wishes. Churchill was now in charge of the Norway business. Indeed, he was more involved in the actual naval planning than was Hitler. Moreover — something often ignored by some of his historians and biographers — by early April he arrived at a stage where harmony and collaboration between him and Chamberlain had reached their peak. On 4 April Downing Street announced that the First Lord of the Admiralty would thereafter preside over the Military Co-ordination Committee, including the Chiefs of Staff. "Among other Service Ministers, who were also members of the War Cabinet, I was 'first among equals' " Churchill would write in his war memoirs. Then he went to considerable extent to explain that "I had, however, no power to take or to enforce decisions." That high committee was, after all, still a committee, a "fluid, friendly, but unfocused circle." All that was true, but the responsibility for the Norway campaign was still his.

On 5 April Chamberlain spoke in the Commons. Of Hitler he said: "one thing is certain: he missed the bus." That unfortunate phrase would haunt him soon.* Late on the seventh, the British mining of Norwegian waters began. During the eighth, news began to accumulate about the northward movement of a German fleet. A larger and more powerful force of the Royal Navy drove toward Norway in a squall. Some of their ships carried a few British units that would land in Norway when needed. They missed the German bus — or, rather, the German fleet. At dawn on the ninth, German troops invaded

---

* Not that Churchill had not said foolish things. In the House of Commons on 11 April: "In my view, which is shared by my skilled advisers, Herr Hitler has committed a grave strategic error. . . . For myself, I consider that Hitler's action in invading Scandinavia is as great a strategic and political error as that which was committed by Napoleon in 1807 when he invaded Spain."

Denmark and landed at Copenhagen, capturing the Danish capital, government and king. At the same time — this was the "impertinent" operation — they landed in various ports of Norway, including Narvik in the far north, where no one, including Churchill, had expected them to go.

Now I must turn to an episode that has not received the attention it deserves. It involved a shot that was not heard round the world but that may have changed the course of history.

The fort of Oscarsborg is a small rock of an island in the long bay leading to Oslo. The battery on its stone parapet consisted of three old, black iron guns, made by Krupp in 1892 and bought by the Swedish government then. (Norway was not yet an independent state.) The three guns bore the Old Testament names of Aaron, Moses and Joshua. The Oscarsborg commander was Colonel Eriksen, a Norwegian officer close to retirement.

The Norwegian government knew that the ominous race for Norway was on. They bent backward to avoid any possible pretext for a German attack. The commanders of the army and of the coastal artillery were told not to fire at anything approaching until further orders. Even on the eighth, when evidence began to assemble about German ships making for Norway, the government refrained from taking any action. A little after midnight an ancient Norwegian minelayer (built in 1858) and an armed whaler were shocked into action as they met the towering forms of German warships entering the Bay of Oslo. Gallantly they drove at the Germans and were then blown to bits.

No sound of their gunfire reached Oscarsborg. At three in the cold, sub-Arctic night Colonel Eriksen walked the parapet. Suddenly he saw a dark shadow blocking the lights of a village three miles down the bay. In a moment he realized that this was the silhouette of a large vessel that was approaching very fast. In a few minutes it would be passing Oscarsborg on the lee side of the narrows. He open-sighted one of the three guns, roughly estimated the distance and, against his instructions and without precise calculations, fired. The black night lit up in a yellow flash. That single shell from Oscarsborg hit the ammunition chamber of the large German cruiser *Blücher*. She was carrying the German occupation troops to Oslo, about two thousand officers and men, including Gestapo and SS units. The *Blücher* moved on. The fire in her holds kept her visible. As she thumped forward in the narrows two coastal torpedoes finished her off. The rest of the German force turned back.

Later, in the northern daylight, German troops landed elsewhere in the bay; by noon airborne troops were in command of Oslo; late in the afternoon they occupied Oscarsborg; Colonel Eriksen was their prisoner. (They allowed him to live with his family in the town of Drøbak across the bay. He died soon after the war, after he had received a high decoration from de Gaulle.) Few historians of World War II know his name. Yet without his shot the *Blücher* would have passed through the narrows, docking in Oslo before seven A.M., still in the dark. What happened earlier that morning in Copenhagen would have happened in Oslo. The Oscarsborg gun made it possible for an alerted king and government to leave the capital for the north that morning, not heeding the demands of the German envoy or the entreaties of another Norwegian colonel, Quisling. Had the king and government been captured in Oslo there would have been no Norwegian campaign, except perhaps for Narvik in the far north.

The Norwegian campaign brought Churchill to power. Without that shot from Oscarsborg the blame might have fallen on Churchill rather than on Chamberlain. "I certainly bore an exceptional measure of responsibility for the brief and disastrous Norwegian campaign — if campaign it can be called," Churchill wrote General Ismay after the war. Yet as that dismal April rolled on, more and more people grew impatient not with Churchill but with Chamberlain, because the response of the Allies to the German invasion was agonizingly slow, ineffective, disheartening. Nearly a fortnight after the German landings British and French troops were put ashore at two small Norwegian ports. As Churchill later put it, their milling around was not much more than "a muddy waddle." They were no match for the Germans. Soon they thought it best to withdraw. Later, after the war, Churchill wrote how "the Germans traversed in seven days the road from Namsos to Mosjoen, which the British and French had declared impassable ... we were each time too late. ... Our finest troops ... were baffled by the vigour, enterprise and training of Hitler's young men." This was the first time Churchill recognized — recognition that would often dominate his strategy and his military choices throughout the war — that the British army now faced an enemy that was superior to it not only in its armaments and organization but in its hardiness, resolve and spirit.

"It was a marvel," he remembered, "that I survived and maintained my position in public esteem and parliamentary confidence." There was a reason behind this "marvel." Many people in Britain, and more and more of their representatives, thought they had had enough of

Chamberlain. They ascribed the Norway fiasco to him, not to Churchill. They saw in Chamberlain an example of an inefficiency the source of which was listlessness and an insufficient resolution to fight. In Churchill they were now inclined to recognize a man who, at least about Hitler, proved his credibility by having been right. They were also inclined to overlook the fact that in Norway Churchill, too, had been wrong.

ON 1 MAY, Wednesday, Chamberlain asked Churchill to come to 10 Downing Street after dinner. It was a cold, blustery day, pouring rain and wind. "If I were the first of May, I should be ashamed of myself," Churchill said to John Colville, Chamberlain's private secretary. Colville, who disliked Churchill heartily (but who soon would change his mind), wrote in his diary: "Personally I think he ought to be ashamed of himself in any case," suggesting thereby that Churchill was intriguing against his chief. He was wrong: Churchill's talk with Chamberlain was sincere and amicable. Two days later the opposition in the House of Commons asked for a debate on the war and leadership. Both Chamberlain and Churchill knew that this was coming. As early as 2 May Churchill said in the Cabinet that he did not wish to discuss the Norway operations in the House, since the enemy might obtain valuable information. It was Chamberlain who said that it was "out of the question to cancel the public debate without incurring the most serious political consequences."

The political developments of the following Tuesday, Wednesday and Thursday, 7, 8 and 9 May, have been described in minute detail so often that for our purposes the shortest summary should suffice. Attacks on Chamberlain's leadership of the war rained down on his head from both sides of the House — even more strongly from certain Conservatives than from the spokesmen of the Labour opposition. On Wednesday the debate assumed the character of a vote of censure. Churchill was very loyal to Chamberlain. Twice he stated that he took full responsibility for what happened in Norway. Lloyd George, who despised Chamberlain, said that Churchill's responsibility was limited, and that Churchill should not allow himself to become an "air-raid shelter" protecting the rest of the government. He demanded that Chamberlain resign, "because there is nothing which can contribute more to victory in this war than that he should sacrifice the seals of office." Then came the vote of confidence. The division revealed that Chamberlain had lost the support of about one hundred members of the Conservative Party. Chamberlain then asked Churchill to come to his room and said that perhaps he, Chamberlain, should not go on. There must be a national government. Later next morning Churchill knew that he would be considered for the prime ministership. There was a crucial meeting between Chamberlain, Halifax and Churchill. Chamberlain inclined to Halifax. Churchill held himself back. "Usually I talk a great deal, but on this occasion I was silent." Halifax said that, being a peer, he could not effectively govern because of the House of Commons. At the end of the day Chips Channon, an enemy of Churchill's, noted in his diary: "Neville still reigns, but only just." Another enemy of Churchill's, Joseph Kennedy, the American ambassador, telegraphed to Washington: "Nobody has the slightest idea of what should be done. Chamberlain, Halifax and Churchill are unquestionably tired men." He was wrong about Churchill.

What happened on the tenth was described in the first pages of this book. That evening Chips Channon wrote in his diary: "Perhaps the darkest day in English history. . . . I sat numb with misery, and mused on this fantastic day." Fantastic it truly was. On this same day Hitler had started the battle on which depended the future of Western civilization. That this milestone — more, that this turning point — in the lives of both Hitler and Churchill happened on the same day was nonetheless a coincidence. "Coincidences," Chesterton once wrote, "are spiritual puns." Coincidences, at the same time, are not the results of nothing; they are the sudden convergences of myriad separate threads. There had been close supporters of Chamberlain, such as Kingsley Wood, who thought it best to abandon him and make clear that they were now working for Churchill's favor. The outcome of that uneasy struggle for power in England reflects much honor on British parliamentary democracy. Parliamentary democracy had for many years, indeed decades, seemed not only unwieldy but unrepresentative and even corrupt, unsuited against the new — and in many ways not unrepresentative — centralized exercise of power by the dictators. Yet during these days it was parliamentary democracy that helped put Churchill in the saddle. On the seventh Harold Nicolson wrote about the climate in the House: "The atmosphere is something more than anxiety, it is one of actual fear but it is a very resolute fear and not hysteria or cowardice in the least. In fact I have seldom admired the spirit of the House so much as I did today." This was the man who wrote on the first page of his diary on New Year's Day, 1940: "In all probability a year of doom." He was Churchill's ally;

but he also knew that the grimmest of times lay ahead. Upon hearing the news of the German invasion of Western Europe on the tenth of May he wrote: "What makes it worse in a way is that it is a beautiful spring day with the bluebells and primroses in flower everywhere."

HITLER'S VIEW of England and the English people was not simple. We have seen that he wanted their alliance, their friendship, or at least their neutrality. But then he was spurned by them, and his desire for a historic accommodation with them eventually turned into bitterness and hate. This suggests that there was more to his desire for English friendship than cold political calculation. At the same time, to speak of Hitler's love-hate relationship with England may be too strong, even though it contains some truth. Hitler — in this respect he differed little from masses of the German people — had a certain sense of inferiority (the kind of inferiority that is a compound of both respect and resentment) toward the English, certainly until 1940. He did not know enough about them — a handicap that was, however, more than counterbalanced by a fearsome asset in the mind of this extraordinary man: a sixth sense with which he often unerringly recognized the weaknesses of his opponents.

Because of this, an incident in Hitler's and Churchill's lives in 1932 may have had great importance for both — and eventually for their duel eight years later. In the summer of that year they had a chance to meet. Hitler was not yet chancellor but a rising power in Germany. Churchill was then a minor political personage in England. He was motoring through Germany, inspecting the battlefields where his great ancestor Marlborough, whose monumental biography he was then writing, had fought. At an evening party at his hotel in Munich Churchill met Hanfstaengl, a genial Bavarian giant of a man speaking perfect English (he had an American mother and knew Franklin Roosevelt from Harvard days), a piano player and Hitler's social secretary at the time. Churchill talked with Hanfstaengl. He would not mind meeting his boss. Late next morning Hanfstaengl saw his boss. Hitler was usually willing, at times even eager, to meet English political figures. Though I have found no mention of Churchill by Hitler before 1932, he surely knew Churchill's name. But Hitler told Hanfstaengl that he did not care to meet Winston Churchill then. I have often thought about that episode. As I wrote above, Hitler had an extraordinary ability to perceive the personal weaknesses of people, including men whose national and social backgrounds were entirely different from his. It was a strong sense, perhaps not entirely unlike the way in which an animal smells fear in a man. It was strong enough for Hitler to bank on it. It was an intuition that could be translated into intelligence, one that carried him to some of his greatest successes. Had he met Churchill in Munich in 1932 he would perhaps have understood him better. (In 1937 Ribbentrop, who was the German ambassador to London then, twice invited Churchill to visit Hitler. Then it was Churchill who declined the invitation.)* As things turned out, during their duel Churchill understood Hitler better than Hitler understood Churchill.

There is much evidence that by late 1937 Hitler was interested in the various forces within English politics. Well before the full development of the Munich crisis he became acutely aware of the deep conflict between Chamberlain and Churchill. During and after Munich he clearly saw where Churchill stood. In September 1938 he said to Josef Goebbels that Chamberlain might one day be succeeded by Churchill, who would start a world war against Germany. Ten days after the Munich settlement Hitler made a speech at Saarbrücken. He said: "It only needs for Mr. Duff Cooper [one of Churchill's friends who resigned from the Chamberlain government after Munich] or Mr. Eden or Mr. Churchill to come to power in Britain in place of Chamberlain, and then we can be quite sure that the aim of these gentlemen would be to start a new world war. They make no bones about it, they speak of it quite openly." It is evident at this point that Hitler wanted to influence English politics. In this he had the enthusiastic support of Goebbels. On 28 October Goebbels issued a circular to the German press. It must "not pass up any opportunity of attacking Churchill, Eden and Duff Cooper . . . the German press is to [describe] these three so that the entire world sees . . . that for such persons to be given high office would be the gravest affront to Germany."

---

* He gave his reasons after the war: "I would gladly have met Hitler with the authority of Britain behind me. But as a private individual I should have placed myself and my country at a disadvantage. If I had agreed with the Dictator-host, I should have misled him. If I had disagreed, he would have been offended, and I should have been accused of spoiling Anglo-German relations. Therefore I declined, or rather let lapse, both invitations. All those Englishmen who visited the German Führer in these years were embarrassed or compromised. No one was more completely misled than Mr. Lloyd George, whose rapturous accounts of his conversations make odd reading today. There is no doubt that Hitler had a power of fascinating men, and the sense of force and authority is apt to assert itself unduly upon the tourist. Unless the terms are equal, it is better to keep away."

Hitler saw Churchill as an arrogant and combative enemy of Germany, an ancient English reactionary. At the same time he knew of Churchill's personal connections and of his group of advisers, among whom were German and other Central European émigrés, including Jews. On 6 November 1938 he spoke at Weimar: "I recently named three of these globetrotting warmongers by name. What hurt them was not the allegation, but my courage in naming them. . . . They are living on the moon. . . . Mr. Churchill has openly pronounced his view that the present regime in Germany must be overthrown by internal forces who are standing gratefully by. . . . If Mr. Churchill would mingle more with Germans and less with émigré circles, with venal traitors in foreign pay, he would see the absurdity and the stupidity of this." By the summer of 1939 the German radio broadcasts spluttered about Churchill in extreme terms. Hans Fritzsche, the main commentator, would on occasion call him "filthy liar" or "gangster" or "puffed-up pig." (He was unaware of Churchill's liking for pigs.)

More important is the fact that Hitler's acute interest in English politics continued after the war had begun. We saw that he had hoped for some response by Chamberlain to his speech offering a settlement after he had conquered Poland. A few days later, on 11 October, Goebbels brought him the translation of an article by George Bernard Shaw in which the latter had made fun of Churchill. Hitler liked it: "Shaw is one of the brightest wits of the world," he said to Goebbels. Nine days later Hitler gave Goebbels instructions — something that he rarely did — "on how to handle Churchill's case. . . . We may perhaps be able to topple him." Goebbels now wrote an enthusiastic article against Churchill, adding in his diary: "This will make a big sensation." (It didn't.) On 12 December Goebbels lunched with Hitler. "He criticizes Churchill very strongly. [Churchill] lives in the sixteenth century and does not understand at all the real needs of the English people."

During the Norwegian campaign Hitler showed his contempt for Churchill. For the tenth of May Goebbels wrote in his diary: "Churchill is now made Premier. The field is clear! That's what we like."

CHURCHILL UNDERSTOOD Hitler very well. This was unusual, since Englishmen, no matter how acute their observations, seldom evince a profound interest in foreigners. Chamberlain, of course, failed to comprehend Hitler for a long time. Even the greatest champions of England, statesmen such as Pitt or Palmerston, whatever their virtues, their understanding of their foreign counterparts and adversaries was not among their principal assets. But Churchill's comprehension of Hitler was different.

To some extent — but only to some extent — Churchill's perceptions of Hitler and of the Germans were inseparable. Very early in his life there is evidence of his Francophilia: a cultural, and not merely political, strain that accompanied him throughout his life, surviving and persisting through his shattering disappointments with France in 1940. In this respect Churchill's early inclination corresponded to the then new, decisive and unprecedented turn in British policy that in the earliest years of the century — more precisely, between 1899 and 1904 — began to consider Germany as the main potential adversary and France as a potential ally of Great Britain. At that time the main instrument of the potential German danger was the German navy. Churchill knew much about navies and sea power. He played the leading part in preparing the British navy for war in 1914. He was a convinced proponent of the effectiveness of sea power, whence his principal advocacy of the Dardanelles operation in 1915, which failed by a hairsbreadth — not because of him; yet that led to his then sudden, and seemingly lasting, political demise.

The ruthless dedication and efficiency of the German effort in World War I made a deep impression on Churchill. At the end of his massive work on World War I (in three volumes, of which the last one was published less than ten years after the end of that war) he felt compelled to write: "It will certainly not fall to this generation to pronounce the final verdict on the Great War. The German people are worthy of better explanations than the shallow tale that they were undermined by enemy propaganda. . . . Yet in the sphere of force, human records contain no manifestation like the eruption of the German volcano."

> For four years Germany fought and defied the five continents of the world by land and sea and air. The German armies upheld their tottering confederates, intervened in every theatre with success, stood everywhere on conquered territory, and inflicted on their enemies more than twice the bloodshed they suffered themselves. To break their strength and science and curb their fury, it was necessary to bring all the greatest nations of mankind into the field against them. Overwhelming populations, unlimited resources, measureless sacrifice, the Sea Blockade, could not prevail for fifty

months. Small states were trampled down in the struggle; a mighty Empire was battered into unrecognizable fragments; and nearly twenty million men perished or shed their blood before the sword was wrested from that terrible hand. Surely, Germans, for history it is enough!

. . . Is this the end? Is it to be merely a chapter in a cruel and senseless story? Will a new generation in their turn be immolated to square the black accounts of Teuton and Gaul? Will our children bleed and gasp again in devastated lands? Or will there spring from the very fires of conflict that reconciliation of the three giant combatants, which would unite their genius and secure to each in safety and freedom a share in rebuilding the glory of Europe?

It took another world war to achieve something like the last prospect.

Churchill's perception of Hitler was a compound of the old and the new. He saw him as a reincarnation of some very ancient evil; at the same time he recognized how Hitler stood for something that was thoroughly untraditional and terribly modern. There is evidence that he became interested in Hitler well before Hitler began to be interested in him. In September 1930 Hitler's party achieved a very considerable success in the German elections. But at that time Hitler was still only a secondary figure on the German political scene. No one except for Hitler himself saw the prospect of his ever becoming chancellor. Yet a month later, when Churchill dined at the German embassy in London, the then counselor of the embassy, a descendant of Bismarck, considered Churchill's words significant enough to report them to Berlin. Churchill was anxious about Hitler. "Hitler of course declared he does not intend starting a world war but Churchill believes that Hitler and his followers will grasp the first chance to resort to arms again." Two and a half years later Hitler was the master of Germany, the Führer of the Third Reich. Thereafter there were plenty of occasions to be reminded of Churchill's early warnings of what this meant and would mean — warnings that were neglected, dismissed and, indeed, unheard by the politicians and representatives of the British people, and by the people at large.

Their insufficient reaction at that time was not always and everywhere due to somnolence, inattention, indifference. There were in 1933, and for some years afterward, Englishmen and Englishwomen who were sympathetic to what Hitler represented — or, more precisely, to what he seemed to represent to them. I am referring not only to Oswald Mosley, his British Fascists or odd devotees of Hitler such as Unity Mitford. There were other, more influential or at least more significant, men and women in Britain who saw in Hitler something new and positive, a vitalizing force to the potential benefit of Europe and of the world order, perhaps even of Britain. These were different people but they had certain inclinations in common. The British Germanophobia of the previous war had died in their minds. They thought, and not without reason, that the vengeful treatment of Germany after the war had been wrong. They recognized that the Germans had been gallant and brave fighters. They disliked the ineffectiveness, the bumbling, the petty corruptions, the hypocrisies and dishonesties of parliamentary politicking, especially in those drab, dust-laden Depression years. Some of them saw Fascism and National Socialism as strong, and perhaps admirable, new alternatives not only to parliamentary democracy but also to Communism. Some of them disliked Jews and what they thought were Jewish influences. At least in 1933 such dissimilar people as the avant-garde writer Wyndham Lewis, the well-connected playwright Enid Bagnold, the novelist Philip Gibbs and the newspaper magnate Lord Rothermere were among those who shared such inclinations, which were also current among some families of the British aristocracy. We shall have to return to them later, since some of them continued to be elements of a British opposition to Churchill even in May 1940.

This is not the place to recount, or even to illustrate, the very large accumulation of Churchill's warnings about Hitler in the 1930s. My purpose here is not to sum up Churchill's record but to describe the elements of his unusual perception. The volume of Churchill's journalism in the thirties was enormous. He depended on that for his living. His articles included passages in which he thought he had to recognize "the enormous dimension" of Adolf Hitler. He composed a portrait of Hitler in 1935: "What manner of man is this grim figure who has performed these superb toils [meaning the raising up of Germany] and loosed these frightful evils [meaning Hitler's persecutions and terror]?" In November 1935 he wrote: "Those who have met Herr Hitler face to face in public business or on social terms have found a highly competent, cool, well-informed functionary with an agreeable manner, a disarming smile, and few have been unaffected by a subtle personal magnetism." As late as September 1937 he wrote: "If our country were defeated I hope we should find a champion as indomitable to restore our courage and lead us back to our place among the nations." There was nothing hypocritical in these phrases. They were not the results of the sometimes undue, and therefore exaggerated, British habit of rhetorical fairness. Nor were they polite phrases masking hate. The hate — if that is what it was — that would animate Churchill against Hitler came later. Even then it was less of a hate for a man than the hate of what that man had wrought. Even after the war, writing about Hitler, Churchill described how Hitler's sufferings in 1918 "did not lead him into Communist ranks. *By an honourable inversion* he cherished all the more an abnormal sense of racial loyalty and a fervent and mystic admiration for Germany and the German people." The italics are mine.

From the very beginning there was a constancy in Churchill's view of Hitler. Even after the war there was a human proportion in his portrait of Hitler in his memoirs. He devoted a chapter to Hitler in the first volume. On the first page of that short chapter, which he dictated walking up and down in his room in Chartwell, Churchill described Hitler's career and his personality astonishingly well. The remarkable quality of those passages was not only the result of Churchill's rhetorical and literary mastery. It was the result of his insight. He recognized, for example, how the decisive element in the formation of Hitler's mind — and not only in his career — came in 1918–19, and not before the war; in Munich, not in Vienna. Yet Hitler in *Mein Kampf* had insisted — and most historians even now accept the thesis — that while his life took a sudden turn in late 1918 and then in Munich, his political ideology had already crystallized in Vienna. Many professional historians, bombinating in their airless circles, tend to ignore or dismiss Churchill the historian. Yet in those pages Churchill's understanding of Hitler is phenomenal.

Aware as Churchill was of Hitler's frequent statements of admiration for England, he also saw that this admiration was not a simple matter, since it included uneasy sentiments of resentment. When, only a few days after Munich, Hitler made a sharp speech at Saarbrücken, for the first time attacking Churchill by name, Churchill noted that; but he noted something else, too — a phrase of Hitler's that he found to be significant. For in the same speech Hitler said: "It would be a good thing if people in Great Britain would gradually drop certain airs. . . . We cannot tolerate any longer *the tutelage of governesses.*" Churchill alone saw the significance of that phrase, so much so that he italicized it in his memoirs. Hitler also said: "I can never admit for a second that anybody in the ranks of our Western opponents has the right to look upon or to imagine himself as superior to us Germans. Nor do I, on that account, suffer in the least from any sort of inferiority complex!" The italics were Churchill's; the exclamation mark was Hitler's. Both are telling.

To me there is something providential that in 1940 Churchill became Hitler's main opponent. I know of no statesman, no national leader in the history of the modern world, who understood a foreign enemy as Churchill understood Hitler. This had brought him to power in England. But understanding and intelligence are only the handmaidens of power. By that time Churchill knew something else, too: that Hitler had brought the energies of the German people to an unprecedented peak. This was before Churchill himself recognized that Hitler's strategy in Western Europe was brilliant and successful, while the military moves of the British and the French (which he himself had supported beforehand) were disastrous and weak. Thereafter his acute comprehension of Hitler went hand in hand with his increasing respect for what the German armed forces were able to accomplish in this war. He would not underestimate either Hitler or the German soldier. He was, however, aware of certain weaknesses in Hitler's view of the world — at the same time when Hitler began to pay more and more attention to what he thought were weaknesses in Churchill's character.

THAT VIEW of the world, those views of the world of the two duelists, were inseparable from their strategies and tactics during their eighty days' duel. Nor were they separable from the formation of their characters.

Hitler's childhood, his relationship to his parents, was painful and difficult. This was true of Churchill's childhood, too. But they came to terms with this in very different ways. Hitler disliked and perhaps even hated his father, who sometimes beat him; but he would obscure this fact publicly, as in *Mein Kampf,* where he wrote about his father respectfully and sentimentally. On rare occasions he would admit to certain people, in private, that he rejected the situation, the career, the standards, the very personality that his father represented. Lord Randolph Churchill's relationship to his son was also far from satisfactory — satisfactory, that is, for a son who wanted affection from his father — but the young Winston, early in life, chose to suppress such frustrations, preferring to respect and admire his father throughout his life, and to follow his political career. Both Hitler and Churchill adored their mothers. A detached observer may say that

Hitler's mother, a sad-eyed, hard-working, long-suffering, warm-hearted woman, deserved more respect than Lady Randolph Churchill, who neglected her infant son and whose beauty and quick intelligence were nonetheless marred by her sensual appetites, revealing weaknesses of character. Yet her son was dedicated and remained loyal to his mother throughout her personal vicissitudes. He was, moreover, both proud of and willing to draw from his mother's American heritage and strove consciously from his earliest youth to pursue and uphold the purpose of Anglo-Americanism that his mother championed.

Hitler was much less emotional than Churchill. His personality was cold, Churchill's was warm. No one had ever seen a tear in Hitler's eyes, whereas tears would often gather in Churchill's, which seem not to have bothered or shamed him at all. It is surely remarkable that Hitler, who loved his mother, as too his mother loved and protected him, bore many of the marks of an unhappy childhood, while Churchill, who was more than often neglected by both of his parents, bore none of those marks at all. Some of this may be ascribed to his English aristocratic attitudes, but surely not all. Very early in his life he must have decided that his childhood was not unhappy, and that was that. There is an element of character — and perhaps the first budding of magnanimity — in such a choice, involving the suppression of unhappy memories; a positive element whose functioning is a living denial of what psychoanalysts tell us about "suppression."

In any event, their mothers played the more important part in Hitler's and Churchill's lives. This brings us, and very briefly, to their relations with women. Sexuality and its appetites seem to have played a less than decisive part in their lives — to use an ungainly word, both of them were undersexed. Much nonsense has been written and said about Hitler's sexual abnormalities. Evidence about such matters is often rare, inauthentic and difficult to judge. In my considered view, a result less of speculations than of more than forty years of reading about Hitler, his relations with women were fairly normal. So were Churchill's, whose marriage, with the possible evidence of one very brief and transitory exception, was a model of loyalty and of that mutual respect that is the foundation and refuge of every good marriage.

There is only one odd element in Hitler's relations with women that I find significant enough to note here. It appears in a recent and not well known memoir of his loyal private secretary, in whose opinion — and from whose observation — the knowledge that all kinds of beautiful women admired him and wished to bed him may have been sufficient for Hitler, who *may,* in his late forties, have wanted to avoid the risk of a sexual malfunction. This hypothesis, at least in my opinion, is confirmed strongly by Fräulein Schroeder's observed evidence (but also by other sources) to the effect that one of the things that affected Hitler's private and public life was "the fear that he might look ridiculous, in this Hitler was morbid [*krankhaft*]." He would, for example, let none of his servants ever see him in his underpants. (He also insisted that none of his photographs should show him wearing glasses.) Churchill had no such fear of being laughed at. This contrast was connected, too, with their respective senses of humor, which in Hitler's case was primitive, infrequent and, when it appeared at all, coarse, whereas Churchill's sense of humor was excellent, suffusing his character and bubbling suddenly forth even at the darkest of times.

Hitler's personal weaknesses may have been few: but, as we have seen, shortly before the war they included some symptoms of hypochondria. Having come to believe that he would not live much longer, he began to ingest an increasing amount and variety of pills, and changed his dietary habits. His only culinary weakness was his fondness for sweet creamy cakes. Churchill smoked cigars, ate well and drank much. We have conflicting evidence about his drinking. In 1940 his secretary John Colville was pleased to notice that the repute of Churchill's alcoholism was exaggerated; he liked to hold a drink in his hand but the whiskey content of his drinks was weak (just as his seemingly ever-present Havana cigars were rarely smoked to their ends). On the other hand people had seen him drunk. For dinner he almost always drank champagne. In April 1939 Lord Rothermere offered him six hundred pounds if he would stop drinking brandy for a year. Whether Churchill did so or not we do not know. What we know is that there is no evidence of anything resembling excessive alcohol consumption during the months of the Duel. We also know that, soon after May 1940, Hitler — who otherwise seldom requested intelligence reports about such details — became very interested in Churchill's drinking habits and wished to obtain minute details about them. It is not only that he began to refer to Churchill more often as "that drunkard"; it is that he obviously wanted to find a personal weakness, a potentially fatal chink in his adversary's armor.

This alone is interesting, since it went contrary to their mental and working habits. It was Churchill who kept his eyes open for all kinds of small but, to him, significant details; it was Hitler who, although having an enormous memory for certain details, read few political reports and trusted his intuition. Yet during their duel it was Hitler who wanted to have more and more information about Churchill and English politics, while Churchill's attention to Hitler consisted of something other than a minute peering into details.

The greatest difference in their characters was the one I mentioned earlier: Hitler was moved by resentments and hate, Churchill was not. I am not saying that magnanimity was *the* principal trait of the latter's character, but it was nonetheless a rare and precious substance within it, whereas it was largely absent in Hitler's. Certainly it is resentment, not magnanimity, that leads to personal obsessions. Hitler had one overall, ever-present, ruling obsession: his hatred of Jews. What we must remark here is that this was not (as is often the case) an outcome, albeit an important outcome, of his racist philosophy of mankind. To the contrary: the latter was consequent to the former. Hitler thought that Jews, even more than race, were a key to history. He was not consistent in his racism: he sometimes spoke well of and welcomed alliances with Chinese, Japanese, Afghans and Arabs, while he had few compunctions in conquering and suppressing Nordic nations. There were inconsistencies in his racial advocacies and policies, while about Jews he was fearfully consistent to the end. With all of his occasional dependence on Jewish friends and associates, and even in view of his early advocacy of the Jewish cause in Palestine, Churchill was neither an ideological philo-Semite nor a calculating one. But not only did he find Hitler's obsessive Judeophobia repulsive from the beginning; he very early saw therein a symptom of evil in Hitler's character.

The obsessive nature of Hitler's vision found expression in his use of the word "fanatic." He demanded a "fanatical" loyalty to the cause of the Party, Germany, the Third Reich. The soldiers and officers must be, he insisted, infused with it. In his, as in his propagandists', view that was a positive adjective. I need not argue that it is a pejorative one in English; but so it is in most of the Latin languages of Europe, including Italian (which is one small indication of the differences not only between Hitler and Mussolini but also between German National Socialism and Italian Fascism). Loyalty to friends, supporters and staff was true of Hitler as well as of Churchill. Appreciation of loyalties or of past acts from which he had benefited were not absent in Hitler. He was capable of friendships. But chivalry was largely absent from his character. This was not true of

Churchill, who on occasion would not only feel but wish to express an appreciation — that is, more than respect — for some of his German enemies. In the earlier mentioned episode of boarding the *Altmark* in a Norwegian fjord, Churchill's order to do so was piratical; yet when he learned that some of the personal belongings of its German captain had been taken he immediately ordered their restitution, in an angry minute (which he found proper to reprint in one of the appendixes of his war memoirs).

Their working habits were different, except for one thing: both rose late and went to bed late. Even there they differed. Hitler would not issue from his bedroom or suite except fully dressed, usually after eleven; Churchill woke up early; after lunch he would retire to bed for a full and refreshing sleep. Hitler was less demanding of his secretaries than was Churchill. Hitler was considerate and sometimes even gallant with them, especially with his female typists. Churchill's gruffness and occasional rudeness were the results of his impatience. He was more impatient than the fanatical Hitler. This is interesting to consider, since we have heard and read much about Hitler the frustrated artist. It is true that he was not only knowledgeable about architecture and music but that these filled some of his spiritual needs, they gave him inspiration. Yet in some ways Churchill was as much of an artist as was Hitler. Again it is noteworthy that while Hitler had been a not untalented painter in his youth, his interest in painting (not only in his own but in that of the great painters of the past) ceased to exist after the great turning point of his life. Churchill, on the other hand, discovered and cultivated the satisfactions of painting in his forties. While he had little ear for music he had an extraordinary sensitivity and retentive memory for poetry of all kinds. If we, then, include their respective use of their languages, then Churchill was surely the greater artist of the two.

This was important, since so much of their duel was fought with their words. The reading of both duelists was vast — in Hitler's case much more extensive than he has been credited with. Yet he was not much interested in the written word. He himself said once that *Mein Kampf* was a book to be spoken, not read. This is no place, and there is perhaps no need, to compare their oratorical talents, surely not for English-speaking readers who may be critical of Churchill's Augustan style here and there but to most of whom Hitler's language sounds frightfully alien. It is remarkable that, with his otherwise astonishing memory for certain details, Hitler wrote little — this was especially so of the time of their duel, indeed, of most of the war — and wrote amazingly few comments on the papers presented to him. He also read few documents, except certain military ones, while Churchill rushed through mounds of reports and papers, devouring them. Churchill found it imperative to express his wishes, all kinds of wishes, on paper. His very habits of speech, public as well as private, had literary qualities of their own of which he was almost always aware. In this, as in other things, he was less secretive than Hitler, who on occasion would tell his secretaries not to write down some things that he had been saying. In sum, Hitler was a non-writer, while Churchill was a writer. There was, however, a disadvantage to the latter, though that disadvantage would not accrue until later in the war, especially involving Churchill's relationship with Roosevelt. Churchill was not immune to the handicap that befalls most writers. Having expressed himself in writing clearly and fully about a subject, he was inclined to feel and think that the matter was accomplished, largely done. (He was not unaware of the obstacles of bureaucracy, that is, of the need to follow things up, whence the custom he created soon after his assumption of the prime ministership: a special label affixed to papers and directives, marked "Action This Day.") But that inclination was nevertheless a handicap. It did not always work. Yet it is a truism that, especially and primarily during the Duel, Churchill's mastery of the English language proved to be a tremendous, though undefinable, asset.

Both he and Hitler had quick minds, but not superficial ones. Hitler's knowledge of history — and also his understanding of certain historical forces — was considerable. Churchill's knowledge of history was of a higher quality — not merely because of his background and education but because it encompassed much more than Hitler's. Intuition played a greater part in Hitler's knowledge of the world than in Churchill's, but at least partly because of his obsessions, not always to his advantage. In any event, Churchill's respect for history was greater than Hitler's, as indeed befitted the mind of a reactionary compared with that of a revolutionary, which Hitler surely was. "Fortune is rightly indignant to those who break with the customs of the past," Churchill once wrote. He was entirely right. Unlike Churchill, Hitler was not a traditionalist. He also believed that many of the customs and institutions of the past deserved to be discarded — indeed, that the time had come for them to be broken, to his and Germany's advantage.

In this respect we ought to note how, with all of his half-American heritage and his great faith in the United States, Churchill was an old-

fashioned Europeanist. This was not true of many of the great statesmen of England, surely not of most of those in the twentieth century,
and absolutely not of the Chamberlainite Conservatives. Among
other matters, this may have been the essential difference between
them and Churchill. In 1935 Rothermere, who was an admirer of
Hitler's (while also respectful of Churchill's abilities), showed
Churchill a letter that Hitler had written him. Churchill answered
Rothermere: "If his [Hitler's] proposal means that we should come to
an understanding with Germany to dominate Europe, I think this
would be contrary to the whole of our history." Moreover — again
unlike many Englishmen — Churchill's vision of Europe, including
its essential inseparability from the destiny of Britain, was more than
strategic or political, it was cultural. In 1940, during their duel, Hitler
(and his propagandists) began to speak of a "new Europe" — that is,
a German-dominated and National Socialist one. But that was not
much more than propaganda at the time. Toward the end of the war
Hitler said that he was Europe's last hope. Did he believe what he was
saying? In any event, he was wrong.

There was one important matter in which Hitler's vision was
clearer than Churchill's. Churchill (and, as we shall see, Roosevelt,
though in a different way) still believed in the supremacy of sea
power. After all, that had made Britain and the Empire great. We also
know how experienced Churchill was in naval strategy, tactics,
equipment and planning. But relatively early in his life Hitler recognized the new and immense potentialities of the internal combustion
engine. He was interested in and liked automobiles throughout his
career. (He was the creator of the Autobahn as well as of the idea of a
"people's car," the Volkswagen.) He also understood something that
dawned on Churchill later: that the horrible slogging matches of mass
armies in the trenches of the First World War were an aberration, that
they would not recur. Hitler realized something that went even further than his recognition of a new warfare whose decisive instruments were to be rapid advances of motorized armor. He saw that
after five centuries the primacy of land power was replacing that of
sea power — in part because it had now become easier and faster to
move troops on land than by sea. Memories of how the British, because of their primacy on the seas, could sail rings around Napoleon's Europe and land in many places with impunity were strong in
Churchill's mind during both world wars. Yet these conditions existed no longer. This — and not only his wish to reach an accommodation with the British — was the main reason why Hitler chose to

limit the size of the German navy in the 1930s. (As late as 1939 the French navy alone was larger than the German one.) Very soon it became evident that Hitler's strategy was effective. Churchill began to recognize this during the Norway fiasco. "We, who had the command of the sea and could pounce anywhere on an undefended coast, were outpaced by the enemy moving by land across very large distances in the face of every obstacle." There is a historical parallel between Napoleon and Hitler standing at the Channel, contemplating an invasion of England from which both of them would recoil; but in Napoleon's time the obstacle to that was the existence of a British navy, whereas in 1940 the navy alone could not prevent a triumphant German landing in England. Of course no one, neither Hitler nor Churchill, saw this absolutely clearly in 1940. There was that other novel element of air power, the effectiveness of which first Hitler and then Churchill would overestimate. But that would not occur until after their eighty days' duel.

BOTH HITLER and Churchill were idealists, but in different ways. With all of his insistence on his personal comforts, with all of his interest and concentration on material factors and technical innovations, Churchill was not a materialist. The historical essence of his vision was so deeply rooted that it provided an excellent compound of idealism and realism (for it is idealism and materialism and not idealism and realism that are the true antitheses). Hitler's idealism was rooted in a certain German tradition, according to which history is the outcome of ideas; yet for many Germans this valuable and by no means untruthful recognition often leads, as in Hitler's case, to a categorical version of an idealist determinism, believing that ideas make men, without stopping to consider how it is men who make ideas. (An indication of how this inclination penetrated even Hitler's deepest obsession may be found in a statement that he made toward the end of his life, when he said that Jews are essentially less of a physical than a "spiritual" race.) In 1940 Hitler thought that the war was but a repetition, on a larger scale, of what had happened in Germany to bring him to power. At that time he and his National Socialists were bound to win, because their ideas were stronger than those of their opponents. The fact that during the street fighting in Weimar Germany a Nazi storm trooper was worth two or three of his Communist or Socialist opponents was a consequence of that. By 1940 Hitler came to believe that, in much the same way, one German soldier was worth two or three Polish or French (or perhaps British) soldiers, not only because of German equipment but because a German soldier of the Third Reich incarnated a national ideology that was stronger and better than those of his enemies.

There was some truth in this but not enough. One of the essential differences between Hitler and Churchill was this: the former was a nationalist, the latter a patriot. (During the last one hundred years these words have become regrettably confused, perhaps especially in American usage, where we speak of a superpatriot when what we mean is a supernationalist.)* There was another, not unrelated difference. Hitler — and this too was a German inclination — had a philosophy of history, whereas Churchill possessed something different, a historical philosophy. A philosophy of history is categorical and systematic; a historical philosophy, because of its very nature, is not. Many people, to this day, have not understood this. In a silly essay, and later in an insubstantial book, two British historians, Professors Rowse and Carr, compared Churchill to Trotsky, to Churchill's detriment, writing that Trotsky had a philosophy of history but Churchill had none. They did not see that it was precisely therefore that Trotsky but not Churchill proved to be a failure. (The great Swiss historian Jakob Burckhardt once wrote that "the philosophy of history is a centaur, a contradiction in terms, for history coordinates, and hence is unphilosophical, while philosophy subordinates, and hence is unhistorical.") We may perhaps go even further. We may recognize that while Hitler was a man of ideas, Churchill was, rather, a man of principles. ("A categorical idea," the old Metternich once wrote in a letter, "is like a fixed gun. . . . It is dangerous for those who stand or move along the line of its trajectory. Principles, on the other hand, may be compared to a gun that can turn around and fire at untruth in every direction.") Throughout the war Churchill's ideas often

---

* When Dr. Johnson said that "patriotism is the last refuge of a scoundrel," he meant nationalism, a word that did not appear in the English language until more than sixty years after his departure from the world. This is no place for a philosophical or philological disquisition of the differences between the two words, except to say that patriotism is essentially defensive, while nationalism is aggressive, and that the former is deeper rooted than the latter. Patriotism is not a substitute for a religious faith, whereas nationalism often is. It often fills the spiritual and even emotional needs of uprooted men. It is often the result of hatred; and as Chesterton wisely said, it is not love (which is personal and particular) but hatred that unites men — something that Hitler instinctively understood. "The jingo nationalist," as Churchill's faithful supporter Alfred Duff Cooper once wrote, "is always the first to denounce his fellow countrymen as traitors" — a truth very applicable to how Hitler and his party saw and dealt with their domestic opponents.

changed, much more than those of Hitler, who was prone to think of ideas as if they were principles, which was not true of Churchill.

When their great duel began, not much of this was clear. What was clear was that Hitler and National Socialist Germany represented more than an enormous and efficient military organization. They represented an armed force of ideas, not entirely unlike the French Revolution a century and a half before. Nevile Henderson, the last British ambassador to Germany, composed his memoirs in late 1939, soon after his departure from Berlin. Much of his book was explanatory and at least indirectly apologetic, since this ambassador had been a principal representative of appeasement, with strong personal pro-German inclinations. Yet it was not for the purpose of explaining himself that in his *Failure of a Mission* Henderson wrote that, much like the French Revolution, German National Socialism amounted to a new and powerful element in the history of Europe and the world. Hitler, of course, believed that, and in some ways so did Churchill. The difference — surely before September 1939 — was that Churchill, unlike Henderson, never for a moment thought that therefore Britain must come to terms with it. This is especially remarkable, since Churchill had been impressed earlier with the many failures of parliamentary democracies, which was one of the reasons why he spoke and wrote in favor of Mussolini in the twenties and extended the benefit of the doubt to him for a long time thereafter. (Hitler, on the other hand, with all of his genuine respect, loyalty and appreciation for Mussolini, was supposed to have said that Fascism was only a half-job.) In 1930 (the same year when we saw evidence of his early recognition of Hitler) Churchill wrote a preface to the London edition of a then timely and interesting book, entitled *Dictatorship on Trial,* by the Austrian political writer Otto Forst de Battaglia, which carried a motto by Mussolini and in which preface Churchill wrote that authoritarian national leaders (such as Mussolini in Italy or Kemal in Turkey or Pilsudski in Poland) might be a new and salutary alternative to the weakening, inefficient and increasingly unrepresentative parliamentary systems in many countries of Europe.

One of the matters Churchill understood was that words are not merely symbols of things; they are symbols of meanings. This brings this chapter, introducing the duel of Hitler and Churchill, to a last remark. The symbolic function of certain words sometimes applies to names of certain people, too. Like Honoré de Balzac and Edgar Allan Poe, this writer has a weakness for cognomology — that is, for the mysterious way in which a person's name becomes a representation of his character. Adolf Hitler himself said at least once that he was thankful for his name. He should have been thankful to his father, who thirteen years before Adolf's birth had changed his name from Schicklgruber (and Hiedler: both family names of his) to Hitler. Early in his youth Hitler said to his friend August Kubizek: "Schicklgruber seemed to him too crude, too peasant-like, and moreover too fussy and impractical. Hiedler was for him too tedious, too weak." A Bavarian-Austrian name such as Schicklgruber would have been a handicap for a politician bent on a German national career. But there was more than that. The name and the sound of Hitler was hard-hitting, direct, determined and cold. It had a cutting and chilly sound, and not only because of what we have come to associate with it.

The very sound and the shape of his name fitted Churchill, too. I thought about this in 1965 when I went to Churchill's funeral and wrote about it, perhaps exaggeratedly: "Pouting, aristocratic, flecked by sunlight. . . . The pout makes it human and humorous rather than churched. The pout merges, in a genial way, into the second syllable. There is nothing chilly about that final syllable; it is short, brilliant, a spring-like sound of a rill. The sound of the full name is both serious and humorous: it has a male charm about it; it is like the baroque fountains of Blenheim The shape of the name, too, like the shape of his body: compact, corpulent, but with the glimmer of a single jewel, jaunty. The fluted cylindrical second syllable giving clear form to the roundness of the first. Wearing his black 1940 hat, he looked like the dome of St. Paul's in 1940. Churchill." I recognize that this may be too much for some of my readers, and not only for historians reluctant to consider poetical expressions of imagination. I only ask them to consider that perhaps these are coincidences, too: "spiritual puns." In any event, in 1940 the names of Hitler and Churchill were becoming familiar to the vast majority of mankind. During the First World War there were millions of people in Europe and Russia (not to speak of the rest of the world) to whom the names of Clemenceau or Lloyd George or Hindenburg or Wilson were unknown. In May 1940 there were very few people in Europe, America and Asia who did not recognize the names of Hitler and Churchill. During the next few weeks more and more of them would recognize that these two men were not only the leading figures of their two warring nations but the two protagonists of the great world war that had at last begun to flame, dazzle and rage.

III

THE SLIPPERY SLOPE

11–31 May

FROM DAWN on the tenth of May the German and British armies were approaching each other. Hour by hour they drew closer. Somewhere in Belgium their first clash was imminent. More than eight months had passed since the declarations of war; yet, save for flashes of fire at sea, some in the air and a few skirmishes in the mountains of Norway, the armed forces of the German and the British peoples had not come face to face with each other. But now the time was fast drawing near to a test, perhaps the ultimate test, of two peoples.

The equipment and the organization of the German armed forces were excellent, better than those of the British and the French — indeed, perhaps the best in the world. That tells us something about Germany in 1940 that goes both beyond and beneath technical analyses of weapons or statistics. Napoleon once said that two thirds of the quality of an army depends on its morale and one third on its equipment. An army is an extrusion, an expression of a nation. That was as true in 1940 as it was 140 years earlier.

The German people were behind Hitler. That simple statement is essentially correct in the sense that it is surely not false. But history and human nature are much more complex than are the definite categories of mathematics or than the kind of logic that is but a verbal mathematics of sorts. The very meaning of "people" suggests — or, more precisely, it should for the historian suggest — a multitude of disputable matters.

The German people were healthy. In the physical sense of the word they were healthier than their opponents. They had recovered from the bloodbath of the First World War better and faster than the French and the English. In 1939 German women bore almost twice as many children as the French. The average age of the German population was younger than that of any other Western European nation. Most of these developments were long-standing: the demographic rise of the German and the relative decline of the French population had begun more than a century earlier. Yet it is also true that the first six years of the Third Reich filled many Germans with a surge of confidence — a condition that was reflected in facts such as the steep rise of their marriage rate, of their birth rate, and the drastic decline of their suicide rate, for example.

They were perhaps the best-educated people in the world. Their schools were excellent, their organization and curricula the models for many nations in Europe. Because of the dismissals of some of the professors after Hitler had come to power, the quality of some of their university faculties may have begun to decline, but their middle schools were not much affected by that. Already in 1871 Ernest Renan wrote that the victory of the Prussians at Sedan was the victory of the German schoolmasters — meaning that the young German soldiers were better educated than the French: an unusual admission by a Frenchman then. In 1918 British soldiers were disillusioned with their own generals, while they were impressed by many of the qualities of their German opponents. During that most murderous Battle of the Somme in 1916 it was not only evident that the German tactics and the organization of German defenses were much better than those of the British but that the standards and comforts of the German trenches were much better, too — in sum, that the soldiers of a repressive militarist autocracy were better cared for than those of a progressive and free empire, so often called "a nation of shopkeepers." Ten years after the war just about all of the British resentment of the Germans had evaporated. In the thirties all kinds of English visitors were impressed with the health, cleanliness and bearing of German youth, impressions that were much stronger than their negative impressions of the Hitlerian dictatorship — and evidences of the latter were apparent only to those who were determined to look for them.

Some of the less agreeable qualities of the German people continued to prevail. The German masses were well schooled, but the question may be raised: were they very intelligent? By this I mean the literal sense of the word — that is, the capacity and the willingness to read between the lines. That quality varied, of course, from person to person and from class to class, but it was not pervasive. The German tradition of the largely unquestioning acceptance of authority, including that of their national government, prevailed. It was an inclination inherited from the past. Their discipline and their rectitude, while most impressive at first sight, also contained a negative quality. That critical and skeptical acceptance of authority by a solitary person which is the mark of true individuality but also that of civic freedom and mental integrity was not among the principal German qualities. Most Germans were obedient because they were unsure of the virtue of individuality. They were also, by and large, a humorless people. There were many exceptions to this: but the sense of humor that is more than a sense of the comic — that is, more than the human need for occasional laughter, for the Germans could roar with laughter as well as any other people — that encompasses a kind of self-knowledge together with its foibles, was not widespread among the Germans. In his *History of Germany in the Nineteenth Century* the great German historian Heinrich von Treitschke wrote this ponderous sentence: "The German jokes with difficulty." Neither he nor his readers thought that such a sentence was funny (or even odd).

Such inclinations, as is often the case with the national characteristics of a people, were long-range and enduring. But in the 1930s Hitler and his rule brought something new to their character and behavior. His achievements filled the German people with a newly found confidence. That confidence was not only the result of his foreign successes and conquests, even though those contributed to the national feeling that being a German meant once again, perhaps even more than before, to be powerful and respected throughout the world. Even before Hitler in 1938 began the territorial expansion of the Third Reich, much of the 1930s were a sunny decade for most Germans. Because of his disdain for economic theories (principally because of his insightful contempt for the idea of Economic Man) Hitler had brought them prosperity, out of the depression and despair of the last Weimar years. That was almost unique in the history of modern dictatorships and surely different from Communism: it was substantial and real. This prosperity spread among all classes of Germans — which was one, though only one, of the reasons why many of the most unquestioning and committed believers in Hitler came from the German working classes. The other, allied reason for that was a characteristic of the Hitler regime that is even now denied or obscured by many historians. It was democratic, and it was modern. It was democratic in the sense that Hitler and the Nazis were votaries of a new classless society; of a state rising out of the *Volk;* of a unified welfare state that was, in almost every sense of the word, anti-traditionalist. Among the Germans the Nazis were both brutal and easygoing. They had none of the punctilious seriousness, none of the rigid frozen faces of the old civil service but, rather, a contemptuous (and, on occasion, contemptible) sense of humor — at the expense of others, of course. It was modern, because Hitler and the Nazis believed in the superb potential of German technology — while their racial philosophy itself was the outcome not of old prejudices but of certain discoveries of "modern" biological science. They propagated the systematic breeding of German children less for the sake of the family than for that of the *Volk;* their vision of a healthy German youth was athletic, open-air, agricultural, yes, but also motorized. During the past fifty years entire libraries have been written about the Hitler era, including many valuable historical analyses. Yet I found one of the most telling observations in the notes of that deeply intelligent English observer and writer, Robert Byron, as he saw from close up the Nuremberg party rally in September 1938:

> One reflects: this is undoubtedly democracy. But it is one which postulates, not the rational being judging questions for himself, but the emotional creature subordinating his judgment to the mass instinct. Both are true, but this system puts humanity on a much lower plane . . . the whole ceremonial is of a remarkable kind. It is certainly that of a democracy rather than of a tyranny — there's no cringing or bowing and a general ease pervaded the Führer's entourage. And it is new in that it incorporates, indeed, is based on, the last resources of the age — floodlighting, relaying, motorcars — and does them without being shoddy, because these devices are the essence of it. I haven't seen a horse — not one. Is this being explained by the fact that the Führer doesn't ride?

(On another ceremonial occasion someone on Hitler's staff suggested that he mount a horse. That was ridiculous, he said. He would arrive in his automobile.)

That Hitler stood for something that was dangerously anti-traditional and very radical occurred to not many among the otherwise tradition-respecting German people, including many of those who ought to have known better. This is what I meant when I wrote of a certain want of discriminating intelligence that would eventually reveal a want of character. Most of the German conservatives went along with Hitler. They would, privately and on occasion, tut-tut about some of his excesses; but more than often they had neither the courage nor the conviction to oppose them. Among all of the traditional institutions in Germany the Catholic Church had, relatively speaking, the most respectable (or, to be more precise, the least disreputable) record during the Hitler era. But Hitler, who had a respect for the influence of the Catholic Church, including masses of German Catholics, knew how to treat its hierarchs. Twenty days before his invasion of Western Europe in 1940 the Conference of German Bishops, meeting in Fulda, led by Cardinal Adolf Bertram of Breslau, sent a fulsome congratulatory telegram to Hitler on the occasion of his fifty-first birthday. Hitler found it both welcome and politic to answer. "I am especially pleased," he wrote, "by the expression of your convictions that the efforts of the Catholic Church to maintain the Christian characteristics of the German people are not in conflict with the program of the National Socialist Party."

It could be argued — and, here and there, even proved — that even in 1940, at the time of his most dazzling successes, not more than a minority of the German people were convinced Hitlerites. But this does not mean that their majority were opposed to Hitler. (Conversely, it may be argued that even though convinced opponents of Hitler were but a very small minority, this does not mean that the majority of the German people were convinced Nazis.) These are matters for which the mathematical formulations of public opinion research are inadequate. Human nature is not as simple as that.

The elemental hate that moved Hitler was shared by few Germans in 1940. They were much less enthusiastic about the war in September 1939 than they and their fathers had been in August 1914. Yet they were inclined to accept what Hitler told them: that this war was an ineluctable struggle against Germany's foreign enemies. And that largely unquestioning acceptance was sufficient for the formidable cohesion and discipline that made the German army in 1940 the most efficient in the history of the modern world, and the most striking, if not altogether irresistible, instrument for the purposes of their national leader.

IN HIS headquarters Hitler contemplated the progress of the German armies. He was confident but also anxious. There were reasons for his confidence. The crushing of Dutch resistance in the north was going in accord with the plans, indeed, running ahead of the original timetable. Even more important was the northward movement of the French and British troops in Belgium. They had not yet met the advancing units of the German army, except in isolated instances, here and there. But they were falling into his trap: the Sickle-Cut would cut them off. But when, and how? In a superbly planned and daring descent German troops had captured the principal Belgian fortress in the east of that country. Through the wooded hills of the Ardennes German armor was threading its way to the west. But it had not yet debouched from those forests and hills. Not until late Monday, perhaps Tuesday, would they come face to face with the French. Hitler hoped that his army would break through them; but he was not yet sure. During those first days of the Western European campaign he spoke relatively little. He depended on his generals; he had to trust them, as he had in Poland eight months before.

On 10 May the British government canceled the Whitsun holiday schedule. Yet there remained something of that long, three-day weekend that was not quite washed away by the torrent of events across the Channel. On Sunday night the hum of traffic in London receded into silence, like the echo of a great bourdon bell. It was not until early on Monday, the thirteenth, that dramatic news began to gather. At five o'clock that morning the telephone woke King George VI. Queen Wilhelmina of Holland called him, pleading for help. She asked for more British planes. The king could do nothing but transmit her message to the government. Later that day the Dutch court and cabinet were fleeing to London. It would be five years before they would return to their country. (In Holland, too, lived the exiled German kaiser William II. That day Churchill offered him a refuge in England. William refused to move. He would soon see a German troop saluting him in his courtyard. He would eventually see the Paris he had not been able to conquer conquered by Hitler's Germans. He showed no sympathy for the tribulations of his hosts, the Dutch, now under German rule. He died a year later.)

Three days had passed since Churchill had become prime minister. That Monday afternoon he addressed the House of Commons in that capacity. It was one of his shortest speeches, of which one famous phrase lives on: "I have nothing to offer but blood, toil, tears and sweat." (There is some evidence that he first said these words to his ministers, whom he had called to Admiralty House that morning.) The historian A. J. P. Taylor wrote about the speech that it "combined echoes of Garibaldi and Clemenceau." Yet what those words, on 13 May 1940, resembled were the words of the then largely unknown George Orwell, who a few weeks before that wrote in an obscure little magazine an article about Hitler and *Mein Kampf.* "Whereas Socialism, and even capitalism in a more grudging way, have said to people, 'I offer you a good time,' Hitler has said to them, 'I offer you struggle, danger and death,' and as a result a whole nation flings itself at his feet." But it is doubtful whether Churchill had read that article.

That he read the mood, and the characteristic temperament, of the English people well enough is fairly clear. (Months later, in October, he remarked: "I always hesitate to say anything of an optimistic nature, because our people do not mind being told the worst.") But he also knew something that in those days (and, as we shall see, for some time thereafter) was equally, or perhaps even more, important. He could read this on the faces of most members of the Conservative Party when he first appeared in the House of Commons that afternoon. They disliked him. The Labour members, by and large, cheered Churchill, but most Conservatives sat on their hands. Churchill was not well received. Chamberlain was. When Chamberlain entered a moment after Churchill, the members "lost their heads; they shouted, they cheered; they waved their Order Papers, and his reception was a regular ovation." The distrust of Churchill was evident even among some of those who five days before had allowed themselves to be carried away by the then sentiments of the House and had not voted for Chamberlain. Some of them were, at least a little, shamefaced; they wished to demonstrate their loyalty to their former prime minister and their party leader. Their dislike of Churchill was at least equal to their affection for Chamberlain.

It would be a mistake to attribute these inclinations solely to a few stodgy members of a stodgy party in Parliament, who had been elected in 1935, at a time when the political climate and the mood of the people had been quite different, in a past that by 1940 had become very remote. Among the governmental and political and social elite of Britain the inclinations to doubt Churchill were more widespread than that. Those inclinations went from a sense of uneasiness to outright loathing; and they existed among people of different positions and situations. The Foreign Office had, generally speaking, a better record in assessing the German danger than other government departments. But even there the stiff Alexander Cadogan, the principal adviser to the foreign secretary (of an aristocratic family, the first earl of which had fought with Churchill's great ancestor Marlborough at Blenheim and Ramillies), wrote in his diary on 9 May that he could not think of a premier who would be better than Chamberlain; and on 11 May: "I'm afraid that Winston will build up a 'Garden City' at No. 10, of the most awful people." R. A. ("Rab") Butler, the undersecretary of state at the Foreign Office, who in November 1939 had told Chamberlain's private secretary that Churchill was "vulgar," now told Colville that Churchill as prime minister was "a disaster. . . . They had weakly surrendered to a half-breed American whose main support was that of inefficient but talkative people of a similar type." Even at the Admiralty, where Churchill was liked, the deputy director of operations of the Home Fleet, a Captain Edwards, wrote: "Winston is Prime Minister. . . . I distrust the man and think it is a tragedy." Maurice Hankey, a minister without portfolio in Chamberlain's government, told Samuel Hoare on Sunday that Churchill was "a rogue elephant," difficult to hold in check. Churchill kept John Colville for his secretary. Soon this charming and well-bred young man would change his mind about Churchill, but not yet. A sentence in his diary of 13 May is telling. The new prime minister "made a brilliant little speech." But also: "I spent the day in a bright blue suit from the Fifty-Shilling Tailors, cheap and sensational looking, which I felt was appropriate to the new Government."

Much of this reluctance to credit Churchill was personal, entertained by men and women who did not like him and his "crowd." Much of this was still the result of the momentum from a past distrust of what they saw as his grandiloquence and unsteadiness. Fortunately for Britain, few of his opponents had gone so far as to question not only his capacity for leadership but the very purpose of the war against Germany. One of these people was David Lloyd George, to whom Churchill now offered the post of minister of agriculture, which he declined. This was curious, since Churchill knew Lloyd George's opposition to the war. After the war Mrs. Churchill said how greatly relieved she had been when Lloyd George did not accept. One may presume that Churchill's offer — which would be repeated later — may have been a result of his loyalty: of memories of his collaboration with Lloyd George a world war earlier, as well as of political calculation.

A measure of magnanimity and of calculation marked Churchill's construction of his new Cabinet. His generous treatment of Neville Chamberlain prevailed. It was not only that Chamberlain remained a principal member of Churchill's War Cabinet. ("To a large extent I am in your hands," Churchill wrote Chamberlain late at night on 10 May.) He also told Chamberlain and Mrs. Chamberlain not to move from 10 Downing Street but to stay there comfortably for at least a month — a fine offer that Churchill tendered before it would appear that Chamberlain was ill. It took Churchill several days to form his new Cabinet, in which twenty-one out of the thirty-six ministerial posts would still be held by Chamberlain appointees. Churchill would not indulge in political revenge, partly because he knew its dangers to national unity, partly because of his character. He booted out very few people. Among them was Chamberlain's gray eminence, the Germanophile appeaser Horace Wilson. Wilson stayed around Downing Street on 11 May, when Churchill let him know that his presence was no longer wanted. (Some people pretended to know that Churchill threatened to appoint Wilson minister of Iceland. He made good use in sending some of his enemies abroad; it was thus, for example, that Samuel Hoare, a great intriguer and opportunist, would be sent as British ambassador to Spain, where he acquitted himself honorably.) But Churchill knew how thin were the ranks of his political supporters. "If one were dependent on the people who had been right in the last few years, what a tiny handful one would have to depend on," he later said. Churchill made himself minister of defence. That was a new post, at which he could control the main course of the war.

Outside political circles he had had enthusiastic supporters among some of the personalities of *tout Londres*. The fact that they included such men as Noël Coward, Ivor Novello and Philip Guedalla, with their reputation of superficial and perhaps frivolous smartness, was held against Churchill by men and women who thought him to be insubstantial and unduly theatrical. There were intellectuals of a high caliber who supported Churchill enthusiastically, but they were depressed by the prospect of defeat, more so than many other people. Among them was Harold Nicolson, who wrote in his diary on 15 May: "What I mind are the mornings. I wake up at dawn and am left alone with all my fears. I am depressed to an extent which I have never been depressed in my life. Is it personal fear? Partly it is. But it is really the fear of defeat." On 14 May Arnold Toynbee wrote to a friend, Abbot Columba: "Well, Hitler has staked everything, and we

must face the possibility that he may win and that Religion and Freedom may be suppressed all over Europe — temporarily, but for a time
that might still run into hundreds of years. If we can stem the tide,
then I should say Germany was certain to collapse before the end of
next winter." He may or may not have been right about the "possibility"; he was surely wrong about the "certainty."

　　Churchill knew that he had the trust of the common people of
Britain — at least for a while. He also knew that he, and they, must be
prepared for the long haul. On 11 May there was a gathering of people around 10 Downing Street, shouting, "Good luck, Winnie. God
bless you." "Poor people," Churchill said softly to Lord Ismay. "I can
give them nothing but disaster for quite a long time." When he entered the building his eyes were rimmed with tears.

IN FIVE days the Germans conquered all of Holland. In six days
they were across half of Belgium. By that time they had broken the
French front. They poured out from the foothills of the Ardennes.
The French Second Army failed to halt their crossing of the broad
Meuse River at Dinant and Sedan. (Only a week before, the commander of that army, General Huntziger, told the mayor of Sedan
that the Germans "will never think of attacking in the sector of
Sedan." A few years before, Marshal Pétain had written that the Ardennes was "impenetrable.") The Germans swept the French aside.
Six days after the tenth of May they were well west of the Meuse,
more than halfway to the Channel, and driving fast. At times their
motorized troops had no time to collect French prisoners; they
waved them off. Such a humiliating scene made Charles de Gaulle
feel "borne up by a limitless fury." In that moment the entire purpose
of his life changed. "All I have managed to do was resolved upon that
day." But he was, as yet, light-years removed from the mastery of
events.

　　This was a new kind of war. The previous one had been fought by
enormous masses of soldiers struggling for a few square miles. During
the First World War the advancing armies picked up the frontier posts
and tried to move them forward, like armed settlers. During the Second World War they were driving ahead, like armed tourists. During
the First World War the spearheads (where they existed at all) were
blunt little spikes closely welded to the massive body of the army.
During the Second World War the spearheads were really spearheads:

they were flying ahead. Their job was to impress that they *were* the conquering armies, en masse — and in many ways they were. Often they succeeded not only in impressing frightened masses of civilians but also masses of bewildered enemy soldiers. This explains the enormous bag of prisoners that small armored and motorized units of infantry could pretend to encircle and then collect. (Thus the Germans would capture 1.9 million French soldiers during the forty days after 10 May.)

Hitler knew that this was a new kind of war. Churchill did not. As early as 1932 Hitler was supposed to have said: "The next war will be quite different from the last world war. Infantry attacks and mass formations are obsolete. Interlocked frontal struggles lasting for years on petrified fronts will not return. I guarantee that. They were a degenerate form of war." After the war Churchill confessed his initial ignorance. "The idea of the line being broken, even on a broad front, did not convey to my mind the appalling consequences that now flowed from it. . . . I did not comprehend the violence of the revolution effected since the last war by the incursion of a mass of fast-moving heavy armour. I knew about it, but it had not altered my inward convictions as it should have done." There was another great handicap in his mind. He deceived himself because of his affection for the French, an inclination swelled further by the sentimental side of his character. In August 1939 he gave an interview in Paris, having returned from the Maginot Line. That line was a guarantee of "absolute security," he said, "against the horrors of invasion, not only through its impregnable fortifications but also through the brave and efficient soldiers who man them. I was particularly struck by the alert and intelligent appearance of the French soldiers." The memory of such statements would haunt him soon. His enemy Hitler disliked, if not altogether hated, the French ever since he had first read about them in his childhood. Later in the war he would underestimate their ability to rise again; but in 1940 his underestimation was warranted.

On the fourteenth of May, Tuesday, Churchill and the War Cabinet began to receive more and more ominous news from northern France. Holland had already fallen; and the left wing of the French army that had moved up there was recoiling fast. These worrisome developments were now replaced by a darker cloud of news about the break of the French front along the Meuse. The War Cabinet met several times that day. The slow bombers of the Royal Air Force had flown out to destroy the German pontoons and other bridges across the Meuse, but they failed. By the end of the day half of the British planes in France had been destroyed. At seven in the evening Paul Reynaud, the French prime minister — a small, dapper, energetic Anglophile political figure who was committed to the British and who trusted and admired Churchill — telephoned with more bad news. His appeals for more British planes put Churchill in a dilemma. Soon those planes would be needed for the defense of Britain. There was the allied consideration that to throw more planes into the skies over the great land battles in France had already proved largely ineffective, especially when the French were losing on the ground and retreating. On the other hand the British government could not afford not to respond to the "incessant, vehement" appeals for help from the French government. What would happen if not only one or two of the French armies but the French government would crack? It was in the British interest to keep the French fighting.

Shortly after seven next morning (the fifteenth) the telephone rang at Churchill's bedside. At that very unaccustomed hour it was Reynaud again. He spoke in English, rapidly. His first sentence was: "We have been defeated." Churchill, hardly awake, was silent at first. Reynaud went on: "We are beaten; we have lost the battle." Churchill started to respond. He tried to calm Reynaud. The French premier repeated the words: "defeated," "lost the battle." He was not only under stress; he was compelled to impress Churchill with the suddenness of an abyss opening up before Paris. Churchill said that he would fly over to Paris.

Next day he flew there in the early afternoon. From the moment he landed he knew that the situation was much worse than he had thought, that Reynaud's phrases were not merely attributable to the excitable temperament of a Frenchman. Two things impressed Churchill particularly. He would return to them often later. One was the black cloud of smoke he saw rising from the courtyard of the French Foreign Ministry on the Quai d'Orsay. It was a beautiful, brilliant day, with a cloudless sky over the sun-stroked walls and streets and stones of Paris; but in that courtyard clerks were burning packets of documents, with black bits of paper fluttering across the Seine. What this meant was that the French government was preparing to leave Paris. This was, then, confirmed to Churchill by the words of General Maurice Gamelin, the French commander in chief, whose cat-like face was frozen rigid by the knowledge of his helplessness. There was nothing between the advancing Germans and Paris, he said. The bulk of the French army? The reserve army? Churchill asked. Where is it? There is none, Gamelin said. Churchill sat, argued, stood up, walked around, "crowned like a volcano by some of his cigars." He kept telling the French — not for the last time — that things were never as bad as they seemed, that England would go on fighting, no matter what happened. Reynaud was grateful for that. He asked for more British fighter squadrons. Churchill had agreed to four — now he raised to ten. But by that time he knew that he would or could offer no more. He realized that, contrary to what the French military were saying, this new kind of motorized warfare could not be defeated from the air. More important, he already knew that in no circumstances could he commit more of the Royal Air Force outside Britain. That morning he had read Air Marshal Hugh Dowding's letter. Dowding wrote that the existence of an adequate fighter force was the only way through which Britain would "be able to carry on the war single-handed for some time, if not indefinitely . . . [but if that] is drained away in desperate attempts to remedy the situation in France, defeat in France will involve the final, complete, and *irremideable* defeat of this country." That crucial word "irremediable" was slightly misspelled in the letter and corrected by Dowding's pen. It was a crucial document, of the greatest importance in the long run.

Churchill kept his composure during this day of disaster. He was fairly good-humored during those dismal hours. He went to bed very late, at two A.M. He told his retinue to be ready to leave at six; but then he kept them waiting in the Paris morning till seven. He had slept soundly. Then they flew home. He met the War Cabinet at the early hour of ten A.M., telling them everything he had learned in Paris. He had learned fast. He said to the Cabinet: "It was now plain why the Allied troops had not been bombed in their advance into Belgium; the Germans had wanted to get us into forward positions in order to effect a break through and turn our flanks." That was exactly what the Sickle-Cut had been about. Churchill had now begun to understand something of the new kind of warfare. He now understood the great design of Hitler's war plan better than the French generals, whose entire careers should have been dedicated to the purpose of understanding it. That was all to the good. But that very comprehension of the power of his opponent, while clarifying his mind, darkened his spirits. After the Cabinet he went to a luncheon at the Japanese embassy. By the end of that full day he was depressed. In the close circle of his secretaries he gave vent to his fears that the once much vaunted French army might crumble and be crushed by the Germans as the Poles had been.

That was the end of that Friday, the seventeenth of May. We now know that it was also the end of what, in essence, was the decisive phase of the Western European campaign. It all happened within a week. The French were routed; and they would not recover. Churchill sensed this strongly now. Hitler did not. The very success of the German advance worried him. It was all too good to be true — including his plan, including his trust in the thrust of German armor. He became restless. He decided, for the first time in this campaign, to see his generals. At one in the afternoon he was driven from the Rock Eyrie to a small airfield and flew to General Gerd von Rundstedt's headquarters (Army Group A), then at Bastogne, the village whose name would enter American history four and a half years later. Hitler impressed some of his generals and surprised others. He said that the rapid advance toward the Channel was not the most important matter. It may even have to be slowed down temporarily. The south side of the German wedge stretching beyond the Meuse was the most important matter. It must be strengthened with "absolutely reliable defensive" measures. There *must* not be an Allied counterattack. The importance of that, he said, went beyond military effects; it was "political and psychological. Under no circumstances must a setback occur . . . that would give a fateful rise to the [spirit] of our enemies, not alone to their military but, above all, to their political leadership." In the absence of such a setback the English would realize that they must leave the Continent. Then he would make peace with them. He spoke briefly, cut the conversation off and returned to the Rock Eyrie before supper. That evening General Franz Halder, his chief of staff, wrote in his diary that "the Führer was nervous. He is worried by his own success, he does not want to risk things further."

He need not have fretted himself. That day the British retreated from Brussels without a fight. A Spanish diplomat negotiated the surrender of the Belgian capital to the Germans. A week had passed: and the British army had not yet had a serious clash with the Germans.

THE PICTURE that many people, including historians, still have of the Duel is that of an impatient Hitler, fired by his successes and ambitions, confronted across the English Channel by a stout Churchill, composed and determined, husbanding his energy for both the long run and for the greatest of tests soon to come. That impression is not altogether false; but for that fateful May in 1940 it is not altogether correct. Long before 1940 some of Churchill's friends remarked that Churchill's main fault was impatience. To that we may add that his impatience was the kind that results from a quickness of mind; and he, unlike most of his countrymen, had a very quick mind. That is often a handicap for a politician, not always an asset for a statesman and rarely an asset for a diplomat — to wit, Talleyrand's famous admonition: *surtout pas trop de zèle,* above all, no excessive enthusiasm, no hurry, please.

Indeed, Churchill was not the best of diplomats. Toward the end of the war his waning physical energy, his occasional impatience and the earlier mentioned innate handicap of a writer whose immediate satisfaction by expressing his concerns in a strong and clear prose compromises his subsequent willingness and energy to pursue these concerns through long and often wearisome negotiations — these were evident in his failures to carry his wishes through against Stalin and especially against Roosevelt. But this was the beginning of the war, and those dynamic bursts of an impatient energy were often advantageous. They were advantageous not only because his impatient insistences were directed, even though in short spurts, to an amazing variety of matters involving the preparation, organization and morale of Britain's defense. They involved, necessarily, matters of the greatest importance, including the relationship of the world's Great Powers to a Britain that seemed to slide with increasing speed down the slope of a great and unprecedented defeat. Less than one week after Hitler's Western European offensive had started, that impression of a Franco-British defeat had begun to gather in the capitals of the world: in Mussolini's Rome first of all, while in Roosevelt's Washington the progress of that perception was more complex and slow.

Perception is a component of reality, and not its subsequent rationalization: a message, not a package. Strange as that seems in retrospect, during the 1930s Mussolini's Italy was a Great Power, indeed, more important than the Soviet Union: because this was what people, including the leading statesmen of the world, had then thought. In 1935 and 1936, for example, the fact that France lost the possible support of Italy in the face of Germany while France concluded an alliance with the Soviet Union was a definite loss in the balance of the Great Powers, not a gain. A Franco-Italian alliance could have obstructed Hitler's annexation of Austria, the first and crucial item on Hitler's agenda of territorial expansion, whereas (as indeed proved to be the case) the Franco-Soviet alliance was entirely ineffective, well before Stalin would choose, in 1939, to make a deal with Hitler.

Churchill in 1935 did not oppose Italy's ambitions to extend its empire in East Africa, including its conquest of Ethiopia, especially if that kind of British acquiescence would keep Mussolini from choosing to side with Hitler. There was more to that too. Churchill respected, in some ways even liked, Mussolini. He had met Mussolini twice in the twenties, when they got along well. In some of his journalism he wrote about Mussolini approvingly. Even after the Second World War, when he had every reason to dismiss or malign him, some of these memories remained. He remembered how, in the early 1920s, he "with difficulty escaped the highest [Italian] decoration" that had been offered him by Mussolini. He never regarded Mussolini's Fascist dictatorship as anything like Hitler's brutal one; he recognized some of its salutary reforms. He also wrote — and in his volume about 1940 — that "in the conflict of Fascism and Bolshevism there was no doubt where my sympathies and convictions lay."

However, Mussolini by 1936 concluded that he had better side with Hitler than with the British and the French. He had, after all, more in common with Hitler's new, modern, nationalist dictatorship than with the corrupt and antiquated parliamentary democracies. He also believed that the British had become brittle and weak. Chamberlain's strenuous and sometimes undue attempt to appease him only fortified that impression. He told his son-in-law Galeazzo Ciano, whom he had made foreign minister, that these were not the same Britons who had made the Empire: they were but the last in a line of tired old men whose virility was hopelessly sapped. In May 1939 the Rome-Berlin Axis (Mussolini's own term) evolved into a military alliance with Germany, a "Pact of Steel."

That was a grandiloquent phrase; and, at least for a while, it did not matter unduly. We have seen earlier that he tried to dissuade Hitler from going to war over Poland. Thus in September 1939 Italy was a nonbelligerent. Then, in March 1940, Mussolini told Hitler that he had decided to bring Italy into the war. Yet as late as 2 May, eight days before the German invasion of Western Europe, the British Cabinet was pleased to learn that the British minister in Rome had just had a "cordial interview" with Count Ciano; they also learned of Ciano's remark to the French ambassador in Rome that "the Allies need not expect Italy to take any action if things went well for them." If, however, Germany had more military successes, "he could promise nothing." All through the month of May men and women of Roman high society, friendly to the West, kept telling their French and British conversants that all the Allies needed to show was one small military triumph, *una piccola vittoria*: that might influence everything, even Mussolini's mind. That mind, however, could be as quick as Churchill's — though, unlike Churchill's, not always to his ultimate advantage. Three days after Hitler's offensive had begun Mussolini made up his mind. He saw what was happening: the French and the British would be defeated; they were already defeated. It was his duty to range Italy with his German ally before it was too late.

Churchill knew what was coming. Whatever the value of his earlier relationship with Mussolini may have been, he discounted that. In this respect it is interesting to note that the historic letter that Churchill composed on 16 May and sent to Mussolini was not a result of his impulse; it was Halifax, his foreign secretary, who two days earlier suggested that he do so. That letter was a curious combination of hardheadedness and romanticism. "Whatever may happen on the Continent, England will go on to the end, even quite alone, as we have done before. . . . Down the ages above all other calls comes the cry that the joint heirs of Latin and Christian civilisation must not be ranged against one another in mortal strife" — an expression of Churchill the European. As Churchill wrote after the war: "The response was hard. It had at least the merits of candour." Mussolini answered instantly. "If it was to honour your signature that your Government declared war on Germany, you will understand that the same sense of honour and of respect for engagements assumed in the Italian-German Treaty guides Italian policy today and tomorrow in the face of any event whatsoever." Stripped of its grandiloquence, that sentence made it clear to Churchill that Italy's entry into the war was irreversible, and coming soon. It also revealed an important element in Mussolini's mind. He knew how the German peoples had not much confidence in Italian military valor, and that in their minds lived the memories of Italian faithlessness that had been shown in Italy's turning against its erstwhile German ally during the First World War — together with the still present Italian nonbelligerence. He had to show that his new Italy was no longer a cunning and calculating secondary partner but a strong and steadfast ally. In this the historian may detect for the first time a subtle, or not so subtle, reversal of the relationship of Mussolini to Hitler. Before that time Hitler's respect for Mussolini was greater than Mussolini's admiration for Hitler. Now Mussolini felt compelled to prove that he was an equal and not an inferior.

Hitler had admired Mussolini ever since the latter had assumed power in Italy in 1922, at a time when Hitler was at the beginning of his political career. In order to maintain Mussolini's friendship Hitler would even abandon a cause that was dear to German and Austrian hearts: despite his insistence on German folkish unity he would not support the German-speaking people in the South Tyrol, which had been allotted to Italy in 1919. In 1938 Mussolini gave his tacit support to Hitler when the latter annexed Austria and his active support during Munich when Hitler destroyed Czechoslovakia. With all of his faults (if that is the *mot juste,* which I fear it is not) Hitler was not devoid of loyalty. When Mussolini accepted Hitler's occupation of Austria, Hitler wrote him: "Mussolini, I shall never forget that." In this he was as good as his word. In 1943 he ordered the daring mission to rescue Mussolini, who was interned on an Italian mountaintop. Yet long before 1943 Hitler's opinion of the quality of his ally Italy had dropped to a very low level. He respected Mussolini; he had no respect for the Italians. Some of this was already evident in May 1940 — that is, before the poor quality of the Italian military would show up in their campaign against France. When on 29 May Mussolini told him that Italy would declare war on France and Britain on 5 June, Hitler acknowledged this with some satisfaction, but he cared little about it. He did not need the Italians to win his war.

HITLER DID not need an ally to prevail in this war; but Churchill did. He needed an ally for a future victory; but in May 1940 that kind of a future had suddenly become remote. Unlike Hitler, Churchill now needed an ally for the sake of survival: for the survival of a Britain that, at least at that time, was a cause inseparable from his own survival as its leader. That ally was no longer France. It was the United States of America. Even without France, Churchill's Britain could — perhaps — survive in the short run. Without the United States — at least in the long run — Britain could not.

Hitler understood much, though not all, of this. It is a common error to believe that Hitler was both ignorant of and indifferent to the United States. He did not care for the political system of the United States (to say the least), but he was well aware of its potential power and of its geopolitical situation. In his early youth he read stories about the American West avidly. There is evidence (to be sure, some of it questionable) that as early as 1931 he knew much more about American politics than he is credited with even now. There is definite evidence that he was both well informed about and interested in various currents in Washington, mostly about the existence of certain influential persons, especially those isolationists who respected his new Germany. He often read the reports of General Friedrich von Boetticher, the German military attaché in Washington, who cultivated excellent contacts with American generals of the Army General Staff there.

At the same time Hitler knew that there was little he could do to influence American political leadership at its highest level. At the latest by January 1939 he became convinced that President Roosevelt was his outright enemy. He was not wrong in thinking that. It was during the winter of 1938–39 that Roosevelt began to take an active interest in European politics. Secretly, surreptitiously working through his confidant ambassadors (foremost among them William C. Bullitt, in Paris), Roosevelt began to intimate his support of politicians in Paris and London who were willing to stand up to Hitler. The latter knew that. By the time the war broke out he was also aware of the contacts between Roosevelt and Churchill. He attributed much of that to the influence of American Jewish circles on Roosevelt. His hatred for Roosevelt grew during the war. What he, at least in May 1940, did not quite comprehend was how much the British depended on the Americans: as yet, less on their material or military support than on the effects — meaning the worldwide perception — of an American commitment to range themselves on the British side, sooner or later.

Roosevelt's inclination to support the British against Hitler preceded his particular relationship with Churchill. As early as June 1939 — during and immediately after the visit of King George VI and Queen Elizabeth to the United States — he suggested a close and clandestine naval cooperation with Britain, in exchange for the British granting the rights to American naval bases on two of their Caribbean islands and on Bermuda. His suggestion took the British by surprise. Neither the Foreign Office nor the State Department were informed of these secret arrangements until later. During the Reluctant War American naval patrols in the western Atlantic passed reports of German ship movements to the British. Chamberlain was aware of this. His earlier skepticism of the United States (and particularly of Roosevelt) vanished as soon as the war had begun. That certain kind of instinct that has always been an important, though hidden, asset among British officials and civil servants (and among the people, too) on all levels — that is, an instinctive understanding of the vital interests of their country on certain occasions — kept functioning during those cloudy months. (One example appears in a memorandum of the British Chiefs of Staff in October 1939 — that is, well before the Soviet attack on Finland. It stated that the Allies could not really help Finland, but "the one strong argument for action was that it would win the sympathy of ... the U.S.A. [which] would outweigh the enmity of Russia." The Chiefs of Staff must have been aware of the ties of an anti-Communist ideology that bound many isolationists, Republicans and the Hearst press together.) At the end of 1939 Churchill himself recognized that the isolationists "gathered unexpected strength" in the United States. By that time his special relationship with Roosevelt, manifest in their secret correspondence, had begun. Secret as it was, Chamberlain knew of this relationship, as did a few high officials in the Foreign Office. Contrary to his earlier inclinations, he did not much mind it by then.

Roosevelt and Churchill had met in London in 1918 when Roosevelt was assistant secretary of the navy. He recalled that meeting in 1939 and 1940 (Churchill seems to have forgotten it — this bothered Roosevelt's vanity, at least for a while). In June 1939 when the king and queen met Roosevelt in the United States, Roosevelt's (at times self-appointed) adviser Justice Felix Frankfurter was in England, where he met Churchill. He was impressed with Churchill's resolution to fight Hitler, if and when he must. Yet it is not clear whether Frankfurter's report to Roosevelt was instrumental in the latter's decision to start a personal correspondence with Churchill in September 1939, after Churchill had become First Lord of the Admiralty in Chamberlain's War Cabinet. Surely it was an unusual practice of a head of state to correspond directly and secretly with a member of the cabinet of another government. On the English side this caused few problems, since this somewhat extraordinary correspondence was conducted with the full knowledge, indeed with the tacit encouragement, of Chamberlain and Halifax. There *were* problems on the American side, to which I shall presently turn.

Before that, we must keep in mind that Roosevelt's assessment of Churchill's character was, as yet, not unequivocal. We saw that Sumner Welles, another Roosevelt confidant, reported in March 1940 that Churchill was unsteady and drinking too much. Five days before the tenth of May Welles talked with Adolf Berle, an assistant secretary of state. Berle thought that Churchill might be too old and "tired"; Welles said that he did not quite trust Churchill's ability to govern. The day after Churchill became prime minister, this news was discussed in the White House. Harold Ickes, the secretary of the interior, noted in his diary: "Apparently Churchill is very unreliable under the influence of drink." Roosevelt said that he "supposed Churchill was the best man England had." But Frances Perkins, his secretary of labor, remembered that Roosevelt was "uncertain" about Churchill, asking his cabinet members "what kind of a man" Churchill really was. Ickes thought that Churchill was "too old." Add to this the view of Mrs. Roosevelt, who thought that Churchill was too conservative, indeed "reactionary." She had gone so far as to ask a friend to impress that upon her husband.

At the same time Roosevelt was very much aware of the influence of American isolationism, together with the anti-British sympathies of many of the isolationists — especially in view of his soon forthcoming and exceptional nomination for a third presidential term. Closely connected with this matter was the problematic character of the American ambassador in London, Joseph P. Kennedy. Roosevelt had appointed Kennedy to that post in 1938. He had owed something to Kennedy for the latter's political support within the Democratic Party; he thought that this was a smart move. In reality, that appointment was woefully shortsighted; indeed, in 1940 it came close to being disastrous. That Kennedy was a new-rich millionaire, with a strong streak of vulgarity running through his mind and character; moreover, a man with an enduring chip on his shoulder, resentful of the older, Anglo-Saxon American elite of the Eastern Seaboard, did not matter much in London, not until the function of an American ambassador there would become much more than largely ceremonial. What then mattered were Kennedy's political ideas, indeed his ideology. He believed that the greatest danger to the world (and especially to his world) was Communism: an insidious danger much greater than Hitler's Germany. The latter was, after all, in some ways a bulwark or at least an obstacle against the spread of Communism. Therefore it was ruinous for Britain to war against Germany, while it would be criminal for the United States to do so. That was the essence of Kennedy's isolationism — so-called, since properly speaking that was no isolationism but the result of a selective ideology; as the careers of most American "isolationists" after the war would demonstrate, they would fight "international Communism" abroad, with relish.

In 1938 Kennedy's anti-Communism, together with his opposition to obstructing Germany, corresponded with the inclinations of certain British Conservatives. After Munich Kennedy spoke and wrote privately of "the Jews starting to mess the thing up . . . Jewish propaganda following Munich." After March 1939 he had fewer British listeners. But more important was the fact that he hated Churchill. He liked Chamberlain — more precisely, to the extent to which Chamberlain's opinions and inclinations accorded with his. As late as 20 July 1939 Chamberlain, talking with Kennedy, discounted Churchill; he said he was not willing to bring him into the Cabinet; Churchill was a "two-handed drinker and his judgment has never proved to be good"; if Churchill had any authority, "England would have been at war before this." (We must keep in mind that these words were Kennedy's version of what Chamberlain was supposed to have said to him — an inaccurate paraphrase at best.)

Even after the war had started Kennedy kept saying (for example, to Leopold Amery in October) that it was a fatal mistake; a defeat of Germany would mean the "Bolshevization of all Europe." In November he wrote the same thing to Roosevelt, adding: "Make no mistake, there is a very definite undercurrent in this country [Britain] for peace." In December he returned to Washington (and Palm Beach) for a couple of months. He told Roosevelt that Churchill's colleagues in the Cabinet disliked him, that Churchill was "ruthless and scheming," wanting to embroil the United States in the war, that Churchill was in touch, "notably, [with] certain strong Jewish leaders." To his colleague Bullitt Kennedy said in March 1940 that Germany would win the war and Britain would "go to hell." But by that time the British had Kennedy's number. In February 1940 they intercepted his telegram from Washington to the American embassy in London, requesting "English pacifist literature." Soon afterward Sir Robert Vansittart wrote a memorandum at the Foreign Office: "Mr. Kennedy is a very foul specimen of double-crosser and defeatist." Someone else in the Foreign Office wrote that Kennedy should no longer be treated "as a kind of honorary member of the cabinet." Halifax commented:

"I should think it is a diminishing temptation." One problem was that the secret Churchill-Roosevelt correspondence went through the channel of the American embassy. The Foreign Office objected to that, but Churchill, for various reasons, continued to use it.

It is significant that during the entire government crisis that brought Churchill to the prime ministership in early May there were no communications between Churchill and Roosevelt at all — an important argument against those (including Hitler) who were inclined to see a great clandestine conspiracy between the two at the time. The messages from the American embassy in London were indifferent and insignificant. The essential character of the Churchill-Roosevelt relationship had not yet matured. They were, as yet, far from being old, or even trusted, friends. Indeed, we have seen that Roosevelt was still unsure about Churchill. But now events were rushing ahead. This must be kept in mind as we contemplate the startling nature of the message that Churchill composed and sent to Roosevelt on 15 May. That message was a milestone in their developing series of messages (the first of which Churchill signed as "Former Naval Person") and in the evolution of their relationship. But its importance is not that. It is the first revelation of Churchill looking ahead, into the abyss, of his recognition that he might be cast aside if Britain was compelled to sue for peace. "As you are no doubt aware, the scene had darkened swiftly," he wrote. "If necessary, we shall continue the war alone and we are not afraid of that. But I trust you realize, Mr. President, that the voice and the force of the United States may count for nothing if they are withheld too long. You may have a completely subjugated, Nazified Europe established with astonishing swiftness, *and the weight may be more than we can bear.*" The italics are mine. Note, too, that this message went out from London at six P.M. on 15 May, a full day before Churchill, in Paris, would come face to face not only with the prospect of a battle lost by a French army but with that of the collapse and surrender of France.

Churchill's message, sent during the darkening hours of that day, then went on to request six items from Roosevelt, "first of all, the loan of forty or fifty of your older destroyers." It was his first mention of this business, the symbolic and political importance of which eventually became greater than its material one. Did Churchill really think that their actual presence in the seas around Britain — something that, with the best of will and effort, would take weeks, perhaps months, to materialize — would be that decisive? That is what the tone and the text of his message suggested, but we cannot be sure. In any event, the original idea was not his. On the fourteenth he said something about the destroyers to Kennedy; but before that it was William C. Bullitt who earlier that day had wired to his then close friend the President that Roosevelt could legalize the sale "to France of twelve old destroyers by having classed them as obsolete; that there were plenty more, if that sale went through, and that if the British government would like some he had mentioned 50 or even 100." That information was discussed in the War Cabinet before Churchill drafted his message to Roosevelt.

Roosevelt answered Churchill's message twelve hours after its receipt. The tone was friendly, but there was not much meat in it. About the destroyers he did not think he could go to Congress "at this moment." He also wrote (correctly) that the transfer of the destroyers would take weeks. Two days later Churchill acknowledged Roosevelt's response in a short letter of five sentences, of which the last three read: "we are determined to persevere to the very end whatever the result of the great battle raging in France may be. We must expect in any case to be attacked here on the Dutch model before very long and we hope to give a good account of ourselves. But if American assistance is to play any part it must be available soon." Two days passed; Roosevelt talked to the British ambassador in Washington, Lord Lothian; and then Churchill decided to send yet another direct message to the President. He drafted it. Then he hesitated whether to send it. In the end he did. He felt compelled to impress upon Roosevelt the awful prospect of what might happen. He, and his administration, could go down in battle, "but in no conceivable circumstances will we consent to surrender." But:

> If members of the present administration were finished and others came into parley amid the ruins, you must not be blind to the fact that the sole remaining bargaining counter with Germany would be the fleet, and if this country was left by the United States to its fate no one would have the right to blame those then responsible if they made the best terms they could for the surviving inhabitants. Excuse me, Mr. President, putting this nightmare bluntly. Evidently I could not answer for my successors who in utter despair and helplessness might well have to accommodate themselves to the German will.

He ended: "However there is happily no need at present to dwell upon such ideas." Happily no need? Perhaps the prospect of such ideas was unthinkable; but the unthinkable must sometimes be thought about; and the time had come to give some thought to it at least. Roosevelt, and Washington, did not realize this fully, or even adequately. His trust and friendship for Churchill were not yet strong enough. There was still a distance between their minds. For almost another month no important messages would pass between them.

Meanwhile a dangerous fracas broke to the surface in London. An official at the American embassy there, the code clerk Tyler Kent, was a convinced isolationist. Not unlike some American isolationists and at least some Republicans, his extreme dislike of Franklin Roosevelt went hand in hand with his anti-Communist and pro-German world view. He had taken hundreds of classified documents from the embassy to his home near Baker Street, including the secret messages from Churchill to Roosevelt and vice versa. He passed some of these to a handful of women and men in London who hated Churchill and who were German sympathizers, the papers going on to a few British Fascists and even to Italian agents. On 20 May British security police broke into the room of this Baker Street Irregular. Then his diplomatic immunity was waived. He was sentenced to seven years in prison. (At the end of the war he was released and returned to the United States.) It is interesting to note that there was nothing unconstitutional in the contents of the Churchill-Roosevelt correspondence at that time. It was fortunate that Roosevelt's ambassador Kennedy, whose political preferences were very similar to Kent's, chose to wash his hands of the latter and would not insist on his immunity. Kennedy the politician chose not to break with Roosevelt before the 1940 election campaign. He did not think that this was the right occasion or the right time to cause open trouble for Roosevelt.

CHURCHILL, ON that twentieth of May, knew that he had to face troubles that were not on the surface. They went beyond and beneath the accumulation of dreadful news from France, where the German Panzer generals had reached the Channel that day. They now stood on the French cliffs across from Dover.

Four days earlier Bullitt, from Paris, had touched on the crucial matter. It was not that of the American destroyers. It was the prospect not only of a French but of an eventual British surrender. "You should have in mind," he wrote to his great friend in Washington, "that the British may install a government of Oswald Mosley." Before such an event Roosevelt should have the British move their fleet to Canada.

On the twenty-first Churchill moved against Mosley. He had to render him harmless. There was a long discussion in the War Cabinet, where Chamberlain, too, was in favor of drastic measures taken against Tyler Kent and one of his confederates, Captain Archibald Ramsay, a Conservative member of Parliament who admired and supported the Third Reich. Next day the government rushed through the so-called 18B Regulations. (On the same day a Mosley follower, a British Fascist, ran for a seat in a by-election, but he polled only 1 percent of the vote.) On the morning of the twenty-third Mosley was arrested and taken to Brixton prison. (His wife, Diana, would be arrested and lodged with him five weeks later.) Another 1,847 men and women were put under arrest during the twenty-third and twenty-fourth.

Sir Oswald Mosley was an attractive, clever, virile political personality. There were politicians (and, later, historians) who said and wrote that he would have made a great prime minister. In 1931, disgusted with the dreary stagnation and political fudging of the Labour Party, he quit it and founded a "New Party," which for a while attracted a few intelligent men and women (among them Harold Nicolson and James Lees-Milne). By 1933 Mosley declared that he was a Fascist and led the British party by that name. This is not the place to sum up his political career, except to say that until the mid-thirties his following was considerable. It may be interesting to note that Roosevelt had met Mosley in America in 1926 and liked him. They exchanged letters even in 1933 — that is, after Mosley had declared his Fascism. Thus before 1939 Roosevelt had more contact with Mosley than he had with Churchill. But that is neither here nor there. By 1940 there were not many people in Britain who trusted Mosley. That is one of the reasons why Churchill's arrest of Mosley in May 1940 was criticized (he would be criticized again from other quarters when he chose to release the Mosleys from prison well before the end of the war). English common law eschews conviction on the basis of potentiality ("Intentions must be judged by acts," as Dr. Johnson said); and Mosley had declared that in the event of an invasion he would fight it as an English patriot. To some people his arrest seemed not only lawless but exaggerated, perhaps even panicky, in retrospect. Yet retrospect is not always, and not necessarily, correct.

To forgive is one thing; to forget is another. We must not forget that Mosley and others of his persuasion were not merely potential opponents of the war government. Nor were they but a new kind of pacifist. Their agitation and propaganda were directed against this war with Germany. There was ample evidence that they admired the political system and the European aims of Hitler's Third Reich. Mosley and his friends were not German agents, as that word is generally employed; but at least in one dictionary sense (*OED*) an agent is "he who operates in a particular direction, who produces an effect." In May 1940 that direction, that effect, endangered the security, nay the stability, of the war effort of the British people. It also endangered Churchill, whose situation was neither secure nor stable.

There was more to that than Mosley. We have seen the extent of a British consensus about Churchill before 1939: brilliant but unstable, wanting in judgment. On the tenth of May much of that was forgotten — or, rather, obscured by the rush of events. But ten days later? Some people, and not only Mosleyites, began to recall the Dardanelles; and Norway; and now France. One catastrophe after another: and now the worst one of all. Churchill the warmonger: he had his chance; and where would it all lead? There were people in Britain who began thinking that way. They were not many; and the habitual British slowness in changing their minds was a good thing. But that potentiality existed; and it was more important, because it went wider, than the potentiality of the Mosleyites for eventual treason. Already on 17 May Alfred Duff Cooper, the newly appointed minister of information, suggested to the Cabinet "that more should be done to inform the general public of the seriousness of the situation, about which most people were in complete ignorance." Cecil Beaton, the society photographer, on his way to America that day, wrote: "My own private courage was badly bruised, and each person one spoke to was more depressing than the last." In his domestic history of Britain during the war Alexander Calder wrote: "A mood of panic was gripping upper-class circles." On the eighteenth Chips Channon put down in his diary that Lloyd George was "jubilant by the turn of political events." Five days later Channon decided to bury his diaries in his garden.

That there was defeatism around, sometimes in the circles of those who were well informed and, not surprisingly, among intellectuals (including some of avant-garde and formerly Leftist persuasions), is undeniable. At the same time the call that Anthony Eden broadcast on the evening of the fourteenth for "Local Defence Volunteers" (Churchill soon renamed it the Home Guard) had an inspiring response, with thousands of men walking up to register at police stations even before Eden's broadcast was over. George Orwell noted that the patriotism of the middle classes was something to build on. He was anxious about the ignorance among masses of people, but there was not much muttering. On 20 May Harold Nicolson dined in Balliol in Oxford. "Communism has practically died out in Oxford and there is not a pacifist practically to be seen. They are all champing their bits to get into uniform."

Hitler was looking for divisions within England. He was inclined to consider its potentialities as if these were actualities. He was not surprised when Churchill had Mosley arrested. Somewhat later he spoke at length about Mosley to his close circle. He did not think much of him as a "personality," but he was a potential leader, the only Englishman who understood "the German-European idea." Hitler was still influenced by what Unity Mitford (Mosley's sister-in-law) in July 1939 had told him about Mosley and the English unreadiness for war — the same Unity Mitford who told Robert Byron in Munich that England "would become a second-rate power unless it saved itself by the proffered alliance [with Germany]. An Anglo-German alliance could dominate the world; otherwise England would go under." But by the twentieth of May in 1940 the option was no longer an "Anglo-German alliance." It was whether England should, or indeed could, go on against Germany, instead of seeking some arrangement with Hitler, if necessary on the latter's terms — and it was not only Unity Mitford (who had tried to kill herself in Munich at the outset of the war and who, badly wounded, was then transported back to England with Hitler's assistance) who was thinking about such terms. The war diary of General Halder recorded some of Hitler's thoughts on 21 May, only days before Dunkirk: "We are seeking contact with England on the basis of a division of the world." Fifty years later this historian is not clear what these contacts were, or whether they existed at all. But what Hitler thought is clear. The English would see the light sooner or later. Then they would get rid of Churchill.

ONCE HITLER'S troops reached the English Channel his nervousness was gone. His loyal confidant General Alfred Jodl wrote in his diary that the Führer was "beside himself" with joy. Hitler had begun to talk about peace negotiations. "The English could have a separate peace any time," he said. "After a return of the [former German] colonies," he added. There was more to this than a sudden change of mood; more even than his well-earned satisfaction with the success of his Sickle-Cut, now that the British Expeditionary Force was cut off from the south, from most of the French. He was thinking of political consequences, not only of military results. As early as 8 September 1939, merely a week after the war had begun, he said to Halder and Jodl that after the Poles were eliminated he would make another peace offer to England. He did not really expect an answer; but "when we get to the Channel, the English may then change their minds."

The Channel was now the key. In 1914 the kaiser and his government should not have gone to war against England; and the German generals then failed not only at the Marne but in the race for the sea; they never took the Channel ports. Now things were different. On 20 May 1940 Hitler was confident enough to mention for the first time that he would bring the French to sign their surrender in the forest clearing at Compiègne, at the very place where they had made the Germans sign the armistice in November 1918. But now Hitler was thinking more about the English than about the French.

His enemy Churchill had gone through a very difficult day. He, too, thought that the Channel was the key. Of course: but his immediate preoccupations were military ones. He was suddenly faced with a dilemma. On Sunday, 19 May, he had thought he could spend some time in his home for the first time since he had become prime minister. It was not to be. He drove down to Chartwell after a War Cabinet meeting in the morning. (Some of his swans had been eaten by foxes, but his favorite black swan was still there, floating calmly, craning and pecking at whatever Churchill threw to him.) Then Churchill had an urgent telephone call from across the Channel, from General Lord Gort. The French army in the west was dissolving; the Germans were racing ahead; a decision had to be made about the fate of the entire British army across the Channel. The views and the plans of General Gort and of General Edmund Ironside (the chief of the Imperial General Staff) differed. Gort thought that the British Expeditionary Force should retire westward, to the Channel ports, among which the name of Dunkirk appeared for the first time. Ironside thought that the British should move southward, to join the French behind the Somme. Churchill's inclination was to Ironside's plan, mainly because he was aware of the necessity of showing more support to the French, not only in words but in action. Abruptly he returned to London. He asked the War Cabinet to meet at four-thirty. Toward the end of the meeting he stood up and said that he was ready to fly over to see Gort immediately. But then this was not deemed necessary. Instead Churchill would fly to Paris in a day or so, where the French had just appointed a new commander in chief, General Maxime Weygand. At least for a day the choice between the Gort and the Ironside plans was postponed.

That night Churchill made his first broadcast to the British people as their prime minister. (He had made his "blood, toil, tears and sweat" speech in the House of Commons.) Many politicians, men as different as Baldwin and Eden and Chamberlain, took up their pens to congratulate him. The tone of that speech was sufficient to allay their doubts, at least for a while. His private secretary, John Colville, who had been skeptical of Churchill's character and judgment but a few days before, now revised his own judgment. He did not admire this particular speech but wrote in his diary that he was much impressed with Churchill: "his spirit is indomitable." He and some of the others no longer minded that Churchill was in the saddle. But behind the horseman sat black care. That night Churchill composed his ominous message to Roosevelt. For once — a rare occasion with him — he did not sleep well. At half past two in the morning he called his secretary to get the text back from the American embassy. He wanted to review it. But then he sent it without any alteration.

With the dissolution of the French army came the dissolution of the dilemma. The British Expeditionary Force had to pull back toward the Channel. The first orders had already gone out to gather all kinds of seaborne craft in the English ports across from the coast of Flanders. The government was well aware of the dangers to London itself — whence not only the arrest of the Mosley people but the first preparations against a possible sudden descent of German parachutists: eight small, sandbag-filled breastworks were erected around government buildings in London, manned by soldiers in full battle dress and with machine guns. Churchill feared, too, that the Germans might manage to put a few thousand men ashore in motorboats and other light craft. Churchill's energy, evident in his attention to countless details, was amazing. But on Tuesday, 21 May, he became depressed as the day wore on. His nerves, his mind, even his composure, were affected by the chaotic breakdown of communications across the Channel. He no longer knew what was going on in Flanders. He even had trouble getting through to Paris. Holding the telephone receiver in his hand, he turned to Colville. "In all the history of war, I have never seen such mismanagement," he said. "I have never seen Winston so depressed," Colville wrote in his diary. Then Churchill revived. Sweeping aside the advice of others, he decided to go to Paris next morning, for the second time in a week, to meet General Weygand and the others. At 1:30 A.M., as he was getting ready for bed, a dispatch came that the French general Gaston Billotte, whom Churchill knew well, had died in a motor accident. When his secretary knocked on the door he found Churchill standing half naked. "Poor man, poor man" was all he would say. Then he climbed into bed.

He flew to Paris next morning. It was another beautiful day: a relentless sun shone over France and England. Listening to Weygand, Churchill allowed himself to be impressed — as it would soon appear, wrongly — by this ancient martinet's energy and resolution. Weygand proposed and he and Churchill spoke of a plan whereby a joint French-British attack would cut across the German corridor near Abbeville, Arras and Amiens, turning the encirclers into the encircled. Churchill dispatched an enthusiastic and quite unrealizable order to the British generals for such a turnaround offensive. Soon all of this dissolved; the French were hopeless. Churchill slept at the embassy. By the time he returned to London it was evident that nothing would come of this ambitious and sadly uncoordinated plan. There were two Cabinet meetings that day. Late that night — 23 May, a Thursday — Churchill decided to report to the king. He told George VI that if the Weygand plan could not come off, he would order the British army back to England. He was compelled to advise his monarch of that grave eventuality. He did not tell the king what he already knew: that the Weygand plan had not, and would not, come off.

That evening Hitler had decided to move his command post forward. His minister of armaments and public works had begun the building of three new barracks for his staff at a new headquarters. They would be ready in ten days. During those ten days evolved the events of Dunkirk.

THE EVENTS of Dunkirk: that is, the rescue of the British army. Historians "must not overestimate its importance," wrote the principal German military and political historian of the Second World War, the recently deceased Professor Andreas Hillgruber. He was wrong; but not because we ought to content ourselves with a heroic and mythical image of Dunkirk. The military importance of that — often, but not always — inspiring and courageous extrication of 340,000 British and French soldiers was decisive; but even more decisive was its political importance for the duel between Churchill and Hitler.

Two days before the British evacuation from Dunkirk was to begin Hitler made a decision the importance of which should not be underestimated. Fifty years later the sources and the origins of that decision are not entirely clear. That is why I am compelled to deal with it at some length. On 24 May, Friday, eighteen minutes before noon, Hitler ordered General Rundstedt to halt the move of his spearheads toward Dunkirk.

Boulogne, Calais, Dunkirk, Ostend: the four ports across the narrow part of the Channel that on 23 May had not yet fallen to the Germans. The last one did not matter; it was too far from the English coast for large troop transports. Boulogne, Calais, Dunkirk: bridgeheads for England on the continent of Europe. They had served such purposes centuries before (and in December 1941 Stalin would tell Anthony Eden in Moscow that the British should think of acquiring some of them after the war). But now Boulogne and Calais were less than bridgeheads. They were crumbling enclaves. The Germans had bypassed them and were besieging them; they were encircled, battered, shrinking by the hour. By the morning of 24 May Boulogne had already fallen. It was the smaller of the two enclaves. After less than two days of resistance its garrison, including British and French troops, was taken off by eight destroyers. It was a small forerunner of what would happen at Dunkirk. No one, including Churchill, foresaw that. But he "regretted that decision." For it was then that an awful realization appeared in his mind. It was not only the French who melted away before the Germans' onslaught. The morale and the leadership of the British army, now for the first time grappling with the German one, were not much better. Despite the relative closeness of the Channel ports to England there was an indescribable and unintelligible confusion.

Dunkirk is about twenty-five miles from Calais. The German spearheads were fifteen miles from Dunkirk when Hitler's order to stop went out, at 11:42 A.M. on the twenty-fourth. It was sent in clear. The British intercepted it. Was it meant to be intercepted by them? Perhaps, though I doubt it. It was not yet known at the Cabinet meeting in London that met in the same hour of the Hitler order. (Besides the five members of the War Cabinet, there was also General A. E. Percival, the assistant chief of the Imperial General Staff, informing the Cabinet of military matters — the same man who would abjectly surrender Singapore to a relatively small Japanese army in February 1942; one of those omens that appear but in retrospect.) In any event, while Churchill did not yet know what Hitler was doing, Hitler thought he knew what the British were doing. He thought they were leaving the Continent. The night before the last troops had embarked from Boulogne for England. Their embarkation was unvexed by German guns. Before dawn on 24 May, at two A.M., the War Office ordered the evacuation of Calais, too, "in principle." At the bright morning hour of nine, the large ship *City of Canterbury,* full of British troops, was moving off the shell-spattered maritime dock of Calais, bound for Dover. Another ship, *Kohistan,* sailed from Calais at half past eleven. The British were destroying some of their tanks on the quays. The Germans could see much of this, and they read some of the War Office signals. Before noon Hitler's order to halt went out. The general pattern of the entire war may have crystallized in his mind. The British were leaving. Let them leave. Is that exactly what he thought? Possibly; even probably; but we cannot be sure. Whatever evidence we have consists of two parts: his actual moves; and his rationalizations.

The night before the twenty-fourth General Rundstedt had slowed down somewhat. He reported that half of his armored spearheads were worn out. He was still worried about the potentiality of a British-French counterattack farther east, behind his advanced lines — the Weygand plan, which as we know had not materialized. Early on the morning of the twenty-fourth — an unusual hour for him — Hitler flew to Rundstedt's new headquarters at Charleville, nearly one hundred miles east of the Channel. He agreed with Rundstedt. The Panzers ought to be saved. Some people would later say that Hitler's memories of the First World War, of the mud and the watercourses in the canal country of the Flanders lowlands, remained vivid in his mind. But then this was the same Hitler who was convinced and said that this would be, as it indeed was, a different kind of war from the last one.

In any event, some (though not all) of his generals were either stunned or dismayed. There was Dunkirk, the last port, within easy striking distance, since the bulk of the British army was still well to the east of it. General Rundstedt (and, it seems, Generals Ewald von

Kleist and Günther von Kluge) were inclined to halt, regroup and ready themselves for eventual counterattacks; others, such as Heinz Guderian and Walther von Brauchitsch, the commander in chief of the army, were surprised and disappointed. From the Hitler order they surmised that Dunkirk was to be left to the Luftwaffe. The next day Brauchitsch suggested to Rundstedt to go ahead after all. Rundstedt would not do so. The decision to start moving again toward Dunkirk came a day later. Even then Rundstedt ordered that the direct advance be mounted carefully and slowly. Even then the main effort would be that of pushing the Allied troops westward *toward* Dunkirk, not a direct thrust *into* Dunkirk itself.

Rundstedt was one of the German generals closest to Hitler at that time. After the war he claimed that he only followed Hitler's instructions: that he understood Hitler, who wanted to let the British go; Dunkirk would be their "golden bridge" for leaving the Continent. Thus would Rundstedt rationalize his decisions that may have cost the Germans their greatest opportunity of the entire war. However, our interests should be directed at Hitler's rationalizations, not Rundstedt's. There were plenty of these to come. Very soon after Dunkirk Hitler talked to a small circle of his closest staff, including his secretaries: "The army is England's backbone. . . . If we destroy it, there goes the British Empire. We would not, nor could not inherit it. . . . My generals did not understand this." Didn't they? At the time, 25 May 1940, General Hans Jeschonnek (a close friend of Göring's), among others, was overheard to say that "the Führer wants to spare the British a humiliating defeat." Hitler may have been trying to explain too much. But he turned to the argument about that golden bridge several times, for the last time near the end of the war, near the end of his life. "Churchill," he said in February 1945 to his close confidants, "was quite unable to appreciate the sporting spirit of which I had given proof by refraining from creating an irreparable breach between the British and ourselves. We did, indeed, refrain from annihilating them at Dunkirk. We ought to have been able to make them realize that their acceptance of the German hegemony in Europe, a state of affairs to the implementation of which they had always been opposed, but which I had implemented without any trouble, would bring them inestimable advantages."

"Sporting spirit," "refrain" and "inestimable advantages" are too much. Churchill was loath to credit Hitler with good will, sporting spirit or golden bridge, whatever that was. In his war memoirs, written eight years after 1940, he took good care to attribute the Halt

Order to Rundstedt's hesitations, not to Hitler's. He was not altogether incorrect. "Golden bridge" was an overstatement, to say the least. But an overstatement, while wanting in precision, is not necessarily altogether devoid of truth. Hitler's purposes were mixed. He was attracted by the prospect of the British army leaving Europe. He would not have minded expediting that. But his Halt Order and all that followed were not meant to be gestures to the British. Nor did he intend to allow them to make the Dunkirk evacuation painless.

There was a crucial element in his tactics that may not have received the attention it deserves. This was his willingness to believe Göring, who three days before the Halt Order tried to convince him that he, Göring, would trap the British at Dunkirk by attacking them from the air. When on 21 May he talked with Hitler, they were closeted together. Even Hitler's headquarter generals Wilhelm Keitel and Alfred Jodl were excluded. Two days later Hitler's adjutant, Major Gerhard Engel, noted in his diary that the Führer talked with Göring by telephone again. "The Field Marshal thinks that the great task of the Luftwaffe is beginning: the annihilation of the British in Northern France. The army will only have to occupy [the ground]. We are angry, the Führer is inspired [*begeistert*]." Note that this occurred before Rundstedt's slowing down before the Aa Canal and before Hitler's Halt Order. Other high German officials were aware of what was in the offing. "Whether the English give in now or whether we make them peace-loving through bombing . . . ;" wrote Ernst von Weizsäcker, the undersecretary of state, in his diary on 23 May. As late as the twenty-seventh Engel noted that Göring reported great air results in the harbor of Dunkirk: "Only a few fishing boats are coming across; one hopes that the Tommies know how to swim." Göring convinced Hitler that the Luftwaffe could do the job at Dunkirk. Hitler was willing to be convinced, in part because of his own preferences and concerns. One year later — by then he was in the midst of the Russian campaign — Hitler spoke to another close group: "Even though Göring had assured him that the Luftwaffe alone could do the job, since Dunkirk he [Hitler] had become a little more skeptical about that." This contradicts the simple golden bridge thesis — suggesting as it does that Hitler then wished he had killed or caught more British at Dunkirk.

FIFTY YEARS after these events the accustomed general belief still prevails. It is that while the French failed, at Dunkirk the British, led by Churchill, succeeded. This either discounts or ignores many things: that, for example, at Boulogne, Calais and Dunkirk, the French fought as well as the British. It also discounts (to say the least) the mortal peril of the latter; its extent and its depth; how close Hitler had come not only to capturing the British army but to winning his entire war; how close Churchill was to being forced onto a slippery slope — his own words, as we shall see.

We know what people in May 1940 did not know: that, like Napoleon, Hitler eventually chose not to risk an invasion of England. But Hitler was very unlike Napoleon. The entire scene was fundamentally different from Napoleon's time. Wellington was supposed to have said that the Battle of Waterloo had been "a close-run thing." But even if Wellington had lost and Napoleon won at Waterloo, Britain's existence, her independence, was not at stake. How different were matters one hundred and twenty-five years later! The prospect was not merely — merely! — the domination of Europe by a dictator; not even his conquest of the entire Lowlands across from England. It was that of the conquest not only of Western Europe but of England. On 21 May Admiral Raeder talked to Hitler about such a potential invasion. At that moment Hitler was still uninterested in it. He thought that the English would have to come to terms without an invasion. At the same time Albert Kesselring, one of the toughest and most Nazified of German generals, said to Göring, even before the battle around Dunkirk would be joined, that the time had come to think of going on to England across the Channel, with gliders and parachute troops perhaps. Churchill was aware of that supreme danger. We saw his decision to set up eight gun posts in London. Without going into details, he — and others, too — did not think that such an invasion was impossible. After all, the Germans were pulling off one incredible military feat after another. Now that the Germans had reached the Channel the immediate question was whether their next thrust would be southward, against the remnant French army, or northwestward, against the British. The latter alternative was becoming more and more evident.

Churchill was not immediately impressed by the halt of the German spearhead at the Aa Canal, fifteen or so miles from Dunkirk. His mind was full of the more immediate awfulness of Calais. The War Office ordered the evacuation of Calais "in principle" at 2 A.M. that morning of the twenty-fourth (it is at least possible that Hitler learned of that order). Churchill rescinded it later on that day. He told the British commander at Calais to keep fighting till the end; the defense of Calais was "of the highest importance to our country and the Army now." But the news filtering through from Calais was as bleak as it was dark. Churchill would say something on the twenty-fifth about "defeatism in the General Staff." Morale at Calais was not very good either. Some of the British dockworkers brought to Calais to help in the loading skulked and refused to work under the sporadic German shelling; officers with pointed guns had to force them to go back to the docks. Brigadier Claude Nicholson, the British commander in Calais, was an admirable soldier. (He would die three years later in German captivity.) His answer to the second and last German offer to surrender was: "The answer is no as it is the British Army's duty to fight as well as it is the German's." These words were recorded in the war diary of the German Tenth Panzer Division, attacking Calais.

The guns fell silent at Calais on the afternoon of 26 May. Churchill would later claim, and write, that the two days of the defense of Calais were of supreme importance in the saving of Dunkirk. This is arguable. The decision by Hitler and his generals to halt on the twenty-fourth and to resume on the twenty-sixth the advance on Dunkirk had something but not much to do with the termination of the Calais episode. Operation Dynamo, the order to begin the evacuation from Dunkirk, was issued by General Gort at seven P.M. on the twenty-sixth. Twenty-four hours later fewer than 8,000 British troops had sailed from Dunkirk, out of an encircled mass of nearly 400,000 British and French soldiers. No one, including Churchill, knew how many of them could be brought back to England.

And now the greatest crisis in nine centuries of English history was at hand — because of what was happening at Dunkirk; but more important, because the distrust of Churchill's leadership had appeared at the highest levels, within his own, recently formed government, voiced by his foreign secretary, who had come to believe that, for the sake of England's survival, the attempt to inquire about peace terms from Hitler should not be avoided.

This is starkly put. Lord Halifax was not a defeatist. Nor was he an intriguer. He was a seasoned watcher of the tides of events, and of the tides of British public opinion. Halifax was a very British type, in the sense that he knew how to adjust his mind to circumstances, rather than attempt to adjust circumstances to his ideas. This does not mean that he was a hypocrite or an opportunist — except in the habitual Anglo-Saxon way, which is not really Machiavellian, since the innate practice of that kind of English hypocrisy often serves purposes that are higher than individual prestige or profit (which is, too, why the Anglophobe phrase "perfidious Albion" is incorrect). What happened was that during three critical days (26, 27 and 28 May, Sunday, Monday and Tuesday) Halifax thought that the time had come — indeed, that it had become imperative — to state his disagreement with Churchill within the War Cabinet.

It is significant that this had come to the surface. Not into the open of the British public: these deliberations in Cabinet were secret; the record — as we shall see, even now somewhat incomplete — would remain so for another thirty years at least. But Halifax was the kind of man who thought he knew when the tide was turning. He would not swim against the tide. To the contrary: he thought that it was his public and patriotic duty to realize the turning and give his considered advice accordingly — again, not necessarily for his personal benefit. There was much evidence of such inclinations in those years, which was perhaps why some people called him Holy Fox. He had supported Chamberlain at the time of Munich; and he advised Chamberlain to hold a national election afterward, to profit from the then overwhelming popular support of the latter. (Had Chamberlain done that, he would have had a House of Commons packed with supporters who owed everything to him; and Churchill could perhaps never have come to power.) In March 1939 Halifax was the first and most important personage to advise Chamberlain that the prime minister must abandon appeasement and declare a British decision to resist any further Hitler aggression, if necessary by war. And now, a fortnight after Churchill had become prime minister, retaining him as his foreign secretary, Halifax chose to confront Churchill, whose single-minded combativeness he thought disastrous. He also knew that in thinking this he was not alone. There is no evidence that Halifax acted as a leader of some kind of cabal, ready and willing to oust Churchill. But he thought that Churchill had to be curbed, to say the least — or, more precisely, diverted from a disastrous course. (Physically, too, Halifax moved closer to the center of events; he had moved temporarily to the then ultramodern Hotel Dorchester in Mayfair, far from his streams and moors, a somewhat atypical residence for this Yorkshire nobleman.)

On Thursday evening, 23 May, he saw Kennedy. The latter was utterly pessimistic about England and volubly critical of Churchill. Kennedy sent a message to Roosevelt in the same vein. The ambassador knew what Bullitt had wired Roosevelt that day, an idea that

Roosevelt adopted next morning. Through his secretary of state, Roosevelt contacted the prime minister of Canada, Mackenzie King, to send a secret representative to Washington to discuss with Roosevelt "certain possible eventualities which could not possibly be mentioned aloud." On the telephone King was referred to as "Mr. Kick," and Roosevelt "Mr. Roberts." King thought that the United States was "trying to save itself at the expense of Britain," and told Roosevelt that he should talk about that to Churchill directly. Roosevelt's idea (and request) was that Canada and the Dominions should press Churchill to send the British fleet across the Atlantic, the sooner the better — that is, before Hitler's peace terms would include the surrender of the fleet. Roosevelt added, too, that Churchill should not be told of the American origin of that proposal. This was significant for two reasons: first, because the realization that Britain might have to sue for peace (that is, surrender) had reached even Washington; the second, suggested earlier, because even at that late date Roosevelt's trust in Churchill was weaker than we have been accustomed to think.

More important in the actual course of events was Halifax's meeting with the Italian ambassador Giuseppe Bastianini on the following day, the twenty-fifth. Halifax knew that Mussolini had already decided to join Hitler in the war. But he knew, too, that eighteen months before, at the brink of another abyss, Mussolini had been instrumental in convincing Hitler to convoke that last-minute conference at Munich. Would Mussolini now state his terms? Would the British government choose to make such an inquiry to Mussolini? The time had come for this, not only because of the catastrophic situation of the British army across the Channel, but because, as Halifax knew, the French were about to ask Mussolini for terms that would actually include changes in the map of the Mediterranean — that is, the cession of some French territories to Italy. Both Halifax and Bastianini knew that there was even more to that: the request for Mussolini's ideas for a general European settlement; the possible role of Mussolini as a middleman, a prestigious broker, between the Western powers and Hitler himself. Halifax told Bastianini that he would meet him again the following day.

That day — 26 May, a Sunday — the French premier flew to London early in the morning. A crucial meeting was already behind him. The previous day in Paris the Comité de Guerre, mostly because of the interventions of General Weygand and Marshal Pétain (the latter, too, had been included in the French government a few days before), suggested strongly that France could no longer go on. Colonel Paul de Villelume, Reynaud's principal military aide, summed it up in one sentence: "We must make peace while we still have an army." The German pressure on the French army had now eased for the time being; it was directed mainly at the British and at those French forces that fought alongside the British in Flanders and in western Belgium. When the War Cabinet met at the unaccustomed hour of nine in the morning, Churchill said that his colleagues must be prepared to face the prospect that the French would give up the fight.

That was largely so. Reynaud was an Anglophile. He admired and respected Churchill. But he knew, and Churchill knew, that his hands were already tied: Weygand and Pétain and, behind them, representative groups of French political figures did not like England and the English alliance. They convinced themselves that the ties binding France to Britain must now be loosened. At the same time these French Anglophobes were Italophiles: they were convinced that Mussolini must be approached. There was, in addition, a disagreement between Churchill and Reynaud. The Frenchman claimed that the Germans were about to turn south, making for Paris. Churchill was convinced that their principal aim now was to move on Dunkirk, against the British. He was right; but at that juncture it did not matter.

After lunch with Reynaud at two P.M. Churchill met his Cabinet again. Now the break between him and Halifax first appeared. Unlike Churchill, Halifax never thought much of the French army. As early as December 1939 — in those suddenly so remote, quieter days of the Reluctant War — he had said in the Cabinet that if ever the French dropped out, "we should not be able to carry on the war by ourselves." On Saturday night, he wrote in his diary how awful the collapse of the French army was: "the one firm rock on which everybody has been willing to build for the last two years." And now he turned to Churchill. The unspoken question had to be spoken. "We had to face the fact that it was not so much now a question of imposing a complete defeat upon Germany but of safeguarding the independence of our Empire . . . we should naturally be prepared to consider any proposals which might lead to this, provided our liberty and independence were assured. . . . If he was satisfied that matters vital to the independence of this country were unaffected," would Churchill be "prepared to discuss such terms"?

Churchill at that moment knew that he could not answer with a categorical no. He said that he "would be thankful to get out of our present difficulties on such terms, provided we retained the essentials and the elements of our vital strength, *even at the cost of some territory.*" (The italics are mine.) He added that he doubted whether such a deal was possible. Chamberlain sat on the fence. The Cabinet decided that Halifax should talk to Reynaud, who waited at the French embassy. At half past four Reynaud explained the French proposal to Halifax. They should approach Mussolini. Within the details of that proposal lay the suggestion that such an approach would amount to more than an attempt to settle British-French relations with Italy. They would ask Mussolini to mediate between them and Hitler.

The members of the French delegation now knew that there was a division within the British Cabinet. That evening Colonel Villelume wrote in his diary: "Halifax . . . shows his understanding; Churchill, prisoner of his habit of blustering [*son attitude de matamore*], was resolutely negative."*

Halifax came back from Reynaud. He wrote out his proposals. Now he would take the bit between his, at least physically remarkable, teeth. The third War Cabinet session that day, meeting informally in Admiralty House, began in conditions of secrecy that had no precedents in the modern history of Britain. The confidential minutes begin with this statement: "The record does not cover the first quarter of an hour of the discussion, during which the Secretary [Sir Edward Bridges] was not present." Halifax said that he thought the approach to Italy should be made. Churchill said that "if France could not defend itself, it was better that she should get out of the war rather than that she should drag us into a settlement which involved intolerable terms. There was no limit to the terms which Germany would impose upon us if she had her way. . . . We must take care not to be forced into a weak position in which we went to Sig-

---

* The French were also divided among themselves: Alexis Léger, the secretary-general of the Foreign Ministry, inclined to Churchill. This did not matter much, though somehow it was made known to the arch-appeaser Horace Wilson, whom Churchill had thrown out from Downing Street a fortnight before, who then wrote that Léger "was violently anti-German, equally violently anti-Italian, and he must bear much of the responsibility for the failure to take advantage of the opportunities offered from time to time, by either Hitler or Mussolini for some kind of rapprochement." That would come to Churchill's knowledge in October 1941, when he was threatened by another potential collapse, that of the Russian army.

nor Mussolini and invited him to go to Herr Hitler and ask him to treat us nicely. We must not get entangled in a position of that kind before we had been involved in any serious fighting." Halifax said that he did not entirely disagree: "but he attached perhaps more importance than the Prime Minister to the desirability of allowing France to try out the possibilities of European equilibrium. He was not quite convinced that the Prime Minister's diagnosis was correct and that it was Herr Hitler's interest to insist on outrageous terms." Chamberlain, on the fence, was now leaning toward Halifax: "If Signor Mussolini was prepared to collaborate with us in getting tolerable terms, then we would be prepared to discuss Italian terms with him."

Churchill said that nothing should be decided until they knew how much of the British Expeditionary Force could be saved. Chamberlain said that the government should not offend the French by turning down "their idea outright." Since Chamberlain never liked the French, this may have been disingenuous. (Cadogan, who attended the meeting for an hour, wrote in his diary that evening: "Settled nothing much. [Churchill] too rambling and romantic and sentimental and temperamental. Old Neville still the best of the lot.") Churchill now retreated slightly. It must be shown to Hitler that he could not conquer Britain. Yet some kind of approach to Mussolini might be made. Arthur Greenwood, one of the two Labour members of the War Cabinet, thought that this would be dangerous. But this time Halifax had the last word. "If we got to the point of discussing terms of a general settlement and found that we could obtain terms which did not postulate the destruction of our independence, we should be foolish if we did not accept them."

The meeting broke up after six o'clock. The War Cabinet would meet again next morning, when Sir Archibald Sinclair, the leader of the Liberal Party, would also attend. Churchill stayed at Admiralty House. With all the dreadful business of that day, he also had to deal with Narvik, the northern Norwegian port that the British and French had at last won back from the Germans but that had to be abandoned anew. That night, too, the first news of a coming Belgian surrender had filtered through to London. The signal of the start of Operation Dynamo, the evacuation of Dunkirk commanded from Dover, came at seven. An hour later Churchill dined with Eden, Ironside and Ismay. He had had to abandon Calais: all the ships were now needed for Dunkirk. Yet he had had to request Brigadier Nicholson to fight till the very end. He was probably unaware that the last posts in Calais had fallen three hours before. For once Churchill's appetite was gone. He ate and drank almost nothing. He sat silently. After dinner he stood up and told his friends that he felt "physically sick." He would mention this in his war memoirs. Lord Ismay remembered that Churchill seemed immensely sad. His spirit was not broken, but the prospect of a British Götterdämmerung was before his eyes.*

When the War Cabinet met next morning (at half past eleven) Churchill thought that he had a little more support. There was the presence of Sinclair, his old friend, who was strongly anti-German, with a respectable record of antiappeasement. Churchill also had a document that he now showed the Cabinet, the essence of which fortified his position. Entitled "British Strategy in a Certain Eventuality" — the eventuality of France dropping out of the war — this was a fairly extensive paper prepared by the Chiefs of Staff about the prospects of Britain carrying on the war alone. As early as 17 May — the day after Churchill's first ominous visit to Paris — Churchill and Chamberlain had asked the Chiefs of Staff to prepare such a paper. Churchill read it on the twenty-fifth, and now presented it to his colleagues. Its essence was that, provided British air superiority could be maintained, Britain could hold out alone, without the French. But not without the United States: the Chiefs of Staff assumed that the United States was "willing to give us full economic and financial support, *without which we do not think we could continue the war with any chance of success.*"

This was underlined in the original version, though it seems that Churchill played it down, as he presented a shorter version to the Cabinet on the twenty-seventh. The reason for this may have been that he expected little from the Americans at that crucial time. He said that the Americans had "given us practically no help in the war,

---

* I chose, probably for the first and last time in my writing career, not to encumber this book with numerous footnotes, but I cannot refrain at this point from including a passage, taken from Martin Gilbert's biography, about Churchill on that twenty-sixth of May. "At times of stress, Churchill often recalled some particular quotation which expressed his feelings. On May 26 he asked John Martin [one of his secretaries] to look up for him a passage in George Borrow's prayer for England at Gibraltar. [George Borrow was the wonderfully eccentric English travel writer of the early nineteenth century; his classic book was *The Bible in Spain.*] Martin gave it to Churchill the following day, and, as he later recalled, 'it matched his mood.' The quotation read: 'Fear not the result, for either shall thy end be a majestic and an enviable one, or God shall perpetuate thy reign upon the waters.' " (Gilbert, vol. VI, p. 406, note 3 [Sir John Martin, letter to the author, 24 October 1982])

and now that they saw how great was the danger, their attitude was that they wanted to keep everything which would help us for their own defence." At the same time Churchill's hand was strengthened by the assumption of the Chiefs of Staff to the effect that the Germans were up against time, since their material and economic resources were bound to diminish precipitously the next winter. That kind of economic assumption was close to Chamberlain's beliefs. The fact that this projection (as indeed the projections of the Ministry of Economic Warfare) was utterly wrong made no difference at that time.

After some discussion the Cabinet agreed with the Chiefs of Staff's assessment. But the situation had worsened again. The king of the Belgians had concluded that the war was lost and that he would seek separate terms from Hitler. "Cabinet as gloomy as ever — see v. little light anywhere," Cadogan wrote. When, at half past four, the War Cabinet assembled again it was Chamberlain who returned to his particular argument of the previous day. The approach to Mussolini might be necessary, if only for the purpose of not disheartening the French further. "Our reply should not be a complete refusal." Greenwood spoke out for British honor: "If it got out that we had sued for terms at the cost of ceding British territory, the consequences would be terrible." *If it got out* ... He was evidently concerned with the prospects of British morale. Churchill agreed. The French must be told that Britain would fight on even without them, till the end. "At the moment our prestige in Europe was very low. The only way we could get it back was by showing the world that Germany had not beaten us. If, after two or three months, we could show that we were still unbeaten, our prestige would return. Even if we were beaten, we should be no worse off than we should be if we were now to abandon the struggle."

> Let us therefore avoid being dragged down the slippery slope with France. The whole of this manoeuvre was intended to get us so deeply involved in negotiations that we should be unable to turn back. . . . The approach proposed was not only futile, but involved us in a deadly danger.

Chamberlain returned to his argument; but he added that some time might be gained until Mussolini's answer to the American President was known. (Roosevelt had sent a message to Mussolini, asking him to keep out of the war. It was wholly ineffective.) But now Halifax went to the root of the matter. He tried to corner Churchill; or at least to pin him down. "There were certain profound differences of points of view which he would like to make clear." "Profound" was a key word. This was no longer a matter of nuances, even though the discord between Halifax and Churchill had often consisted in nuances of wording. But, then, history is often made — and not only written — with words. Hadn't Churchill said the day before that "if he was satisfied that matters vital to the independence of this country were unaffected, he would be prepared to discuss terms. . . . On the present occasion, however, the Prime Minister seemed to suggest that under no conditions would we contemplate any course except fighting to a finish." Churchill answered that the issue "was quite unreal and was most unlikely to arise. If Herr Hitler was prepared to make peace on the terms of the restoration of the German colonies and the overlordship of Central Europe, that was one thing. But it was quite unlikely that he would make such an offer." Halifax kept pressing on. If Hitler offered peace terms to the French and the French said that they would have to consult with their allies, would Churchill then be prepared to discuss such terms, presented to France and to Britain? Churchill said that "he would not join France in asking for terms; but if he were told what the terms offered were, he would be prepared to consider them."

That was as far as he went. At half past four the meeting broke up. Halifax told Cadogan, who had again attended some of the meeting: "I can't work with Winston any longer." Cadogan told him to keep cool; Halifax must not let Churchill's "rodomontades" vex him unduly; in any event, Cadogan advised, don't do anything before consulting Chamberlain. Then Halifax decided to ask Churchill for a private stroll in the garden. What they said to each other we do not know. It appears that Churchill charmed Halifax; but he did not convince him. Halifax had come close to threatening to resign. He wrote in his diary that night: "I thought Winston talked the most frightful rot, also Greenwood, and after bearing it for some time I said exactly what I thought of them, adding that, if that was really their view, and if it came to the point, our ways must separate. . . . I despair when [Churchill] works himself up to a passion of emotion when he ought to make his brain think and reason."

Despite the secrecy of the War Cabinet meetings, a fair amount of what had happened there filtered out to London. John Colville wrote in his diary: "there are signs that Halifax is being defeatist. He says our aim can no longer be to crush Germany, but rather to preserve our own integrity and independence." Stanley Bruce, the Australian high commissioner in London, told Chamberlain of his conviction that the time to approach Mussolini and Hitler had come — something that Chamberlain found necessary to mention to the Cabinet. Kennedy, who was apparently well informed, sent a message to Roosevelt at night: "I suspect that the Germans would be willing to make peace with both the French and the British now — of course on their own terms, but on terms that would be a great deal better than they would be if the war continues" — the opposite of what Churchill thought and said. At ten P.M. there was another meeting of the War Cabinet, the third that day. They discussed the meaning of the Belgian surrender. The news from Dunkirk was grim. The rescue of the British troops had barely begun. Yet Churchill's spirits were better than the night before. He retired at midnight, after having asked for a "very weak" whiskey and soda. But his situation was not secure. After two days of protracted and exhausting debates his resolution had not, after all, carried the day.

Next morning he went to Westminster Abbey. There are days when the contrast between the bright beauty of the morning and the darkness of one's own concerns is especially poignant. This must have been one of them. In the Abbey "there was a short service of intercession and prayer. The English are loath to expose their feelings, but in my stall in the choir I could feel the pent-up, passionate emotion, and also the fear of the congregation, not of death or wounds or material loss, but of defeat and the final ruin of Britain," Churchill wrote. Then he went to the House of Commons for the first time in a week. He gave a summary of the "heavy tidings" about what was happening at Dunkirk, also about the Belgian surrender, without criticizing the Belgian king severely.

At four in the afternoon the five members of the War Cabinet assembled again, in secrecy, now in one of the rooms of the Parliament. Churchill used the term "slippery slope" again. The government's answer to the French was still due. Churchill said that "Monsieur Reynaud wants to get us to the conference table with Herr Hitler." (This was true of some people in the French government, though not quite fair to Reynaud.) Halifax now changed the main thrust of his argument somewhat. There might be no real need to act in concert with the French. "We might get better terms before France went out of the war." He still "did not see what there was in the French suggestion of trying out the possibilities of mediation which the Prime Minister felt was so wrong." Chamberlain was wobbling. "He did not see what we should lose if we said openly that, while we would fight to the end to preserve our independence, we were ready to consider decent terms if such were offered to us." He went on: "in a dispassionate survey, it was right to remember that the alternative to fighting on nevertheless involved a considerable gamble." On the one hand he, Chamberlain, "felt bound to say that he was in agreement with the Foreign Secretary in taking the view that if we thought it was possible that we could now get terms which, although grievous, would not threaten our independence, we should be right to consider such terms." On the other hand, "looking at the matter realistically, this may not be the time." In any event, this was not the rigid, obstinate Chamberlain of the recent past. His incipient fatal illness may have already sapped his strength. But it is also reasonable to surmise that Churchill's magnanimous treatment of him had had its effect. He was in the middle between Churchill and Halifax, but no longer necessarily closer to the latter than to the former. It was then that Churchill said that "nations which went down fighting rose again, but those which surrendered tamely were finished." He was supported by the two Labour ministers, Clement Attlee and Greenwood, with arguments that may have made an impression. Both said that they were deeply concerned with British morale, especially among the industrial classes. The very news of negotiations could become a disaster.

And still no definite decision had been taken. The War Cabinet meeting broke up at six. They would meet again in an hour. Churchill looked tired. But then he took an extraordinary step. Whether he had planned it much ahead we do not know. Perhaps he did: the fact that this time the Cabinet had met in the Parliament building may have had something to do with it. Now that the five members of the War Cabinet had left the room, Churchill asked the other ministers, about twenty-five of them, to enter. He spoke to them about the situation at Dunkirk. Then he said that the Italians and the Germans might offer terms but they must be declined.

> I have thought carefully in these last days whether it was part of my duty to consider entering into negotiations with That Man. But it was idle to think that, if we tried to make peace now, we should get better terms than if we fought it out. The Germans would demand our fleet — that would be called "disarmament" — our naval bases, and much else. We should become a slave state, though a British government which would be Hitler's puppet would be set up, under

Mosley or some such person. And where should we be at the end of all that?

Then he said — as he recalled in his war memoirs, "quite casually, and not treating it as a point of special significance: 'Of course, whatever happens at Dunkirk, we shall fight on.' " These words brought about a sudden explosion of feeling. The ministers shouted their approval, they surrounded the prime minister, some of them patted him on the back. They must have known something of the divisions within the War Cabinet; more, of the considerations about negotiations at the highest level. Now their suppressed anxieties were resolved.

Churchill may have planned this meeting to strengthen his hand in the War Cabinet. In any event, he was heartened by this. His tiredness had melted away. He must have sensed that this was a turning point. The entire thing lasted not more than a half hour. At seven the War Cabinet returned again. Chamberlain and Halifax had their draft answer to Reynaud ready. Churchill agreed to the text. He also thought that an appeal to the United States at the present time would be "altogether premature. If we made a bold stand against Germany, that would command their admiration and respect; but a grovelling appeal, if made now, would have the worst possible effect." It appeared now that Chamberlain was on Churchill's side.

No negotiations at this time.

He had come through. He had worn down Halifax. That evening Chips Channon wrote in his diary: "I think there is a definite plot afoot to oust Halifax, and all the gentlemen of England, from the Government, and even from the House of Commons. Sam Hoare warned Rab [Butler] of this scheme only yesterday, before leaving today to be our Ambassador in Spain." There was no such plot; and Halifax would come around to serving Churchill loyally. There was another item of news that, if not entirely good, was at least promising. More than twenty-five thousand troops had been ferried home from Dunkirk during the day. Before midnight Churchill dictated another message to Reynaud. "In my view if we both stand out we may yet save ourselves from the fate of Denmark or Poland. Our success must depend first on our unity, then on our courage and endurance." In Paris Reynaud, too, was heartened by Churchill's resolve: but unlike Churchill, he continued to face an increasingly divided government.

"Our courage and endurance," yes; but wasn't that a singular usage of the plural? The crux of the matter was British morale — the morale of the British people, even more than the morale of the troops around Dunkirk. Those Cabinet meetings of the three days of the slippery slope, 26, 27 and 28 May, were decisive. I cannot improve here on the calm, impressive summary of Philip Bell, in a book whose subject was not British morale but British relations with France at the time: "There can be no doubt that if the War Cabinet had agreed to the French proposal, and approached Mussolini with a view to mediation, they could not have gone back on that decision. Once the possibility of negotiation had been opened, it could not have been closed, and the government could not have continued to lead the country in outright defiance of German power." Churchill was not only a patriot and a fighter and a man who knew Hitler; he understood the supreme importance of national morale. On the one hand he told the Cabinet to prepare for the worst: "No countenance should be given publicly to the view that France might collapse, but we must not allow ourselves to be taken by surprise by any event." But he also found time to issue a general, strictly confidential directive during that crowded day: "In these dark days the Prime Minister would be grateful if all his colleagues in the government, as well as important officials, would maintain a high morale in their circles; not minimising the gravity of events, but showing confidence in our ability and inflexible resolve to continue the war till we have broken the will of the enemy to bring all Europe under his domination."

Yet, in concluding this description of those three fateful days, there remains one episode — if that is what it was — for our consideration. On 28 May Churchill, for the second time, wrote to Lloyd George, inviting him into the Cabinet. He found time for that, too, during the harried, dramatic, exceptionally eventful day. The composition of that letter could not have been easy. Churchill put in a condition: the War Cabinet, including Chamberlain, must be unanimous in such an invitation. Why did he do this? After all, it was Lloyd George who, after having met Hitler in September 1936, pronounced him as "the greatest living German." In October 1939 Lloyd George said openly in Parliament that Hitler's peace offers must be taken seriously. There can be only two possible explanations for Churchill's move. He owed nothing to Lloyd George — except for his loyal memories of their mutual esteem and collaboration in the past, especially after he, Churchill, had been dismissed from the government because of the Dardanelles fiasco in 1915. To include Lloyd George in the government now might further enhance the impression of a broad national unity. That is one explanation. The other is that Churchill — privately, not publicly — was well aware of the possibility that one military disaster (including one at Dunkirk) might yet follow another, and that the time might come when he would be forced to give up the combat and give way to a government that would have to negotiate with Hitler — and then Churchill would prefer that such a government be led by someone like Lloyd George, not by someone like Mosley.

We do not know. Next day Lloyd George refused the offer. He would not work with Chamberlain, whom he despised. (Later in June, he said to his secretary that he was "not going with this gang. There will be a change. The country does not realize the peril it is in.")

On that day, 29 May, Churchill was encouraged by the news of increased withdrawals from Dunkirk. He was also encouraged by a letter of support from Cardinal Hinsley, the Roman Catholic primate of England. "The Cardinal is vigorous and tough, and I cannot see that it would do any harm if he made it absolutely clear to his brethren over the water that, whatever happened, we are going on to the end." At least for the time being, the political crisis was over. On 31 May Churchill flew to Paris again. He even impressed the French, at least some of them. The news from Dunkirk was not too bad. On 1 June the Italian ambassador in London, Halifax's former conversant, reported to Rome that "during the last two days the sense of confidence in London seems to have largely risen." That day Churchill directed that there must be no plans about some future evacuation of the royal family to Canada, nor that of some of the paintings in the National Gallery. "No. Bury them in caves and cellars. None must go. We are going to beat them." Having returned from Paris, for the first time since he had become premier he was able to spend a partial weekend at Chartwell.

Some people were still worried about Halifax. Oliver Harvey, at the Paris embassy, wrote in his diary on 31 May: "It looks as if Halifax may have evolved some scheme for mediation by Italy. . . . I cannot put it past him. It would be fatal." Three days later: "Halifax, as I had suspected, had been anxiously exploring peace proposals . . . but P. M. had flatly turned them down." He need not have worried by then. It is interesting and perhaps amusing to note that two weeks later Halifax himself, whether consciously or not, would use Churchill's own phrase. On 13 June in the Cabinet Halifax said that if the French were to ask for an armistice, "they would embark on a slippery slope, which would lead to the loss of their fleet, and eventually of their liberty." At the end of May Churchill had avoided the slippery slope. But the course of the war was still hurtling downward for him and for his people.

LITTLE ABOUT these critical days in London evoked the attention of Hitler. He (and Mussolini) were more aware of the divided opinions in Paris. A fortnight later Hitler would become more interested in what was happening to Churchill. The end of May was perhaps the first crucial period when Churchill understood the prospects of the war better than Hitler understood Churchill. Whatever happens at Dunkirk, Churchill kept repeating, the British will fight on. Whatever happens at Dunkirk, Hitler thought and on occasion said, the British will be forced to make a deal. He did not realize what the British evacuation of 250,000 of their troops would mean to British morale and to Churchill's prestige.

After Dunkirk Churchill said, properly and honestly, that "wars are not won by evacuations." Hitler would have wholly agreed. Months had to pass until it dawned on him that Dunkirk was more of a turning point than he had thought at the time. He saw it as but another milestone on the downward path of Allied and British failures. If it was a historical turning point at all, it marked the final expulsion of the British from the continent of Europe. It mattered not much to him whether that was an expulsion or a retreat. With all of the conundrum of who (and how, and why) was responsible for that Halt Order on 24 May, Hitler did not understand the British well enough. During the Dunkirk days he made a remark that the sight of a beaten army often breaks the spirit of an entire people. That is often true. Yet the British did not really see the returning soldiers as those of a beaten army. Hitler did not see the pictures of Englishmen and Englishwomen cheering and waving and handing mugs of tea and glasses of lemonade to the soldiers leaning out of the narrow windows of the Southern Railway trains on the sun-washed platforms of Kentish village stations all along the line, coming home from Dunkirk and Dover.

Even *after* 26 May — that is, when Rundstedt's push toward Dunkirk resumed — Hitler did not (unlike on so many other occasions) urge his generals to push on. On 31 May General Fedor von Bock, one of those few old-Prussian types who stood by Hitler till the end, exclaimed in his diary: "When we finally arrive at Dunkirk [the English] will be gone!" Rundstedt had told him that he must be careful not to wear down his troops in close fighting around the bridgehead. Bock did not trust that argument. He believed that Rundstedt had influenced Hitler. But that influence was reciprocal. Hitler and Rundstedt were very close in 1940: the latter was then, and for some time he would remain, Hitler's favorite general, trusted with the command of the most important portions of the front.

In the last days of May — at the time when Churchill, in London, had weathered the worst and when the scene at Dunkirk had brightened a little for him — Hitler's optimism had risen high. He was much heartened by what was happening at Narvik, which British, French and Polish troops had finally captured but without seriously damaging the German mountain regiments led by a very able general (Eduard Dietl); and now the Allies, so sorely pressed in their homelands, were about to give up Narvik again, and all of northern Norway with it. Hitler had earlier said that if he were Churchill, Narvik would mean an entire campaign for him. For a moment another negotiator appeared in the wings. The Swede Birger Dahlerus, the amateur intermediary in 1939 between Berlin and London, proposed — in agreement with the Swedish government — that northern Norway might be left unoccupied by both Germans and British. But neither Hitler nor Churchill was interested in that now.

On 28 May Hitler talked for the first time of his idea of restructuring — that is, reducing — the German army after the war, to a substantial force of 120 divisions, of which no fewer than 30 were to be motorized. Next day he said that he wanted to take a tour of northwestern France and Flanders. He also dictated a letter to Mussolini, asking him to postpone his entry into the war by a week or so. In that letter Hitler was employing military arguments that were unconvincing. Did he do this because he hoped for some kind of signal from London before Mussolini would make his fatal move to extend the war further? We do not know.

Mussolini's answer stated that Italy would enter the war in ten days, on 11 June. That reached Hitler when he had arrived back at his headquarters from his tour — a strange tour that had relatively little to do with military decisions, even though it took place on the very days when the Dunkirk evacuation rose to its highest totals (including now not only British but French troops rescued from the beaches). On the morning of 1 June Hitler flew to Brussels. He met three of his generals. Then he was driven westward, to visit some of the places where he had soldiered during World War I. He spent the night in a château near Lille. He did not visit the front, and spent less than an hour with his troops when he attended their midday meal at a field kitchen next day. Then he went to Rundstedt's headquarters, where they talked for an hour. By that time most of the British had sailed from Dunkirk; but this seemed not to matter much to either of them. Hitler made a curious remark that was recorded the next day by General Halder (or, more precisely, by Halder's representative, General Hasso von Etzdorf, in Rundstedt's headquarters). He said that there was "a slight difference [*ein kleiner Gegensatz*] between Italy and Germany. Italy's main enemy had become England. Germany's main enemy was France." Then he said that the British would soon be ready for his "reasonable peace [*vernünftigen Friedensschluss*]." There is some reason to speculate that, after nine days had passed, this was Hitler's first rationalization to his generals of his Halt Order before Dunkirk and of its consequences. To say, however — as stated by the principal German historian of the Second World War, in what is still often regarded as his indispensable book on Hitler's strategy in 1940 and 1941 — that "from his viewpoint" Hitler's offers to Britain were "seriously meant" and "subjectively, honest" are German exaggerations.

Hitler returned to his headquarters in Germany early the evening of Sunday, 2 June. Packing there had already begun for the transfer to a new billet, a château in Bruly-la-Pêche, a few miles from Rocroi, just inside Belgium. The site had been selected for him by Rundstedt. Churchill had just returned to London from Chequers.

IV

ALONE?

31 May–30 June

IN THE first days of June 1940 there came a subtle change in the nature of the duel between Hitler and Churchill. Hitler realized that his conquest of Western Europe would be achieved even faster than he and his generals had planned. He thought that with the retreat of the last of the British from Dunkirk the corner had been turned. Churchill thought that, too; but the views and the moods of the two duelists were different. Hitler believed (and his successes seemed to confirm it) that not only the remaining campaign in France but the entire war would be short, because that was the way wars were now being fought. Churchill, who for a while had also thought that this war would be short, and that time was working against Hitler because of the constraints of the German war economy, had begun to change his mind: because of many things, very much including the German occupation of Western Europe, the war would be long. Having survived a most serious challenge to his leadership, having avoided a British catastrophe at Dunkirk, his resolution (perhaps more than his confidence) was as strong as, if not stronger than, before. Hitler's confidence was stronger than his resolution. He was still speculating about what the English might do. In that, too, we may detect a subtle change in his interests. When, in May, he talked occasionally about forcing the English to make peace, he spoke in general terms, while he was interested only in military intelligence. After 2 June he began more and more to look at fragments of political intelligence put before him. Ribbentrop, his foreign minister, had appointed his personal representative to Hitler's headquarters; now Hitler included this man, Walther Hewel, in almost all of his staff conferences. Hitler now read the "brown sheets" (so-called because of the color of the paper on which they were mimeographed or type-written), the products of a special service containing confidential information and intelligence, including the secret wiretaps of telephone conversations. (At that time these were prepared by a Forschungsamt, the research bureau of the Luftwaffe, not yet by Himmler's Security Service.) In May Hitler's contempt for Churchill was such that he paid relatively little attention to Churchill's person. In June his hatred for Churchill began to activate his interest. He wanted to know more about Churchill — more precisely, about his political and personal weaknesses.

Hitler's was not, by nature, an optimistic temperament. Convinced (and often perspicacious) about the weaknesses of his opponents, throughout his career he despised most of them; but a man with such powerful hatreds as Hitler could not be an optimist, since it is in the nature of hatred to expect the worst from one's enemies. Yet his confidence in the rightness of his own vision was such that in crucial instances and in the short run it was suffused with optimism — which was the case this time. Even before the great southward German offensive on 5 June began he did not doubt that the conquest of France would be accomplished in a few weeks. In June 1940 Hitler saw the war in Europe in much the same way as he saw the political struggle in Germany from 1930 to 1933, before he had reached power. It is amazing (the clearest evidence of this is in Goebbels's diaries) how Hitler, a political outsider in more than one way, and a leader of what was then still a relatively small and extremist party, had never flinched in his belief that he would come to power, sooner rather than later — which is what actually happened, because he not only outwitted his opponents but convinced the German conservatives of his popularity, and also of his respectability. In 1940 Hitler saw the collapse of the Western European democracies, and particularly that of the weak and corrupt French republic, as something similar to the collapse of his socialist and democratic opponents in Germany eight years before. The British, to him, were somewhat like the German conservatives had been then: they would soon realize that they would have to make a deal with him, and largely on his terms.

He moved to his new headquarters, Bruly-la-Pêche ("Wolfs-

schanze," Wolf's Redoubt, a name he had chosen instead of the original "Waldwiese," Forest Clearing, a château and outbuildings, some
of which had no running water for his staff), on 5 June, the day after
the last ships had sailed from Dunkirk. He ordered a national celebra-
tion in the Reich on that day: all buildings beflagged, church bells
ringing. The communiqué he had the army draft was unusually grandiloquent, exaggerating the extent of the victory at Dunkirk, describ-
ing it as one of the greatest battles ever fought and won. Yet we saw
that he had paid relatively little attention to the fighting around Dunkirk, and that three days earlier he had found it necessary to rationalize to his generals his reasons for the Halt Order on 24 May.

It was then that he made the remark that while Italy's main enemy
seemed to be England, Germany's main enemy was France. Even before the generals assembled for that conference in Rundstedt's headquarters Hitler made another unexpected remark. As he was walking
up and down with some of the generals, talking to them informally,
he said that he expected England to come to "reasonable terms" —
and after that he would be free for his main task, the defeat of Bol-
shevist Russia. ("The problem is only: how will I then explain it to my
people.") There is something curious about that statement. (There
may even be a question of its authenticity. Its source is the recollec-
tion of a single person, General Georg von Sodenstern, Rundstedt's
chief of staff, to a German and then to an American historian as late
as 1954; none of the other generals present recalled that surprising
statement in their memoirs.)* In any case, Hitler's words were contrary to the directive he had issued a few days earlier: that in view of
the coming peace, plans for the reduction of the army should be
made. I am inclined to think — that is, if he made that statement on 2
June at all — that it was part and parcel of his rationalizations about
Dunkirk. Hitler — who had profited throughout his entire career
from the custom of explaining his decisions by referring to their ultimate motive of anti-Communism — wanted to impress his generals
with his political wisdom. The English would soon see the light; then
he would go on to conquer Russia. (We shall see that two months
later his priorities would be reversed: he would tell some of his generals that Russia might have to be conquered first, in order to make

* We must also consider the tendency of some of the German generals, in the early
1950s, to impress Americans by telling them that the main purpose of the Third Reich had
been the war against Communist Russia, not against England.

the British, and the Americans, see the light.) The generals were now inclined to think that with the defeat of France the war in the west would come to its end. There was as yet no plan to go on to England. A few days later a general in Rundstedt's headquarters did ask an intelligence officer, Lieutenant (later General) Alfred Philippi, to prepare a paper about possible plans for a landing in England across from Calais, but it was presented neither to Hitler nor to his chief army adviser, General Jodl.

There was another change in Hitler's argumentation. As early as 23 January Rudolf Hess noted that the Führer "decided that work should begin on the recovery of [the former German] colonies." On 20 May Hitler told General Jodl that he would be ready to make peace with England after the return of some of those colonies. Yet on 2 June General Wilhelm Ritter von Leeb wrote in his diary what he had heard Hitler say: "Since we do not have a navy comparable to the English one, we cannot expect to occupy their colonies. Hence it should be easy to find a basis for negotiating a peace with the English." Hitler had not only the British but also the Americans in mind. By that time he was more and more aware of Churchill's relationship with Roosevelt. He paid increasing attention to the reports of the German military attaché in Washington: Boetticher "knows how to see behind the scenes." Hitler and Goebbels had decided to tone down anti-American propaganda in the German press and radio. On 21 May, having learned that the French naval command in the Antilles had occupied the Dutch island of Aruba, Hitler ordered German submarines that "for the time being the Aruban oil installations must not be fired at, because of consideration of American interests." He was preparing to impress Americans with his respect for the Monroe Doctrine.

Thus Hitler wished to impress, not only himself, not only his generals, but — at least indirectly — the outside world that the time for peace was near. The German Foreign Ministry took up the cue. This is significant for two reasons: because it was headed by Ribbentrop, who was Hitler's most faithful minion, indeed his toady; and because Ribbentrop (partly for personal reasons, going back to his unimpressive experiences in London) hated the English. But now he was willing to establish contacts with them. Prince Max Hohenlohe, a somewhat unusual member of that most ramified and extensive family of nobles, had served the interests of the Third Reich well, before the Munich crisis, when he had impressed Lord Runciman, and also the other Chamberlainites, with the German case in Czechoslovakia (the prince's estate was in the Sudetenland). On 3 June Hohenlohe met Ribbentrop in Berlin. A few days earlier he had written to Hewel. On 6 June he left for Switzerland (where he had also been a few weeks before) and for Spain. In Switzerland he planned to meet either certain English diplomats or influential persons, including Carl Burckhardt, or both. On 31 May Count Teleki, the Hungarian prime minister, made an extraordinary statement to a group of journalists he had convoked in the Hungarian parliament building. He said that while until recently the world had expected a long war, the impressive German victories, "surprising their friends and enemies alike," made it probable that the war would not last long; indeed, that it might be much shorter than had been thought. Teleki was a conservative, not a Nazi sympathizer. He tried to maintain his contacts with Britain and the United States. The Germans knew that. It seems that Teleki made that somewhat extraordinary statement after he had talked with the German minister to Budapest, Otto von Erdmansdorff — who also knew that the British minister to Budapest, Owen O'Malley, was well connected in British Tory circles. (Erdmansdorff did not know that thirteen years earlier O'Malley had been close to Churchill, working as his private research assistant.) In November 1940 Hitler himself would say something to Teleki about Russia, presumably wishing to have that leak to Britain through O'Malley.

The notion that the war might be coming to an end was filtering through the Nazi hierarchy. One indication of that was the paper Himmler presented to Hitler as early as 25 May, about plans to transport the Jews of Europe to Africa. Hitler marked his agreement on it. On 3 June Rademacher, the "Judenreferent" (Jewish expert) installed in the Foreign Ministry by Ribbentrop, presented for the first time the Madagascar Plan: to establish a state for all of the Jews of Europe, who would be deported to that large tropical island, under German supervision, after the surrender of France.

HITLER'S MIND was more complicated than Churchill's. At first sight such a statement may seem strange. Hitler was single-minded; but his self-confidence together with the ideological bent of his mind would, at times, compromise his concentration. Churchill's mind would flit from one subject to another with astonishing rapidity (and later in the war his very powers of concentration became impaired);

but in 1940 he could hardly have been more single-minded. One evening, after one of the worst days in June, he was unusually impatient with his new private secretary, John Martin. "At last he rose wearily to go upstairs to bed but not before he had laid his hand kindly on my shoulder and said he was sorry there had been no time in the rush of those days to get to know me. 'You know,' he added, 'I may seem to be very fierce, but I am fierce only with one man — Hitler.' "

In more than one way the plebeian Hitler was more complicated than the aristocratic Churchill. Besides the different qualities of their respective rhetoric, they used speech for different purposes — which, in turn, tells us something of their respective characters. Hitler was more secretive than Churchill. When Hitler spoke in public, he was voluble, speaking at times for hours, gushing forth a torrent of harsh words, in order to inspire his auditors with his confidence. When he spoke to his circle, to foreign visitors and at times to his generals he was talkative, ranging from one subject to another, in order to inspire them with his insights and foresight. And yet he was a very secretive man. He kept some of his most important thoughts to himself. General Jodl knew that. He would write in his cell in Nuremberg that Hitler of course knew, before most others, that the war would be lost; but how could he have been expected to tell that to the German people? There were many matters (including the progress of the extermination of the Jews, or of certain contacts with the enemy) about which Hitler preferred to read nothing, hear nothing and say nothing. Speech, for Hitler, was seldom primarily a function of self-expression. It was to influence — to inspire and to impress — others.

Churchill was less secretive. Churchill, too, would make public speeches in order to inspire people, withholding his worries and anxieties (though, as we have seen before, he knew that the English people were ready and willing to accept bad news as well as good). He was also statesman and politician enough to know that certain significant, or even important, matters must be held in secrecy. There were, of course, differences between the public and the private Churchill, but they were not at all as sharp as in the case of Hitler. All in all, there was more unity in the character of the epicurean and the heroic, of the self-indulgent and the indomitable, of the sentimental and the hardheaded, of the cosmopolitan and the patriotic, of the half-American Churchill than in that of the fanatical, valley-Austrian Hitler. There was contradiction in Churchill's character; but there was no split-mindedness in it. He was much more moody than Hitler, but there were no great differences between Churchill's public and private opinions and sentiments. In both public and private life he used (and often enjoyed) words for the same purposes. He was certainly voluble, but less voluble than Hitler. His most famous speeches were shorter than Hitler's. Sir Edward Bridges, the secretary of the War Cabinet, remembered how "significant are the frankness and freedom with which he would discuss things with us, or in our presence. When his mind was occupied with some important issue, he would often discuss it off and on for two or three days with those who happened to be summoned to his work-room. . . . In this sort of discussion he would keep nothing back. He would express the most outspoken views about the public reactions or attitudes of the most important persons, or about the various ways in which the situation might be expected to develop. And these confidences were not prefixed by 'You must not repeat this.'" Hitler, on the other hand, would occasionally remark to his secretaries: "Don't write that down."

Churchill's character was pleasanter than Hitler's. There is nothing very startling in that. But were Churchill's virtues sufficient to defeat Hitler or, at least, to thwart him? By 1 June Churchill had survived a serious challenge from behind. His hands were, perhaps temporarily, free. But his real opponent was Hitler, not Halifax. One's hands may be free, but one's arm might not be strong enough. During the first days of June Churchill knew that very well. Those convoluted discussions with Halifax had now faded away — though, as we shall see, their meaning had not entirely disappeared from his mind. What loomed before him was the prospect of Hitler conquerant: conquerant of France, and then of Britain? Churchill had to struggle against both, in that order of consequence. It is of inestimable importance that even at that time, aware as he was of the low point of Britain's fortunes, he read Hitler's strategy well. On 2 June his long minute to General Ismay closed with "a general observation. As I have personally felt less afraid of a German attempt at invasion than of the piercing of the French line on the Somme or Aisne and the fall of Paris, I have naturally believed the Germans will choose the latter." Churchill thought that the Germans would not attempt a direct attack on England before they had conquered France. He dictated a variety of orders against the dangers of some sudden German descent on England. He warned that the long coastline of the island was not, and indeed never had been, entirely immune to some kind of surprise landing. But he was mainly concerned with France. He was right — but at the same time he was wrong in thinking that the French army might still hold the Germans, on the Somme or somewhere within France. He believed, both during and even after Dunkirk, that the British military commitment of fighting along with the French, *within* France, must neither weaken nor cease. That, together with his customary generosity, made him insist that the British army and navy must carry on at Dunkirk until not only the last British but the French troops were rescued. "The British Army would have to stick it out as long as possible so that the evacuation of the French could continue." It is significant that he said this on 30 May — that is, before he would fly to Paris again to hearten the French.

On that day, in Paris, the French were surprised to learn how many of the troops were being lifted off from Dunkirk. At least Reynaud was impressed, again, by the strength of Churchill's resolution. But at the end of their meeting Churchill coupled his rhetoric of indomitable British resolve with a somber statement of his own prospect of a Götterdämmerung (or call it *Untergang des Abendlandes*): "If Germany defeated *either* ally or both, she would give no mercy; we should be reduced to the status of vassals and slaves *forever*. It would be better far that the civilisation of Western Europe with all of its achievements should come to a tragic but splendid end than that the two great democracies should linger on, stripped of all that made life worth living." The italics are mine. Note the *forever*. It corresponded with Churchill's mood. Note the *either*. This was not mere rhetoric: Churchill, at that moment, still felt that the prospects of the war were perhaps indissolubly bound to the continued resistance of France. He did not change his mind about that for some time. On 2 June he still insisted at the War Cabinet that more British units must be sent to France, since otherwise the French "will not continue in the war." It was then that for the first time he spoke of forming a British bridgehead in Brittany, where troops would hold a line even if Paris were to fall — a most impractical plan.

On 4 June he made one of his great speeches in Parliament. It was not a long speech, hardly more than thirty minutes. Some of his phrases were historic. "We are told that Herr Hitler has a plan for invading the British Isles. This has often been thought of before." It was the "we shall never surrender" speech, ending with an evocation of America. "We shall fight on the beaches, we shall fight on the landing grounds, we shall fight in the fields and in the streets, we shall fight in the hills; we shall never surrender, and even if, which I do not for a moment believe, this island or a large part of it were subjugated or starving, then our Empire beyond the seas, armed and guarded by the British Fleet, would carry on the struggle, until, in God's good time, the new world, with all its power and might, steps forth to the rescue and the liberation of the old." The speech was a great success; it inspired even those who had disliked and distrusted him in the past, Chips Channon, for one. (Later that day the speech was broadcast to the British people.)

At the same time Churchill was deeply worried, not only about the potential collapse of France but about the inefficiency of the British army, and then about British morale. He was careful to state in that otherwise inspiring speech that, with all of the enthusiasm produced by what had happened at Dunkirk, "wars are not won by evacuations." He was aware of the bitterness that many of the troops at Dunkirk felt as they thought that the Royal Air Force had given them insufficient help in warding off the German planes that kept attacking them on the beaches. "Many of our soldiers coming back have not seen the Air Force at work; they saw only the bombers which escaped its protective attack. They underrate its achievements. I have heard much talk of this; that is why I go out of my way to say this." During one of those days Churchill met the later famous general Bernard Law Montgomery for the first time. Montgomery said that he was disgusted with how many people saw Dunkirk as a victory. He criticized the shoulder ribbons issued to the troops, marked "Dunkirk." They were not "heroes." "If it was not understood" that the army suffered a defeat at Dunkirk, then "our island home was now in grave danger." The secretary to the War Cabinet said that "evacuation is becoming our greatest national industry." In his paper to the Chiefs of Staff on 2 June Churchill himself seemed to recognize that Hitler, in a way, had held off at Dunkirk, from where the returning troops were men "whose mettle [the Germans] had already tested, and from whom they have recoiled, *not daring seriously to molest their departure.*" (The italics are mine.) On 4 June, the same day of his great "we shall never surrender" speech, Churchill sent a minute to Ismay: "An effort must be made to shake off the mental and moral prostration to the will and initiative of the enemy from which we suffer." (It must be added that this somber admonition was preceded by a sentence in which Churchill for the first time — and on the very first day after the British departure from Europe — exhorted the Chiefs of Staff to think about returning to the Continent by attacking the Germans at various points of its coasts.) On

6 June he wrote to Eden: "We are indeed the victims of a feeble and weary departmentalism." Compared to the First World War, he found "weakness, slowness, lack of grip and drive"; among other things, it was high time "to lift our affairs in the Middle East out of the catalepsy by which they are smitten." In another memo he wrote: "We seem quite incapable of *action*." He underlined the last word.

Churchill was worried about British morale. He understood that at least for the time being his own position was stronger than it had been before Dunkirk, and so was British morale. What made him anxious now was the sense that the people did not really understand the dangers immediately ahead of them. They were slow to respond. Others noted that too. During the worst days of Dunkirk George Orwell was stunned to find how many people in the pubs showed no interest in the nine o'clock news on the radio. There were defeatist mutterings in some intellectual circles; but they do not seem to have filtered down to the people at large. Churchill's main purpose at the time was not only the strengthening of national confidence but also that of national unity. On 6 June he returned to his idea of inviting Lloyd George into the Cabinet. He spoke to Halifax about this. That evening Halifax wrote in his diary: "We shall see whether he accepts. Winston told me that he meant to put him through an inquisition at first. By this he means, so he explained to me, *adopting a formula I suggested to him* [my italics] that any peace terms now, as hereafter, must not be destructive of our independence." Here was the story of the slippery slope reversed: it was now Churchill who used a phrase that Halifax had employed earlier on a crucial occasion. Churchill had already gone to Chamberlain, asking him to put personal feelings aside and agree to the inclusion of Lloyd George for the sake of national unity. If Lloyd George remained "an outcast," he would become "a focus for regathering discontents" with the war. Chamberlain's reply (Churchill had first talked to him and then wrote him) was reasonable. He would agree, on two conditions. The first was that, in order to work in the War Cabinet together, Lloyd George would "drop his personal feud and prejudice against me." The second was that the recently appearing attacks in some of the press against Chamberlain must be halted before Lloyd George's inclusion in the Cabinet was announced, since that inclusion must not look as if it were "part of a bargain between you and me in return for which you have agreed to protect me."

What is significant in this matter is not only the complete loyalty and cooperation that now existed between Churchill and Chamberlain (itself one guarantee of national unity) but, even more, Churchill's purpose to be able to count on Lloyd George in the event of a great national crisis. He knew that Lloyd George was a potential spokesman for a compromise peace with Hitler. But Lloyd George refused again. At the same time Churchill acted on Chamberlain's second condition. After Dunkirk some of the newspapers had begun to attack Chamberlain and the Chamberlainites, at times with the epithet "Guilty Men." Churchill was very much against that. On 7 June he spoke to some of the owners of these newspapers, requesting that they stop those attacks. He said that most of the members of Parliament were, after all, people who had been Chamberlain's strong supporters. They may no longer be typical representatives of British opinion or feeling. But the House of Commons still ruled the country. "If [he] trampled on these men . . . they would set themselves against him, and in such internecine strife lay the Germans' best chance for victory."

So "the Germans' best chance for victory," to Churchill, was a break in the national unity of England. But when he said this, on 7 June, the Germans' military fortunes had made another decisive advance. On 5 June, the day that the German people celebrated the great victory in Flanders, their army rolled into action again, across the Somme; two days later they had broken what remained of the French (and British) lines; the French (and British) units were in full retreat. General von Bock, who had been so impatient with Rundstedt at Dunkirk, now rushed ahead on the coastal flank, pushing the remaining British units toward Rouen and Le Havre and eventually capturing most of them there.

And now it was the United States that, together with France, began to preoccupy Churchill's mind. He had invoked "the new world" at the end of his speech on 4 June. That was not mere rhetoric. He had some knowledge about new stirrings in American public opinion, as the American people, and especially their social and political elite, began to react to the incredible events across the Atlantic in France. But Churchill had not much to go on. He was downcast by American slowness and by what he saw as Roosevelt's mistaken calculations about the British fleet. By this time Churchill was well aware of Roosevelt's trying to work through the Canadian prime minister. On the day of his great speech, with his invocation of the New World, Churchill had learned that some American supplies were slowly coming through the pipeline but that Roosevelt "could not spare any" of the destroyers. Next day — and what a full day that was — Churchill sent a message to Mackenzie King. "I do not know whether it will be possible to keep France in the war or not. I hope they will, even at the worst, maintain a gigantic guerrilla." (That idea of a great French guerrilla was something that Churchill would repeat often during the next few days, after which it would fade from his mind.) But:

> We must be careful not to let Americans view too complacently the prospect of a British collapse, out of which they would get the British Fleet and the guardianship of the British Empire, minus Great Britain ... if America continued neutral, and we were overpowered, I cannot tell what policy might be adopted by a pro-German administration such as would undoubtedly be set up.
>
> Although President is our best friend, no practical help has [reached us] from the United States yet. . . .

Four days later Churchill expressed himself even more strongly to Lord Lothian, the British ambassador in Washington. A pro-German government might surrender the fleet. "This dastard deed would not be done by His Majesty's present advisers, but if Mosley were Prime Minister or some other Quisling Government set up, it is exactly what they would do, and perhaps the only thing they could do, and the President should bear this very clearly in mind." (Note that Mosley was in Brixton prison at the time.) Lothian should discourage "any complacent assumption" in Washington that they would "pick up the debris of the British Empire" by their present policy. "If we go down Hitler has a very good chance of conquering the world." It is interesting to note that in the last moment Churchill struck out the phrase "if Mosley were Prime Minister."

Kennedy, ever distrustful of Churchill, wired the American secretary of state that talk of going to Canada had faded in London, "which made him suspicious." Bullitt, in Paris, incensed temporarily by the British decision not to send more planes to France, wrote to his friend Roosevelt that he suspected the British would negotiate: they "might be conserving their Air Force and Fleet so as to use them as bargaining points in negotiations with Hitler." In his memoirs Cordell Hull wrote that he and Roosevelt had not thought that, because they were impressed with Churchill's speeches. Whether this was true or not, on 10 June Roosevelt made his first definitely unneutral statement. That was the day Mussolini declared war on Britain and France. Roosevelt was about to deliver the commencement address at the University of Virginia in Charlottesville. On the way down he

added a few strong phrases to the text of the speech that had been
prepared for him by the State Department:

> Some indeed still hold to the now obvious delusion that we of this
> United States can safely permit the United States to become a lone
> island in a world dominated by the philosophy of force. Such an is-
> land may be the dream of those who still talk and vote as isolation-
> ists. Such an island represents to me and to the overwhelming ma-
> jority of Americans today a helpless nightmare, the helpless
> nightmare of a people lodged in prison, handcuffed, hungry, and
> fed through the bars from day to day by the contemptuous, unpity-
> ing masters of other continents. . . .
> . . . Let us not hesitate — all of us — to proclaim certain truths.
> Overwhelmingly we, as a nation — and this applies to all the other
> American nations — are convinced that military and naval victory
> for the gods of force and hate would endanger the institutions of
> democracy in the Western World, and that equally, therefore, the
> whole of our sympathies lies with those nations that are giving their
> life blood in combat against these forces. . . .
> . . . On this tenth day of June, 1940, the hand that held the dag-
> ger has stuck it into the back of its neighbor. . . .

Churchill had been in a very bad temper that day. At night, listening to Roosevelt's speech, he and his colleagues breathed a "deep
growl of satisfaction." He immediately sent a message to Roosevelt
next morning. He asked for the destroyers again. But the key sentence of his message was that "everything must be done to keep
France in the fight and to prevent any idea of the fall of Paris, should
it occur, becoming the occasion of any kind of parley."

The fall of Paris . . . When Churchill wrote that, the French government had already left the capital for a temporary lodgment in the valley of the Loire. There was yet another catastrophe that Churchill
had to face. On top of the evacuation of what was left of northern
Norway the German battleship *Scharnhorst* sank the British aircraft
carrier *Glorious* and two destroyers. During that week of new disasters Churchill's mood varied. On 4 June he wrote to the king, ending
with "Better days will come — though not yet," and to former Prime
Minister Stanley Baldwin: "I do not feel the burden too heavily, but I
cannot say that I have enjoyed being Prime Minister vy much so far."
Five days later he wrote to his friend General Jan Christiaan Smuts of
South Africa: "I see only one way through now, to wit, that Hitler

should attack this country, and in so doing break his air weapon." He added that the full entry of the United States in the war had become "vital." But that was still far away. In another week Britain would be alone. The French would drop out of the war, and the Americans would not come into it.

IT WAS at this moment — after Roosevelt's Charlottesville speech — that Hitler realized how important the American factor had become. He had planned a war in Europe, not a world war. In this, as well as in its methods, the present war would be different from the First World War. His aim was that of a great continental German Reich, dominating most of Europe, especially its east. Some Americans were beginning to say that he wanted to rule the world. That was not true. That Roosevelt was a main enemy of his he had realized a year and a half before. On 30 January 1939, on the occasion of the sixth anniversary of his coming to power, Hitler made a speech, the ominous importance of which appears only in retrospect. It was the first time that he spoke of something more drastic than the expulsion of Jews from the Reich. In that speech, too, he referred for the first time to American hostility to the Third Reich. He warned the Jews "inside and outside Europe" that if they were to "succeed" in bringing about another world war, the result would be "the annihilation of the Jewish race throughout Europe." He could not lay his hands on America's Jews. They had better watch out: the Jews in Europe were the hostages of their behavior; God help them if their brethren in America would mobilize the United States against him. By June 1940 he saw this matter — according to his lights — clearly. Behind Churchill stood Roosevelt; and behind Roosevelt stood the Jews. It had now become important to impress the Americans, and especially Roosevelt's opponents, about the war. It was not enough to impress them that Germany was winning the war, that indeed his Germany was invincible. They had to understand that the continuation of the war made no sense at all. He had no interests in America, in the Atlantic or even in the British Empire overseas. That was what Roosevelt's isolationist opponents believed. He would now give them some ammunition.

On 13 June Karl von Wiegand, an American journalist, arrived in the Wolf's Redoubt. That was an extraordinary event. During the entire war Hitler gave no interviews to journalists, certainly none in his military headquarters. Von Wiegand was a man of German-American origin to whom Hitler had given three interviews during the 1930s. He was the chief European correspondent of the *New York Journal-American,* the principal isolationist paper of the Hearst press; and Hearst had turned from a supporter of Roosevelt's to a determined opponent. Hearst was an isolationist. Hitler knew that. He also knew that toward the end of May Wiegand had talked to a German general, suggesting that Germany ought to propose a "broadminded" or "generous" peace settlement. The importance of the Wiegand interview appears from the fact that Ribbentrop, the foreign minister, came from Berlin to be present at it.

It was more than a propaganda move. (Goebbels, the minister of propaganda, stayed in Berlin.) Even more unusual was the condition that Hitler chose to add to the interview by speaking to Wiegand "off the record." The extensive text of the interview was then carefully examined, and not released until the following day. Off the record Hitler, echoed by Ribbentrop, told Wiegand that he would not like to see the war prolonged by American intervention. He even added that he was pleased because Roosevelt, in Charlottesville, had not mentioned American participation in the war. What he, Hitler, wanted was to reassure American opinion. Now, as in the past, Germany had no interests in either North or South America. (He emphasized the latter, since Roosevelt and others had already shown their concern with "fifth column" activities there.) Hitler praised the Monroe Doctrine and Washington's foreign policy of nonintervention in European affairs. "I say, therefore: America for the Americans, Europe for the Europeans!" (He added the exclamation mark in the typed final version.) He was not concerned with the American program of rearmament. In any event — he answered Wiegand's question to that effect — American supplies of war materiel to England could not change the outcome of this war. He spoke at considerable length, ridiculing the American belief about fifth columns. That was the way to incite public opinion against opponents of American intervention. It was nothing but a dishonest instrument used by certain politicians against others whom they could not oppose honestly. (By the latter Hitler meant the isolationists. It is interesting that in one instance he — rather accurately — referred to them as "radical [American] nationalists.")

It is not because of "Fifth Columnists" in their midst that our enemies will lose this war: but because their politicians are corrupt, unscrupulous, mentally limited men. They will lose it, because their military organization is bad, and because their strategy is truly miserable. Germany will win this war, because the German people know that their cause is just, because the German military organization and leadership are the better ones, with the best army and the best equipment.

Hitler went on to say that it was never his aim to destroy the British Empire. "But now, when England has lost battle after battle, the rulers of England, with tears in their eyes, turn to America and declare that Germany threatens the British Empire with destruction. What will be destroyed in this war is a capitalist clique that was and remains willing to annihilate millions of men for the sake of their despicable personal interests. But they will be destroyed — of this I am certain — not by us but by their own peoples."

More important than their effect on America is what these statements reveal about Hitler's thinking at the time. They show, among other things, that Hitler was fairly well informed of the existence of those various American elements whose opposition to Roosevelt had now coalesced into their so-called isolationism. Hitler now hoped to profit from divisions not only in England but also in the United States. The text had some influence among American isolationists, but its immediate effect was overshadowed by the more dramatic event of the fall of Paris on the day of its publication. About Paris, too, Hitler had given orders to treat the American ambassador there with care. Following tradition (Washburn in 1870 and 1871, and Herrick in 1914), Bullitt elected to stay in Paris and face the Germans. They approached the American embassy with calculated courtesies, to which Bullitt responded with all the tact and reserve of a great envoy of classical stamp.

The fall of Paris had been foreseeable for a week at least. Hitler made no particular remark about it that day. He was privately critical of Mussolini for having resorted to a formal declaration of war on 10 June. Declarations of war were an antiquated and hypocritical practice. "That will be the last declaration of war in the history of the world. . . . Attack and march! That is the right and healthy way. I shall never sign a declaration of war. I shall act." He also foresaw that the French would fight well against the Italians, which is what happened.

As early as 15 June — the day after Paris fell and two days before the news of the French request for an armistice would come — Hitler ordered Colonel H. Boehme on his staff to prepare a text for the armistice conditions. Ten days before that Hitler had still thought the war in France might last another five or six weeks. But now he had the French in his hands. For once he showed a remarkable diplomatic talent. His terms were hard but not impossible. (The British ambassador to France would call them "diabolically clever.") The Boehme draft called for the total occupation of metropolitan France. Hitler would leave two fifths of France unoccupied, though the entire Atlantic coast would remain in German hands. The French fleet would not be surrendered to the victors but remain immobilized in French harbors, supervised by the Germans and Italians. The British would not get the French fleet. Hitler knew that this was their main concern.

Thus for the second time (the first was Norway) Hitler had bested Churchill. He not only defeated the French; he divided them from the British. He would give them a "golden bridge" for a way out. What Hitler called a golden bridge was, in reality, a cul-de-sac, a sordid little passage behind a wall. The French had no desire to be pressed against the wall; and in that cul-de-sac some of their politicians would gather.

Hitler watched for British reactions. Besides the "brown sheets," Hewel now presented him every day with excerpts of news from Britain, typed on Hitler's special large-lettered typewriter (Hitler's eyes had become far-sighted; but he wished to wear glasses — and to be seen wearing them — as little as possible). He was getting restless. On the seventeenth, immediately after the news of the French armistice request, he decided to meet Mussolini in Munich.

The German people were stunned. To foreign observers in Berlin their behavior reflected amazement rather than jubilation. Most Germans hoped that the war would now end. It took some time until their appreciation of the great victories of their armies would congeal with their less attractive wish to see England punished for continuing the war. On 17 June their former emperor, William II, sent from his exile in Holland a fulsome telegram of congratulations to Hitler. (Hitler would thank him in a matter-of-fact manner a week later.) The kaiser's phrases were full of the sounds of the grandiloquent, trumpet-and-cymbal Prussian-German military language of 1870 and 1914. But he belonged to that generation, of course.

THIS WEEK, from the tenth to the seventeenth of June, was Churchill's worst during his duel with Hitler. His stubbornness was, for once, of no great help. It had not degenerated into obstinacy: for obstinacy is often blind, and Churchill was not that. But he still hoped that the French might not give up the fight, and he tried to encourage and succor them. He did not see clearly enough that he had almost nothing to offer them.

At two-thirty on Tuesday afternoon, 11 June, he flew to meet the French leaders again. The air journey took longer than before. The pilot had to fly along a southward arc, away from the advancing Germans, to the Loire Valley, where in a château at Briare the French government now huddled. His companions saw Churchill silent, brooding in the plane. The very scene of their arrival was depressing. It was not until seven that the session began in a house named after a lily of the valley, Château Muguet, "May-lily," surely inappropriate now. (It was inappropriate in another way, too: the only telephone was in the toilet.) There were General Weygand and Marshal Pétain, unrepentant, Anglophobe and hostile. Churchill knew that his expressions of encouragement, and of the British resolve to fight on, were not enough. Yet whatever promises of further British support he could offer to the French were unimpressive, even vague. Weygand said that the decisive moment had come: the British should not keep their fighter planes in England. They should be sent to France. Churchill denied this. (Knowing the sentimental side of his character, knowing also how he felt that the French had deserved more support from the British all along, his staff feared that Churchill would offer more British planes for what remained of the battle of France, at the gravest risk to Britain. They were relieved when he did not do so.) Churchill hammered away on his main theme. Even if France were to fall, the British would fight on and break Hitler's might in time. Some of his phrases impressed some of the French. They amounted to flickers of light, but not enough to kindle the fire of the resistance of the French anew. "Darkness, rather than light," wrote General Edward Spears, "was being shed from the now lighted chandeliers. A miasma of despond had fallen on the conference like a fog. No one appeared to see his way."

Churchill was true to himself. A dinner was to be served at the conference table; but he said that he required a bath and change before dinner. Then there was "a moment of drama." "As we were taking our places," Anthony Eden remembered,

> a tall and somewhat angular figure in uniform walked by on my side of the table. This was General Charles de Gaulle, Undersecretary

for Defence, whom I had met only once before. Weygand invited
him pleasantly to take a place at his left. De Gaulle replied, curtly as
I thought, that he had instructions to sit next to the British Prime
Minister. Weygand flushed up, but made no comment, and so the
meal began.

Churchill had noticed de Gaulle before. The dinner went on without recrimination. Churchill was firm but not abrasive. All during
that awful week he would show his concern and sympathy for the
French. After dinner — it was very late — Reynaud told Churchill
that Marshal Pétain was calling for an armistice with the Germans.
Pétain had a paper ready: but he was not yet quite ready — or, in
Reynaud's words, he was "ashamed" — to present it. (Eight years
later Churchill would write in his war memoirs: "he ought also to
have been ashamed to support even tacitly Weygand's demand for
our last twenty-five squadrons of fighters, when he had made up his
mind that all was lost and that France should give in.")

Churchill slept late. Around eight in the morning he appeared in a
red silk kimono; he demanded his bath. Then there was a breakfast
meeting. Churchill ended it with a momentous statement. The
French must call him to come to France again at once, before they
would consider calling for an armistice. When the meeting broke up,
he walked over to Admiral Jean-François Darlan. "Darlan, I hope you
will never surrender the Fleet." Darlan assured him of that.

Flying back to London, Churchill saw Le Havre burning. He reported to the War Cabinet. He mentioned de Gaulle and his plans for
a Brittany bridgehead. But these were slender reeds. After midnight
Reynaud rang him up again. The connection crackled and broke. The
government was moving to the city of Tours. He asked that Churchill
come over again. He came, on 13 June 1940, his fifth visit to France
within a month, his sixth meeting with Reynaud. Four years would
pass before he would see France again. But that he did not know. The
weather was bad. They landed at the Tours airfield in driving rain. No
one met them. They had to rustle up lunch for themselves. It was not
until three-thirty that the British and French statesmen met in an un-
inspiring room of the Tours prefecture.

The meeting was not a long one. Reynaud had cabled to President
Roosevelt, pleading with him to make a definitive statement committing the United States on the French side. Churchill said that he, too,
would telegraph Roosevelt. The British delegation asked for a recess.
They went out, walking up and down in the dripping garden of that

provincial government building. There Churchill (mostly on Beaver-brook's insistence) decided not to waste their time any longer. They would not argue with the French until Roosevelt's answer came. (Perhaps that was a mistake. The full French cabinet was at another château, Cangé, twenty miles away. Had Churchill gone on to address them personally, that might have made a difference. Many in that French cabinet were still for struggling on. But now Churchill's insistence on fighting on and the news about his messages to Roosevelt had to be conveyed to the cabinet by Reynaud, and that was not enough.) At half past five Churchill and his party left for England. He had met with the French for less than two hours. It was "an abominable conference," as de Gaulle wrote later. Nothing had been accomplished, save for trying to delay matters by passing the buck to Roosevelt.

Churchill landed in London late in the evening, after a wearisome journey in the air that lasted nearly three hours. He asked the War Cabinet to assemble at half past ten. In the meantime the text of Roosevelt's answer to Reynaud's earlier message (of 10 June) had arrived. It sounded positive — more positive than, in reality, it was. Beaverbrook went so far as to say that it was now inevitable that the United States "would declare war." Churchill, too, was momentarily carried away by a wave of optimism. He said to the Cabinet that Hitler would now "no doubt . . . offer very spacious terms to the French, but these we could not permit them to accept. . . . When Hitler found that he could get no peace in this way, his only course would be to try and smash this island. He would probably make the attempt, very quickly, perhaps within a fortnight; but before the United States of America would be in the war on our side." It is remarkable how three days before Hitler drafted his armistice terms Churchill foresaw what Hitler would do with the French. Yet at the same time Churchill misread what Roosevelt would or could do. That began to appear within minutes. The American secretary of state opposed the publication of Roosevelt's phrases to Reynaud. Churchill now sat down to draft his own message to Roosevelt. He worked on it until two in the morning. It was "absolutely vital" that Roosevelt's message to Reynaud be published immediately, "in order that it may play the decisive part in turning the course of world history. It will I am sure decide the French to deny Hitler a patched-up peace with France. He needs this peace in order to destroy us and take a long step forward to world mastery. . . ."

That was not to be. Roosevelt did not agree to the publication of his message. The reasons for his reluctance were, of course, political. He was aware of his domestic opposition: of the isolationists among the Republicans but also of those within his own party, on whom he would soon have to depend for his nomination for an unprecedented third term. There was another long-range reason for his reluctance to commit the United States immediately. Roosevelt still believed that "naval power in world affairs still carries the lessons of history." He also suggested that even if the French should capitulate, that would not commit their navy — which was not the case.

That day, 14 June, Friday, the German army entered Paris. Next day Churchill drafted another crucial message to Roosevelt, evoking the worst of eventualities. "I understand all your difficulties with American public opinion and Congress, but events are moving downward at a pace where they will pass beyond the control of American public opinion when at last it is ripened. Have you considered what offers Hitler may choose to make France? . . ." A declaration that the United States will, if necessary, enter the war might save France. This was hoping against hope. Churchill knew that it would not happen. But he felt compelled to make Roosevelt aware of the worst:

> Although the present government and I personally would never fail to send the fleet across the Atlantic if resistance was beaten down here, a point may be reached in the struggle where the present ministers no longer have control of affairs and when very easy terms could be obtained for the British islands by their becoming a vassal state of the Hitler empire. A pro-German government would certainly be called into being to make peace and might present to a shattered or starving nation an almost irresistible case for entire submission to the Nazi will. The fate of the British fleet as I have already mentioned to you would be decisive on the future of the United States because if it were joined to the fleets of Japan, France, and Italy, and the great resources of German industry, overwhelming sea power would be in Hitler's hands. He might, of course, use it with a merciful moderation. On the other hand he might not. This revolution in sea power might happen very quickly and certainly long before the United States would be able to prepare against it. . . .

This was an exceptionally long message, ending with a plea for the American destroyers. Ninety minutes later Churchill sent another, shorter message to Roosevelt about the impending French armistice. But Churchill was now convinced that direct messages to the President were not decisive. He would keep in contact through the British ambassador in Washington. He composed no direct message to Roosevelt for another twenty days (one which then he decided not to send). Almost a month would pass until Churchill again wrote to Roosevelt directly.

IT WAS on the day that Paris fell that Churchill moved from Admiralty House to Downing Street. Chamberlain and his wife had finally moved to their home. Churchill was now physically lodged at the center of British government. In May he had to stay in London during the weekends. But now he would go down to Chequers, the prime minister's weekend residence, with its large terrace and rose garden surrounded by one thousand acres. He drove there in a Daimler or in a smaller Humber. (Later he would travel in an armored Lanchester automobile.) It took some time until Churchill's later famous War Room would be constructed and ready for him. Otherwise there was little change in his working habits: going through his dispatch boxes in bed, insisting on his bath (sometimes twice a day), sleeping long after lunch, staying up late after dinner. His mind worked best after he woke in the morning and again when he came down from his afternoon nap, before and during dinner. He was a good sleeper, fresh and vibrant in the morning. But there were days, as he would tell Eden later, when "I woke up with dread in my heart."

Surely that must have been so on the sixteenth of June, the most dreadful day of that most dreadful week, perhaps the most dreadful in Churchill's whole career. He was at Chequers; it was a dark gray morning, the rain pouring outside. All night telegrams of the greatest urgency had sparked and sputtered across a now lengthening distance between London and Bordeaux, whereto a broken French government had fled with little hope of repair, and where increasingly hostile authorities were trying to hold the British ambassador at arm's length. The previous night the French government at Bordeaux had adopted a sinuous compromise proposal by Camille Chautemps, a seasoned politician: inquire about the German armistice conditions, but reject them if they were to be incompatible with the remnant sovereignty and honor of France. (Eight years later the familiar phrase came again to Churchill's mind: "It was not of course possible to embark on that slippery slope and stop.") At seven in the morning of 16 June Reynaud's telegram about this armistice request reached

Churchill. Immediately he called for a meeting with the War Cabinet. He drove to London in the rain. Everything was dark: the news, its prospects, the sky, his mien. Yet he kept dictating one directive after another in the car, dealing with the most varied matters.

The next few hours of that tragic day were so full of dramatic details and so confused that historians even now, fifty years later, are not certain about the precise sequence and the whereabouts of crucial telegrams. Above and beneath everything stood the question of what would happen to the French fleet: a mass of modern warships that in 1940 was larger and more powerful than the navy of the German Reich. The first response of the War Cabinet was relatively simple. Until that morning they had considered what Churchill on one occasion called a "Dutch solution": that, as had happened in Holland, the French army might capitulate but the government and the navy would go on fighting, retreating either to Britain or to French territories in North Africa or to both. Because of the growing influence of the armistice party in the French cabinet this solution was no longer possible — if it ever was. So the British government was willing to tell the French government that the latter would be released from its obligation (which had been set down in an Anglo-French treaty in March) not to enter into separate negotiations with Germany "provided, but only provided, that the French Fleet is sailed forthwith to British harbours pending negotiations."

There was something unusually hasty in that message to the French. You can sue for peace; but let us have the fleet. It was not an argument that would impress Pétain and his supporters. Whether Churchill had realized how far the French government had slid down the slippery slope is not quite clear. Nor did he immediately realize how this British release would play into the hands of the armistice party. He surely did not realize (this is strange in view of his knowledge of naval affairs) that such a move would empty the Mediterranean of a French fleet, abandoning at least a portion of that inland sea to the Italian navy. During the next few hours the confused sequence of events is reflected in the confusion of its documentary evidence, including messages sent to the British ambassador in Bordeaux and their subsequent withdrawal.

For in the meantime Churchill had a last card to play. Or, more precisely, a new deck of cards. The entire dreadful debris on the table would be swept aside. A Union between France and Britain would come into existence. Not a new kind of alliance, not a confederation; a Union. A Union of their governments, states, peoples, empires (and of course of their ships). "Breathtaking," for once, is not a worn or tired cliché. It was the most drastic plan involving Great Britain in perhaps a thousand years.

The original idea was not Churchill's. It had been discussed and bruited about by a handful of Frenchmen and Englishmen for some weeks. On 15 June their discussions speeded up. Churchill first heard of the definite plan on that day. On the sixteenth de Gaulle was in London; Churchill lunched with him at the Carlton Club. By that time the telegram releasing the French in exchange for their fleet had gone to Bordeaux. De Gaulle was against this, but in that moment he was emphatically for the Union project. "The two governments declare that France and Great Britain shall no longer be two nations, but one Franco-British Union. . . . Every citizen of France will enjoy immediate citizenship of Great Britain, every British subject will become a citizen of France." Thus read part of the text. Churchill was buoyed up by de Gaulle's enthusiasm. At three he was back with the War Cabinet. He said that "his first instinct had been against the idea, but in this grave crisis we must not let ourselves be accused of a lack of imagination. Some dramatic announcement was clearly necessary to keep the French going." He read to the Cabinet the Union proposal that four others (Sir Robert Vansittart, Jean Monnet, René Pleven, Major Desmond Morton) had drafted, not he. That he would put this forth and that the War Cabinet would accept it in a matter of minutes were a measure of the depth of their fearful alarms on that day. Now they decided to instruct Sir Ronald Campbell in Bordeaux to withhold the telegram releasing the French.

At four o'clock the final draft was approved. De Gaulle took it upon himself to telephone the text to Reynaud. The latter's spirit rose. He, too, thought that such a tremendous offer would make all the difference. But Pétain, Weygand and others rejected it with unmitigated contempt. To them it was a desperate, perhaps even dishonest, attempt. Pétain: "A fusion with a corpse." Jean Ybarnégaray, a French nationalist: "Better be a Nazi province. At least we know what that means." It was a scheme "to put France under British tutelage." When Georges Mandel, one of Reynaud's few supporters, asked: "Would you rather be a German district than a British Dominion?" they looked at him with cold disdain. That night Pétain formed a new government. He immediately chose to have the French armistice plea transmitted to the Germans.

Churchill did not know that until later. In the afternoon he and the Cabinet decided on yet another urgent mission to France. De Gaulle had flown to Bordeaux with the Union document. Churchill would leave by train for Southampton and then sail on a fast cruiser to meet Reynaud and the French in Brittany next noon. From Westminister Churchill drove straight to Waterloo station. He boarded his train, impatient to start. But the engine did not move. One of his secretaries had arrived from Downing Street. He brought a telegram from Bordeaux. Reynaud was about to resign. The Brittany meeting was off. Churchill "returned to Downing Street with a heavy heart."

That was the end of a week when Hitler had bested Churchill, perhaps decisively. Hitler was now the master of almost all of Europe. Italy had come into the war on Hitler's side. Churchill could not bring the United States into the war. He could neither halt nor prevent the surrender of France.

THE EIGHTEENTH of June in 1940 was the 125th anniversary of the Battle of Waterloo. That was the last battle of the world wars that had been fought for more than a century between France and Britain. After Waterloo Germany grew and France declined. One hundred years after Waterloo France and Britain fought side by side against the Germans. Now, in 1940, France fell to the Germans and Britain was alone, facing perils immeasurably greater than those at the time of Waterloo. There was another historical coincidence in 1940. Late at night on Waterloo Day Hitler returned from Munich to his headquarters, Wolf's Redoubt, a few miles from the French frontier town of Rocroi. Rocroi was a grim, gray little town. (When the English historian Veronica Wedgwood visited it in the thirties, a tired little French barmaid told her that things might liven up: "We are promised a garrison." Four years later she got a garrison, but not the one she would have wanted.) If France's world power declined after Waterloo, that power had risen at Rocroi. There, 297 years before 1940, one of the most decisive battles in the history of Europe had been fought. At Rocroi in 1643 the French beat the formidable Spanish infantry. With that victory they became the greatest power in Europe, indeed in the Western world. For the Spanish the defeat of their army at Rocroi was as decisive as the defeat of their Armada in the English Channel in 1588 had been. They did not find their place in the Modern Age. But now, in 1940, it seemed as if the entire Western European Enlightenment, that principal feature of the Modern Age, was coming to a sudden end. Spain played a minor role in that. The French request for Hitler's armistice terms was transmitted by Don

José Lequerica, the eager Spanish ambassador in Bordeaux, and not by the United States (as had been Reynaud's and Chautemps's choice the day before). Pétain preferred Franco's Spain.

Hitler's spirits were high. When Pétain's armistice request had reached him he stepped out of his headquarters. In front of his secretaries and staff he exclaimed and slapped his thigh. That somewhat low-bred, Austro-German gesture was later transformed, by cinematic and photographic trickery, into a jig; and the legend that Hitler danced a jig (whether on that day at his headquarters or five days later in the forest clearing of Compiègne) has since entered the textbooks and the histories and the pictorial and cinematic archives of the world. It does not matter (save for those who are silly enough to believe that a picture is worth a thousand words). He was in high spirits, all right. On the morning of the eighteenth he met Göring at Frankfurt Airport. They embraced each other. From there he flew to Munich to meet Mussolini. The Duce was disappointed. France had fallen too soon, without the Italians having been able to contribute much, if anything, to the victory. (As Hitler had foreseen, a small French force held off the Italians along their entire Alpine and Riviera fronts.) Mussolini wished there had been more war. (As Churchill later said, soon he would get all the war he wanted.) For once the rigid and extreme Ribbentrop, as Mussolini's son-in-law and foreign minister, Ciano, noted, was "exceptionally moderate." He was in favor of "peace." Ribbentrop told Ciano that he did not want "to push their conversation further" until they talked with Hitler. He ended their talk by referring to "a German project to round up and send the Jews to Madagascar."*

Then they joined Mussolini and Hitler. Ciano, who did not like Hitler, was impressed. He understood very well that what Hitler wanted to avoid was for the French fleet to go over to the English.

---

* We have seen (see page 110) that his Foreign Ministry began to occupy itself with the Madagascar Plan on 3 June. Then, on 24 June, Reinhard Heydrich of the German Security Service sent a memorandum to Ribbentrop. According to Heydrich, the Jewish problem "can no longer be solved by emigration. A territorial final solution [*Endlösung*] becomes therefore necessary." To the best of my knowledge, this is the first time that that ominous phrase appears in German documents — not in 1941, as most historians believe. To this add that Hitler talked of the Madagascar Plan on 20 June — and as late as 2 February 1941: "The question is only how to get them there. He has now other ideas, too, not very kind ones, to be sure. [*Er dachte über manches jetzt anders, nicht gerade freundlicher.*]" The significance of the date and the language of this statement is great — overlooked as it has been by almost all biographers of Hitler and by historians of the extermination of the Jews.

"From all that he says it is clear that he wants to act quickly to end it all. Hitler is now the gambler who has made a big scoop and would like to get up from the table, risking nothing more. Today he speaks with a reserve and a perspicacity which, after such a victory, are really astonishing. I cannot be accused of excessive tenderness toward him, but today I truly admire him." Their conference was short. At night Hitler returned to Wolf's Redoubt. Soon he would leave it for good; next day plans were laid before him for another headquarters, now back in Germany, "Tannenberg."

He was full of confidence, for which he thought that he had additional reasons. The first news of a break in London had reached Berlin twenty-four hours before. R. A. Butler, the undersecretary of state for foreign affairs, had met Björn Prytz, the Swedish minister to London, in St. James's Park. He then asked Prytz to come up to his office. Butler disliked Churchill. He disagreed with him. In November 1939 he had told the Italian ambassador, Bastianini, "Churchill only speaks for himself." Now Butler told the Swede that "no opportunity would be neglected for concluding a compromise peace if the chance offered on reasonable conditions . . . the so-called die-hards [suggesting Churchill] would not be allowed to stand in the way of negotiations." Prytz was still in Butler's office when Butler went to see Halifax. When he came back to the room, Butler told Prytz that Halifax had a message for him. "Common sense and not bravado would dictate the British government's policy," even though Prytz should not interpret that to mean peace at any price. In his urgent telegram to Stockholm Prytz added that his conversations with other prominent Englishmen — mostly certain members of Parliament — suggested that Halifax might replace Churchill at the head of the government in about ten days. The news began immediately to circulate in Stockholm. It was reported to King Gustav V, who was known to favor a compromise peace between Britain and Germany. It came to the attention of Francesco Fransoni, the Italian minister to Sweden, who called Rome to report that the British government was ready ("*è disposto*") to discuss peace. The news reached Berlin, too, within hours. At Munich Ribbentrop told it to Ciano and, of course, to Hitler.

The report was not quite correct. Fransoni thought that it was the British minister to Stockholm who had asked for an audience with the Swedish foreign minister about peace negotiations, which was not the case. (When the latter asked the British minister to confirm the essence of Prytz's report, Sir Victor Mallet said that the guiding light remained Churchill's, "to continue the war with all our strength.") Next day Prytz wired Stockholm that Butler and Halifax represented "personal views," and that the attitude of the British government had not "crystallized." Halifax sent a message to Mallet that "certainly no hint was intended." Whether Hitler knew of these corrective details is not clear. On 20 June Hewel informed him that in Conservative circles in London "voices are being raised against Churchill." Three days later Hewel brought another report to Hitler, from Prince Max Hohenlohe, who had returned to Switzerland. There was an anti-Churchill group in London, "especially Butler, who was overwhelmed by pessimism and looks desperately for a way out." The Spanish minister in Bern, who knew Butler, confirmed this to Hohenlohe. Carl Burckhardt — a Swiss patrician and former League of Nations high commissioner in Danzig, whom Hitler had earlier used to convey hints to London — told Hohenlohe that in his opinion, too, the British were attempting to establish some kind of contact with the Germans. On 20 June Hitler met with his commanding generals and with Admiral Raeder, the commander in chief of the German navy. They proposed to proceed with plans for an invasion of England, provided the English were not ready to make peace before long. Hitler was "skeptical: he considers England so weak that large-scale landings might not become necessary"; bombing England would do the job; the army's task might be that of occupation measures. This was presumably what Göring had told him in Frankfurt three days earlier. Hitler ended the conference by saying that the English would eat humble pie soon, in one way or another ("*dass die jetzt so oder so klein begeben werden*"). Then he turned to something pleasant, to the preparations for his coming visit to Paris, accompanied by his favorite architects and artists.

Before that came the ceremony of the French armistice — more exactly, the French surrender. On his orders the French delegation was brought to the forest clearing at Compiègne, where the German generals had been brought to sign their armistice on 11 November 1918. There stood the Wagon-Lits dining car WL 2519, preserved by the French; a commemorative obelisk; and a statue of Marshal Foch. The ceremony was short, about forty minutes. Hitler did not speak a word to the French. He ordered that the obelisk be destroyed but that the statue of Foch be preserved — one of his rare chivalrous gestures. WL 2519 was to be brought to Berlin and displayed in a museum. (It was destroyed in early 1945 during one of the mass bombings of Berlin.) From Compiègne Hitler flew back to Rocroi-Bruly in one of the giant four-motored Condor planes, arranged by Göring.

Two days later he flew to Paris at the unaccustomed hour of half past three in the morning. He brought his favorite sculptor, Arno Breker, and his favorite architect, Albert Speer, with him. They made a fast tour of an empty Paris during the morning hours. Hitler astonished his entourage by his familiarity with some of the buildings, especially the Opéra, where his detailed knowledge surprised the dignified French functionary who had been corralled to guide them through the corridors. It was a strange, furtive, restless tour. By ten in the morning they were back at the Wolf's Redoubt. For days afterward Hitler talked about the beauty of Paris, which he had now seen for the first time. In the meantime he was still waiting for more news from London. Then he went off with his old cronies to visit some of the battlefields where he had served during the First World War. Next day, the twenty-seventh, he left Wolf's Redoubt for his new headquarters near Knibis, in the Black Forest of Germany.

DURING THE last week of May Churchill's leadership had been seriously questioned in the War Cabinet; but at the same time the morale of the British people presented no problem, if only because they had not yet grasped the seriousness of the situation. Three weeks later these circumstances were reversed. The morale of the people could not but be affected by the surrender of France; yet within the government, despite the French disaster, Churchill's authority had grown stronger.

Churchill knew that — an important asset for his unremitting resolve. The other important asset was his insight into what Hitler would or would not do. He did not think that Hitler was either ready or willing to invade England — at least not yet. Preparations for the defense of the island against any invasion attempt were of course of the highest priority. But he knew that Hitler was still undecided. The source of that knowledge was not intelligence reports or decodings of German signals. It was Churchill's insight. Hitler could, or indeed might, offer very tempting terms to England. To resist that temptation Churchill had to keep up the morale of England. That was his principal concern of the moment. That was his duty. During the last fortnight of June Churchill, who was fifteen years older than Hitler, worked ceaselessly, while Hitler did not. On that frantic and catastrophic day, 16 June, for example, during the half hour when nothing less than the Union proposal with France was being prepared, Churchill left the War Cabinet to dictate a long letter to the prime ministers of the Dominions. Considering what was happening that day, the spirit of the letter is remarkable. It began: "I do not regard the situation as having passed beyond our strength. It is by no means certain that the French will not fight on in Africa and at sea, but, whatever they do, Hitler will have to break us in this island or lose the war." It ended with another statement of resolute optimism. In his memoirs Churchill related that as he was dictating this the sun shone benevolent and bright. He may or may not have remembered how that day had begun, with pelting rain.

But next morning he knew that all was lost with the French. Britain was alone. There came the news of another catastrophe. The Germans sank the liner *Lancastria,* carrying five thousand British soldiers and civilians from a French Atlantic port. Three thousand were drowned. Churchill forbade the publication of this dreadful news (and forgot to rescind that order for some weeks to come). The newspapers had quite enough disaster for the day, he said. Yet his spirits were good, and his energy unbroken. That afternoon he made a short statement on the radio. "The news from France is very bad, and I grieve for the gallant French people who have fallen into this terrible misfortune. . . . What has happened in France makes no difference to our actions and purpose. We have become the sole champions now in arms to defend the world cause. We shall do our best to be worthy of this high honour. . . ." Late that Monday night he sent a message to Pétain and Weygand, "our comrades in two great wars," convinced that they "will not injure their ally by delivering over to the enemy the fine French fleet. Such an act would scarify their names for a thousand years of history." They did not answer him.

On the morning of Waterloo Day Charles de Gaulle flew to London from Bordeaux in the nick of time. He left behind his country, governed and represented by some of his worst enemies. He arrived in a foreign city, alone. He had crossed something more than the English Channel; he had stepped over the Rubicon of his life. That afternoon, unaccompanied, he sat down before a microphone in Studio B-2 of the British Broadcasting Corporation. "The flame of French resistance cannot go out," he said. "It will not go out." "France has lost a battle. She has not lost the war." Like Churchill on the tenth of May, de Gaulle on the eighteenth of June felt as if he were walking with destiny, and that all of his past life had been but a preparation for this hour and for this trial. It was a milestone in the history of two great nations. De Gaulle would have many a quarrel with Churchill during the five years that followed. Like all statesmen, de Gaulle had to resort, on occasion, to ingratitude. But, as he wrote about Churchill in his memoirs: "What could I have done without his help?" De Gaulle survived Churchill by five years. Each year he wrote a letter to Lady Churchill on the anniversary of her husband's death.

On the afternoon of Waterloo Day Churchill made his most famous speech in the House of Commons. This was the "finest hour" speech. It has a curious history. We have seen that the day before he had addressed the British people with a short, two-minute statement. Now he spoke again. The speech lasted less than thirty minutes in Parliament. The members were impressed, though he sounded somewhat tired. But sometime later that afternoon some people told Churchill that for the sake of national morale he ought to speak to the nation. So four hours later Churchill reread his speech on the BBC. He did not like doing that; he was tired; many people thought that it did not sound good. The newspaper owner Cecil King wrote in his diary: "Whether [Churchill] was drunk or in, from sheer fatigue, I don't know, but it was the poorest possible effort." Churchill's admirer Harold Nicolson wrote: "How I wish Winston would not talk on the wireless unless he is feeling in good form. He hates the microphone, and when we bullied him into speaking last night, he just sulked and read his House of Commons speech over again. Now, as delivered in the House of Commons, that speech was magnificent, especially the concluding sentence. But it sounded ghastly on the wireless. All the great vigour he put into it seemed to evaporate."

At this point the historian must say something about the effect of Churchill's speeches that summer. Their reception was less unequivocal than we have been accustomed to believe. There were intelligent men, such as Evelyn Waugh and Malcolm Muggeridge, who disliked them. They were too grandiloquent, sham-Augustan, for their tastes. Other people's minds were divided, as, for example, Chips Channon's: "Winston wound up with his usual brilliance and out-of-place levity. His command of English is magnificent; but strangely enough, although he makes me laugh, he leaves me unmoved." Yet George Orwell, writing in his diary of 24 June, agreed with his wife that "uneducated people are often moved by a speech in solemn language that they don't actually understand but feel to be impressive, e.g. Mrs. A is impressed by Churchill's speeches, though not understanding them word by word." De Gaulle, too, esteemed Churchill's ability to "stir up the heavy dough of the English" (*"remuer la lourde pâte anglaise,"* an inimitable French phrase). A report, "Public Opinion on the Present Crisis," prepared by the Home Intelligence Department of the Ministry of Information on 19 June, said, among other things, that the prime minister's speech was anxiously awaited, and evoked varied reactions: "it was considered courageous and hopeful, giving bad news frankly; but there was comment on his delivery."

The question was not, of course, the stylistic quality of those speeches but their effect. The question was political: that of English morale — or, more precisely, that of national unity. Churchill was aware of that. In his "finest hour" speech on 18 June he warned again that there must be no recrimination against those who may have been responsible for the unpreparedness of Britain in the past: "If we open a quarrel between the past and the present, we shall find that we have lost the future." Next morning Churchill renewed his offer to Lloyd George. He sent Brendan Bracken, his close confidant, on that mission; but Lloyd George refused again. Hitler did not know of this, though he said later in one of his table talks that Churchill's "real opponent was Lloyd George. Unfortunately he is twenty years too old."

National unity, national morale, public opinion, popular sentiment — these are matters that any responsible historian must consider, especially in our democratic age. But they are matters of quality rather than quantity; evidence of them has to be culled from the widest variety of often unaccustomed sources; and such evidence is by its nature fragmentary and contradictory on occasion. Sometimes the comments of perspicacious foreigners remind us of essentials. On 12 June André Maurois, visiting London, thought that his English friends did not yet comprehend the realities of the war; he felt that he was "a being from another planet." De Gaulle was impressed by the calm of a city still inviolate and unharmed: he would remember the imposing façades of the luxury hotels with their splendid doormen, the shining elegance of the Mayfair streets. Sometimes the penetrating eye of a novelist records something of the atmosphere. Graham Greene, in *The End of the Affair,* ten years later wrote of the early summer of 1940, which, "like a corpse, was sweet with the smell of doom." Yet others remembered "the sweet scent of crushed grass" in their canteen tents, happily tired after drill. On the crucial day of 17 June Orwell was impressed with the behavior of the common people in London; and when on 21 June he had his first drill with his platoon of the Home Guard (then still named Local Defence Volunteers), he wrote: "They were really admirable. . . . Some officers who were there and had, I think, come to scoff were quite impressed." In *Put Out More Flags,* written in 1941 and published in 1942, Evelyn Waugh made "Sir Joseph" say in June 1940: "There's a new spirit abroad. I see it on every side." "And, poor booby, he was bang right"; but in *Officers and Gentlemen,* published in 1955, Waugh wrote about a corporal who in June 1940 asked for leave because he had inscribed himself in a dance competition with his girl. On 13 June Nicolson wrote in his diary: "Some defeatism about." At the morning Cabinet on 16 June Eden said that he had seen a report from the Ministry of Information about public opinion which was "not very encouraging." Yet next day Churchill said to the Cabinet that "the mass of our population remained remarkably cheerful under adversity." Lord Normanbrook recalled that when France had fallen "there was confusion and perplexity, and in some quarters morale was brittle." Sometime between 16 and 26 June "a feeling of gloom and apprehension was reported in the country as a whole." The Ministry of Information observed on the seventeenth that "unless there was a strong lead from the Prime Minister defeatism was certain to gain ground, and there would be a serious division between government and people." (This was why Duff Cooper and his friends implored Churchill on the eighteenth to speak on the BBC.) Other reports on 19 and 20 June "spoke of defeatism amidst a general determination to see it through; among the working and lower middle classes there were some comments that they would be just as well off under Hitler." At the same time such different men as C. S. Lewis and Arnold Toynbee felt a sense of exhilaration. Miss Vere Hodgson, a middle-class Englishwoman, wrote in her diary on the day of the French collapse that Londoners were now "rather like a quarrelsome family faced by a death in the house; and reunited by it."

On 14 June Joseph Kennedy telegraphed to Roosevelt: "For the first time this morning many people [in London] realize that they are in for a terrible time . . . they are beginning to say we have everything to lose and nothing to gain, and what is the use of fighting. If the English people thought there was a chance of peace on any decent terms, an upheaval against the government might come." A week later Kennedy told a newly arrived American, General Raymond E. Lee, that "the British are going to be beaten." Yet by the end of the month the Anglophile Lee, "trying to evaluate all the alarmist and defeatist talk I have been hearing," thought that the British would hold up, even though "there must be people here who are scheming to unseat Churchill."

But during the ten days after the French collapse Churchill's stock in political circles rose. Every day that now passed without a new

German success, without a heavy German bombing attack or of course without invasion worked in his favor. Even some of the Chamberlainites in the House of Commons began to think that Churchill was more solid and steady than they had thought before, that his indomitability was the result of strength rather than bravado. His secret speech to the Commons on 20 June, when he had gone into considerable detail about the war and its prospects, was quite successful. He still fretted about what he saw as unnecessary retreats — on 19 June he found "repugnant" the decision of the Admiralty to abandon the Channel Islands, "British territory which had been in the possession of the Crown since the Norman Conquest." He refused to make any compromise concerning Gibraltar. The terms of the French armistice did not especially depress him. He had expected the worst, and began to make plans for going after some of the French capital ships, if need be.

He was overworked, to say the least, and at times rude and overbearing with his staff. On the evening of 22 June his wife wrote him a letter. "My Darling. I hope you will forgive me if I tell you something that I feel you ought to know. . . . My Darling Winston — I must confess that I have noticed a deterioration in your manner, & you are not so kind as you used to be. It is for you to give the Orders & if they are bungled — except for the king, the Archbishop of Canterbury & the Speaker you can sack anyone & everyone. Therefore with this terrific power you must combine urbanity, kindness & if possible Olympic calm. You used to quote — 'On ne règne sur les âmes que par le calme' — I cannot bear that those who serve the country & yourself should not love you as well as admire and respect you. . . ." Clementine Churchill then tore up the letter. "Four days later she pieced it together again and gave it to her husband."

That day, 26 June, Churchill found it necessary to remind Halifax that his government was committed to the House of Commons to "fight on to death" and that therefore "any suspicion of lukewarmness in Butler" must be eliminated. We do not know exactly when the Butler conversation with the minister of Sweden had come to Churchill's notice; but Halifax defended Butler, who had written him on the same day, assuring Halifax of his loyalty to Churchill. On that day Harold Nicolson wrote in an unpublished entry of his diary that when he and Duff Cooper had returned to the duty room of the Ministry of Information, "we find a flash to the effect that Hitler is going to offer us sensationally generous terms. I doubt whether our opinion is strong enough to resist this temptation." We do not know where that "flash" had come from; nor do we know whether it was discussed in the Cabinet; but we must note that an important portion of the minutes of that Cabinet meeting (Folio 328) "is not open for public inspection, and has not been filmed" (the same holds for Item 5 of the Cabinet session of 18 June). On 27 June Sir Stafford Cripps, the British ambassador newly arrived in Moscow, wrote a very pessimistic long message to Halifax in which he foresaw the necessity of preparing British public opinion for an eventual transfer of the government from London to Canada.

However, we can ascertain that by 26 June Churchill's second greatest crisis had, by and large, receded. He and his people had survived the shock of the surrender of France.

There was, at the same time, a difference between Churchill and the people of Britain — though not the kind of difference Hitler had in mind. The British people did not seem to mind having been left to themselves, alone. Yet their only chance of winning the war, or even of surviving, was that of *not* being alone — that is, of gaining an ally in the war, another great power in the fight against Hitler. And this they, unlike Churchill, did not yet comprehend.

IN HIS secret speech to the House on 20 June Churchill, for the first time, spoke at some length about the American prospect. He did not speak from a text but only from notes. "Attitude of the United States . . . Nothing will stir them like fighting in England. . . . The heroic struggle of Britain best chance of bringing them in. . . . All depends upon our resolute bearing and holding out until Election issues are settled there." In that event, the "whole English-speaking world will be in line together." Yet he was deeply worried about American hesitation and American slowness. He had reason to be. At that late date no American munitions, arms or airplanes had yet arrived in British ports. On the twenty-fourth, a week after the French collapse, he found it necessary to repeat his warning to Mackenzie King. It was evidently meant for Roosevelt: "I shall myself never enter into any peace negotiations with Hitler, but obviously I cannot bind a future Government, which, if we were deserted by the United States and beaten down here, might easily be a kind of Quisling affair ready to accept German overlordship and protection." The day before, the first large shipment of British gold reserves was loaded onto a liner leaving for Canada. On 25 June Churchill repeated his argument to the British ambassador in Washington, who urged him to make a speech in order to influence American opinion. Churchill said that he would not do that, since "I don't think words count for much now." He added: "Never cease to impress on President and others that if this country were successfully invaded and largely occupied . . . some Quisling government would be formed to make peace on the basis of our becoming a German protectorate. In this case the British Fleet would be the solid contribution with which this Peace Government would buy terms. Feeling in England against the United States would be similar to French bitterness against us now. We have really not had any help worth speaking of from the United States so far."

In Washington on 27 June the Joint Planners of the War and Navy departments (including General Marshall, who was sympathetic to the British) submitted to President Roosevelt their conclusion, according to which no further American war materiel should be sold or sent to Britain, since the survival of the British was very much open to question: the Germans might invade England and overrun it. Churchill did not know about the Joint Planners' report. There was another American matter of which he was inadequately aware. This was the increasing coalescence of the American isolationists — more precisely, of those Americans who opposed any American commitment to the British cause. From his early life Churchill trusted in the existence of those Americans who, mostly because of their ancestry, felt a strong kinship with Britain and had a sense of community with the English-speaking peoples. This was in part due to his sentimental and historical attachment to the concept of such a community; and also to the fact that most of his American friends and connections consisted of such members of the American elite.

In June 1940 those other Americans who were deeply suspicious of Roosevelt's inclinations toward Britain were beginning to band together. Their main organization, the America First Committee, was not yet formed (its constitution would not be announced until September), but some of their supporters and constituents were becoming active, openly as well as secretly. They were the men and women who thought, and said, that American support of Britain was illegal, futile and wrong. The leader of this movement was Charles A. Lindbergh, a great American hero. Its actual members were recognizable, while its potential popularity was not measurable. It is wrong to consider America First as if it were a fluke, a conventicle of reactionaries and extremists. There were many respectable Americans who opposed Roosevelt and who were loath to engage the United States on the British side. They included Herbert Hoover and John Foster Dulles, with whom the Lindberghs dined on 16 June. They were impressed with the Wiegand interview of Hitler. On 19 June these people took particular notice of Roosevelt's dismissal of Harry Woodring, his isolationist secretary of the army. They were angered at the President's appointment of two Anglophile Republicans, Henry L. Stimson and Frank Knox, to the posts of secretary of war and of the navy on 20 June — Roosevelt's first attempt at a kind of national unity and a "bipartisan" foreign policy. Mrs. Lindbergh (Anne Morrow Lindbergh), a woman of considerable intelligence and refinement, was about to publish her book *The Wave of the Future,* arguing that the old world of liberal individualism and parliamentary democracy was being replaced by something new. Another book, written in part by John Kennedy, the ambassador's second son, a Harvard undergraduate, was also in the making. His conclusions in *Why England Slept* were more cautious than Anne Lindbergh's, but some of its underlying suggestions were not entirely different. (Few historians know, even now, that John Kennedy was a secret contributor to America First.)

There were isolationists among Democrats, too; but most of their prominent spokesmen were Republicans. That Churchill knew. He was also wise enough to recall how the revelations of exaggerated and at times unscrupulous British propaganda activities in the United States during the First World War left unpleasant memories in the minds of many Americans. Churchill knew that Roosevelt would seek and probably receive the Democratic nomination for a third term. In his telegram to Lothian he wrote: "We know President is our best friend, but it is no use to dance attendance upon Republican and Democratic Conventions. . . . Your mood should be bland and phlegmatic. No-one is downhearted here. . . ."

When Churchill dictated these lines on 28 June, he did not know that at that moment a great stroke of fortune occurred for the British cause across the ocean, in the very city where American independence from Britain had been declared 164 years before. This was the presidential nomination of Wendell Willkie by the convention of the Republican Party. That convention had assembled in Philadelphia two days after the surrender of France. Its principal candidates were isolationists, Senators Robert A. Taft and Arthur Vandenberg. (Herbert Hoover, too, was an actual candidate that year, the same Hoover who a few months later said to Joseph Kennedy that he was appalled that the British would not accept Hitler's peace terms.) The leading contender was Taft, who as late as January 1941 said that he felt "very strongly that Hitler's defeat is not vital to us." Had someone like Taft been chosen as the Republican candidate, during the next months (and probably even after the election) the American people would have been sorely and dangerously divided; Roosevelt would have been constrained to go slow, very slow; constrained to deny his own convictions, to the mortal peril of Britain; his cautious hands, ever ready to move surreptitiously, would have been tied. Yet Taft was deprived of his nomination, because of two factors. In the strongly Republican and isolationist midwestern states the German invasion of Denmark and Norway had turned a considerable portion of Scandinavian Americans against Hitler. The major factor was the influence of a then still important (and now nearly extinct) element in the Republican Party in 1940. It engineered the nomination of Willkie, whose inclinations in foreign policy were similar to those of Roosevelt — that is, a willingness to stand by Britain; the difference between the world views of Willkie and Roosevelt was one of degree, not of kind. Willkie's nomination was the achievement of the internationally minded, anti-populist, financial and social leadership of East Coast Republicans, of readers of the *New York Herald Tribune* over those of the *Chicago Tribune,* of Anglophiles over Anglophobes. The isolationist conviction was still a strong current among the milling Republican delegates on the floor of that boiling hot arena of Philadelphia's Convention Hall. But a carefully arranged and orchestrated effort, with the galleries chanting "We want Willkie," carried the day.

Four days later Taft hauled Secretary Stimson before the Military Affairs Committee of the Senate. He asked him point-blank: wasn't it true that Stimson favored American entrance into the war "to prevent the defeat of England"? Stimson refused to answer directly. Had Taft been the Republican candidate for President, Stimson — and Roosevelt — would have been very vulnerable; but now that mattered less.

HITLER, LIKE Churchill, was not unaware of these American political developments. There was, however, another coincidence of their attention in those days. At the same moment the minds of the two duelists turned from the prospect of America to the prospect of Russia. That prospect was not yet their main concern. But the significance of its appearance in their considerations calls for a careful inquest into its sources.

We know what few people knew in the summer of 1940: that Hitler, instead of invading the British island that year, would invade Russia a year later. We also know, from overabundant evidence of his statements, spoken and written, including *Mein Kampf,* that Hitler was not only a determined enemy of Bolshevism but that he exhorted the German people to conquer much of Eastern Europe and even European Russia. Yet neither hindsight nor ideological evidence ought to obscure the circumstances in which he found himself in the summer of 1940. The main obstacle in the way of winning his war was not Russia but England. His main opponent was not Stalin but Churchill.

In August 1939, nine days before the Second World War began, he, the self-appointed archangel of anti-Communism, had made a pact with Stalin. The main purpose of that pact was to free his hands for the approaching war with the Western democracies, to frighten them into acquiescence to his conquest of Poland and to avoid the prospect of a Germany threatened by opponents on both sides. The pact marked Hitler the statesman, not Hitler the ideologue. Its important feature was not only the German-Russian nonaggression agreement. It was the division of much of Eastern Europe among themselves, along a line that was then confirmed by their Secret Protocol (and by its consequent minor alterations). That pact served Hitler and Stalin very well. It was followed by economic agreements, among other things, whereby the material needs of the German Reich at war were replenished by all kinds of raw materials, furnished by the Russian government with unusual precision and care. In other matters, too, Stalin's loyalty to the German alliance was nearly impeccable — indeed, assiduous and explicit to the extent of being at times unctuous and craven. His foreign commissar, Molotov, congratulated the Germans on their conquest of Denmark and Norway. On 18 June he congratulated them on their "splendid success" in having conquered France. Stalin wanted Hitler to know that the Soviet Union was Germany's friend. He admired Germany much more than England. Conversely, Hitler had developed a kind of respect for Stalin, probably as early as 1937 — in spite of his contempt for Communism and for the Slavic peoples — a respect he would express privately throughout the war. But that respect was not sufficient to override his speculations about the need to eliminate the power of Russia.

We cannot tell exactly when the idea of eliminating Russia appeared first in Hitler's mind. One of the earliest instances was the previously mentioned recollections of General von Sodenstern on 2 June — which, as I said, should be treated with some caution. However, it is unquestionable that around the time of the French surrender Hitler was beginning to gather evidence that the Soviet Union had dangerous ambitions of its own. He was beginning to convince himself, to accumulate reasons in his mind, that he might have to move against Russia sooner or later.

He was irritated by some of Stalin's moves. A source of that irritation was the imprecise language of the Secret Protocol. The lines of that protocol were precise: an exact demarcation of the German-Russian spheres of interest across Eastern Europe. The language was not: it spoke only of "spheres of interest." (This should remind us of parts of the Yalta Declarations in which some new frontiers were defined but that left the Russian predominance in much of Eastern Europe unchallenged, because the conditions of that predominance were undefined — whence the development of the cold war.) In early October 1939 Stalin forced the Baltic states to allow the stationing of Soviet troops within their territories — in essence, the partial reduction of the independence of those states. Two months later, dissatisfied with the Finnish unwillingness to agree to his demands, Stalin attacked Finland. Hitler said nothing, and the German government offered no support to the unfortunate states behind the Secret Protocol line. But on the very day that Paris fell to the Germans, the Russians presented an ultimatum to the then still semi-independent government of Lithuania, and then to Latvia and Estonia. They were to be wholly occupied by Soviet troops; their governments had to resign (the president of Lithuania fled across the East Prussian frontier to Germany); brutally and fraudulently pro-Soviet governments were forced upon them. Three days after the French armistice the Russians delivered another cruel ultimatum, to Rumania. They demanded the immediate surrender of the former Russian province of Bessarabia. Bessarabia was included on the Russian side at the southern extremity of the Secret Protocol, but Molotov's crude pencil went beyond that line; he demanded that the Rumanians surrender another small province too. That week Moscow, for the first time since the conclusion of the Winter War, began to address new requests to Finland (involving the management of the Petsamo nickel mines in the extreme north).

This was what Churchill would later call the rush for the spoils: "After the Jackal [Mussolini] Came the Bear." As a matter of fact, the bear had already indicated its willingness to get together with the jackal, to divide some of the Balkans: a Russian-Italian agreement perhaps similar in nature to the German-Russian one. Hitler knew that. He told Mussolini that he was contemptuous of Slavs. More important, he was vexed by what he saw as Stalin's greed, even though he had permitted those lands to fall within the Russian "sphere of interest." A few days later a staff officer in Hitler's new headquarters was told to gather some maps of European Russia.

Churchill, too, had begun to speculate about Hitler's turning against Russia in the future. Because he was a statesman and not an ideologue, his contempt for Communism neither hampered nor confused his considerations. Twenty years earlier he had been the principal spokesman of what at that time was a losing cause: for a more determined British intervention in the Russian civil war, making it feasible for the Russian White generals to conquer Lenin's Communists. But the latter won the Russian civil war. They came to represent the Russian state. That was the existing reality. Because of his disdain for revolutionary ideologues Churchill did not think much of Trotsky (he wrote an inimitable article about Trotsky in the 1930s), while he developed a grudging appreciation for the new tsar of Russia, that is, Stalin. Churchill saw Stalin as a statesman, not an ideologue — the view that he was to maintain throughout the war, even beyond Yalta and his famous "iron curtain" speech in 1946. Because of his own statesmanship Churchill would at times credit Stalin with the kind of realism that is the mental armament of a statesman. In this he was largely right — yet sometimes wrong. At times his trust in the influence and in the sincerity of Ivan Maisky, the Soviet ambassador in London, was excessive. We have seen that at the time of Munich, and indeed for many years thereafter, he believed that Stalin would have been the ally of the Western democracies in going to war against Hitler then, which was not the case. In the summer of 1939 Churchill pressed for the conclusion of a British-French-Russian alliance, without realizing that Stalin could (and would) get more from Hitler than what the Western democracies could offer him. In October 1939 Churchill made a speech in which he suggested that the

Russian advances into eastern Poland and the Baltic states might be seen as a Russian defense measure against a future German invasion — which perhaps credited Stalin's purposes with more than was their due.

When he became prime minister, during the dark days of May 1940, he gave Stalin and Russia little thought. His first move in that regard came on 18 May. Perhaps the time had come to do something about the then very unsatisfactory relationship between London and Moscow. He now made a rather unfortunate choice. He would send Sir Stafford Cripps as British ambassador to Moscow. A thin and tweedy teetotaler; abstemious, puritanical, vegetarian; a man of rectitude but also something of an ideologue, Cripps's temperament was the very opposite of Churchill's. He was, however, a convinced proponent of propitious relations with the Soviet Union who had passed through Moscow on his return from China in the spring. It took Churchill some time to recognize that precisely because of his Left-Labour ideas Cripps was the wrong man to represent Britain in Moscow, where Stalin preferred to deal with imperialists. It is interesting to note that the idea of sending Cripps was not Churchill's but Halifax's, and that it was supported by the Tories, whereas the Labourite Hugh Dalton, Churchill's minister of economic warfare, was skeptical about Cripps's judgment. Yet by early June Dalton told Churchill that he, for one, would give Russia much, including even India, if only Russia came over to the British side.

During the week after the French collapse Churchill began to think that if Britain held out, Hitler might recoil eastward and attack Russia. Whether the memories of Napoleon in 1803–1805 played in his mind we cannot tell. Again it was not his but Halifax's idea to send a message to Stalin. On the night of 24 June Churchill wrote a letter that Cripps was directed to deliver personally to the Soviet dictator. It was a state paper of the highest quality. "At this time, when the face of Europe is changing hourly, I should like to take the opportunity of your receiving His Majesty's new Ambassador to ask the latter to convey to you a message from myself."

> Geographically our two countries lie at the opposite extremities of Europe, and from the point of view of systems of government it may be said that they stand for widely differing systems of political thought. But I trust that these facts need not prevent the relations between our two countries in the international sphere from being harmonious and mutually beneficial.
>
> In the past — indeed the recent past — our relations have, it

must be acknowledged, been hampered by mutual suspicions; and last August the Soviet government decided that the interests of the Soviet Union required that they should break off negotiations with us and enter into a close relation with Germany. Thus Germany became your friend almost at the same moment as she became our enemy.

But since then a new factor has arisen which I venture to think makes it desirable that both our countries should re-establish our previous contact. . . . At the present moment the problem before all Europe — our two countries included — is how the States and peoples of Europe are going to react towards the prospect of Germany establishing a hegemony over the Continent.

The fact that both our countries lie not in Europe but on her extremities puts them in a special position. We are better enabled than others less fortunately placed to resist Germany's hegemony, and as you know the British government certainly intend to use their geographical position and their great resources to this end.

In fact, Great Britain's policy is concentrated on two objects — one, to save herself from German domination, which the Nazi Government wishes to impose, and the other, to free the rest of Europe from the domination which Germany is now in process of imposing on it.

The Soviet Union is alone in a position to judge whether Germany's present bid for the hegemony of Europe threatens the interests of the Soviet Union, and if so how best these interests can be safeguarded. But I have felt that the crisis through which Europe, and indeed the world, is passing is so grave as to warrant my laying before you frankly the position as it presents itself to the British government.

"There was no answer, of course," Churchill recalled in his memoirs. "I did not expect one." Stalin received Cripps on 1 July. He said that he did not see Germany's hegemony in the same light as Churchill did. Molotov made sure that the Germans received a full report of the Churchill message and of its reception, emphasizing Stalin's refusal to agree with the British views. Cripps had developed a friendship with the Greek minister to Moscow, who reported the essence of the Cripps-Stalin talk to Athens; a pro-German agent in the Greek Foreign Ministry communicated it to Berlin five days later.

ON THE night of 24 June — perhaps at the same hour when Churchill was writing his letter to Stalin — Hitler explained his view of the world to his closest circle. "The war in the West is over. France has been defeated, and with England I shall reach an understanding very shortly. There will remain our settling of our accounts with the East. But that is a task that opens global problems, such as the relationship with Japan and the balance of power in the Pacific, problems that we may not be able to tackle perhaps before ten years; perhaps I shall have to leave that to my successor. Now we'll have our hands full, for years, to digest and consolidate what we have achieved in Europe." Thus Hitler was yet undecided about Russia. But that was exactly what he now wanted the English to know. There is a discrepancy between that statement and the one on 2 June when, as we have seen, he hoped that the British would make peace, after which his hands would be free for his settling of accounts with Bolshevism. By 24 June Hitler realized that the prospect of a German war with Russia would encourage the British to keep on fighting. He, Hitler, now wanted to rob Churchill of the hope of a German embroilment with Russia.

That day Goebbels saw Hitler, and asked him when the attack on England "that is now demanded by the entire people" would begin; "but he [Hitler] is not yet decided about this." The Luftwaffe proposed a mass attack of 220 German bombers against Southampton. Hitler canceled that. On 25 June the Luftwaffe High Command noted that the Führer was not yet ready to consider crossing the Channel. Back in Berlin, Goebbels repeated in his diary: Hitler "not yet decided whether he wants to go at England." He wanted a settlement. "There are already indirect negotiations about that. Whether they'll succeed or not, is not yet known. We may have to wait a bit." 26 June: "Are the English giving in? No sure signs visible yet. Churchill still talks big. But then he is not England." 27 June: "The great question: how does it now go on against England? The Führer does not want it yet, but perhaps he will have to. If Churchill stays, surely, but that isn't certain." 28 June: Churchill speaks, "but behind that there is pale fear. This begins to appear very clearly. There are two parties: a war-party and a peace-party. They struggle for power. Churchill's stock is not high. Through Sweden and Spain there already are feelers. Perhaps the Führer will make a last offer to London in a Reichstag speech."

So Hitler waited for news from London. Churchill was the obstacle in his way. He wanted to drive a wedge between Churchill and England. He kept his eye peeled for any kind of crack there. For a while (contrary to his habits) he paid attention to the reports of all kinds of clandestine agents. The British denial of the Prytz report to Stockholm did not entirely discourage him. He showed some interest in the movements of the duke of Windsor, a matter to which we shall return in a moment. He was informed about the activities of the newly arrived Spanish press attaché in London. That man, Ángel Alcazar de Velasco, was one of the more colorful spies and liars of the Second World War. From a low-grade bullfighter Velasco turned into a political intriguer and a convinced National Socialist; during the Spanish Civil War he had some trouble with Franco, but he was trusted and liked by Franco's son-in-law, the Germanophile and Falangist Serrano Suñer. He offered his services to the Germans, who trained him in their school of secret counterintelligence agents. In 1940 Velasco succeeded in misleading Sir Samuel Hoare, the newly arrived British ambassador to Spain. Having been informed about Velasco's former troubles with the Franco government, Hoare trusted him, at least for a while, and agreed to his posting in London as press attaché. In London Velasco began immediately to spin his contacts and information network. Among other matters, German counterintelligence knew Hitler's interest in Churchill's personal habits — for instance, whether Churchill was truly an alcoholic or not. (One of Velasco's friends in London attempted to assess the number of bottles discarded each morning in the common trash bins of 10 Downing Street.) But soon the British secret services were aware of Velasco's business. They let him pass intelligence to Berlin through Madrid, since most of Velasco's contacts were (or had become) double agents.

Yet Hitler was doing more than waiting. He was at least considering that the war with England might somehow peter out. The English had no hope of defeating him anywhere. They had not the slightest chance of ever returning to Europe. Perhaps there would be no need for a German invasion of England.

On the last day of June Hitler took yet another vacation. He went on a tour of eastern Alsace.

DURING THESE last days of June Churchill knew that there were many pressures on the government to wind up the war. But now the suggestions to negotiate with Hitler no longer came from within England. They came from abroad. He would dismiss them; but he also had to pay some attention to their details. He was irritated at Sweden because of the Prytz affair. Anchored in the Faeroe Islands (they were occupied by the British after the German conquest of Denmark) were four new small Swedish warships, built in Italy, ready to cross the North Sea on the last leg of their journey to Sweden. Churchill ordered them held back. (Halifax and Chamberlain opposed him about that.) Five days later, after the Stockholm peace rumors had simmered down, Churchill agreed to let the ships go. He also refused to give any credence to a Swedish intermediary.

On 22 June General Franco, the head of the Spanish state and government, gave his first audience to Sir Samuel Hoare. "Why don't you end the war?" Franco said. "You cannot win it." Ten days before, he had sent Spanish troops to occupy Tangier. After the fall of Paris he suggested to Mussolini and Hitler that Spain might enter the war, in which case Spain would demand Gibraltar and much of French Morocco and Algeria. He sent a Spanish general to Hitler's headquarters on 16 June. Hitler was not interested at that time. He did not need the Spanish; and he did not want to stiffen French resistance in Africa (or, perhaps, British resistance because of Gibraltar).

At the end of June the muddle of the Windsors began to moil. In November 1936, at the time of the abdication, Churchill had championed Edward VIII and his marriage to Mrs. Simpson. In 1937 the Windsors visited Hitler and, like Lloyd George, were evidently impressed with him. The Windsors lived in useless luxury in France. At the time of the French collapse they were on the Riviera. The duke telegraphed Churchill, requesting that a British warship be sent for them. Churchill replied that this was no longer possible, but that he would arrange for a flying boat at Lisbon to bring them back to England. Instead of that, the ducal pair elected to remain for ten days in a buzzing Madrid. (The duke had also left a message for Rome, asking the Italian occupation authorities on the Riviera to protect his villa.) Hoare in Madrid knew that. Churchill pressed him to make the Windsors proceed to Lisbon, a much less pro-German and more pro-British capital city than was Madrid. What Hoare did not know was what the duke was telling some Americans in Madrid: that the war should end before thousands of people were "killed or maimed to save the faces of a few politicians" — expressions that soon came to the notice of Ribbentrop and Hitler.

On 28 June Pope Pius XII attempted a peace initiative, communicating a text prepared by Cardinal Maglione, his secretary of state (and then revised by the pope himself), to the nuncios of the belligerent nations. The German envoy to the Holy See wrote to Berlin that he found it possible that the pope had been influenced by what the Führer stated to Wiegand in his interview (the text of which was urged on the Vatican by the American minister to Belgium, John Cudahy, an isolationist and Joseph Kennedy's friend). The papal nuncio in Switzerland was anxious to establish some kind of contact between the belligerents. But Churchill immediately told Halifax to make it clear to the nuncio in Bern, whom the British trusted, "that we do not desire to make any enquiries as to terms of peace with Hitler."

Churchill was still exercised by the dangers of slippery slopes. At the same time he was much concerned with the inadequacy of Britain's defenses. There was a discrepancy between the actual state of those defenses and the rising strength of the British army, about which Churchill made many statements after Dunkirk. "In these days my principal fear was of German tanks coming ashore. Since my mind was attracted to landing tanks on their coasts, I naturally thought they might have the same idea." When he visited some of the beaches near Dover he was appalled by the lack of antitank guns and the paucity of ordinary ammunition. He excoriated the officers who took him to lunch, instead of inspecting the troops at exercise. In the broad sense he was inclined to think that Hitler was not ready to launch an invasion, but still the most urgent precautions were in order. The Germans had proved how capable they were of surprise. On 26 June Churchill had to agree to the final version of the secret plan "Black Move," whereby the high government would be moved to Spetchley House in Worcestershire in the event of a successful German landing.

It was around that time, too, that English cryptographers at Bletchley began to provide Churchill with the most secret information gathered by having broken the code of the Luftwaffe's "Enigma" machines — the story that later became inflated into "Ultra." These messages were sent from Bletchley to the MI6 office in London; selected items were then brought to Churchill in a special buff-colored box, to which Churchill alone had the key. During the Duel of the Eighty Days there were few of these decodings, and they seldom contained important items. Late on the evening of 29 June a deciphered Luftwaffe order made British air intelligence conclude that "the opening of the Offensive against this country must be anticipated from July 1st onwards." Next morning — the last day of June,

Sunday — Churchill was awake at Chequers at half past seven, requesting the charts of tides in southeastern England in order to ascertain the days favorable to landings. He then told General Ismay to "investigate the question of drenching the beaches with mustard gas. [Churchill] considers that gas warfare would be justified if the Germans land."

So determined was Churchill at the end of that momentous, tragic, dramatic month of June — while, as we have seen, Hitler was still undecided. Yet he had almost all of Europe. He was not alone; he had Italy on his side, as well as those governments of the Continent who wished to side with Germany, as well as others who thought that they had no choice but to do so. Churchill was alone. Pétain had not answered him. Stalin would not answer him. From Roosevelt he had no direct message for more than a fortnight.

I began this chapter by writing that early in June a subtle change in the nature of the duel between Hitler and Churchill had begun; and now, at the end of the month, there was another subtle change. This involved their sense of time. In 1939 Hitler began the war because he had convinced himself that time was working against him: as time went on, the superiority of German armament would erode because the British and the French had begun their own rearmament. He was wrong (as we have seen earlier, his friend Mussolini had tried to dissuade him, but in vain). At that time Churchill, too, had been ridden with anxiety: he wanted to speed up the military readiness of the Western allies. But now, in June 1940, Hitler was waiting, at least for a while. Churchill recognized this. He also knew that he desperately needed time. Hitler's expectations, with a now suddenly impatient people behind him, still centered on England. Churchill's expectations centered on the United States. Now — again because he understood Hitler better than Hitler understood him — Churchill began to play for time, in more than one way. Generally speaking, he insisted on high spirits at home; he also instructed all British posts, embassies and legations abroad to show their high spirits. In the particular case of Switzerland, he instructed Sir David Kelly, the British minister, to seem "very gay and confident and have noisy parties of our own." In Madrid Hoare gave "the biggest cocktail party in a year." At the same time Churchill may not have been immune to the temptation to throw out some small bait to Hitler, to encourage or extend Hitler's expectations a little longer. We have seen that on 28 June he instructed Sir David Kelly to tell the nuncio in Bern "that all our agents are strictly forbidden to entertain" any inquiries about German peace terms. Yet at the end of June the German consul general in Zurich reported that an English agent was about to contact him, with the full authorization of the British consul general in Geneva.

That was immediately reported to Ribbentrop, to the Abwehr and, through Hewel, presumably to Hitler. It took another fortnight until Hitler thought that he saw through the ruse: he let Ribbentrop know that he was not interested in that small agents' stuff. He would make a great speech instead — and invade England, if he must.

V

GREAT
EXPECTATIONS
1–30 July

ON THE last day of June in Hitler's headquarters the planning for the armed conquest of England began. This meant a change in his expectations. The change was not entire or sudden; it was gradual, and to some extent even reluctant. He had hoped that the British would consider making peace with him — naturally on his terms. Now he was not certain that this would happen. The time was coming to force them to do so. During the month of July these two expectations existed side by side in his mind. He still hoped that the British would no longer listen to Churchill. But through July Hitler realized that his earlier expectations had not borne results. His conquest of Western Europe, the expulsion of the British from the Continent and a war of nerves were not sufficient to dislodge Churchill from the field. They had not weakened the will of his opponent. Their war of nerves was, after all, a war of wills as much as it was a war of minds. Now Hitler's expectations had begun to change: but their ultimate purpose was the same.

At this point this historian thinks he is compelled to address himself, no matter how briefly, to the larger question. What did Hitler want? We must disabuse our minds of certain ideas that otherwise flow from what we know about Hitler's monstrosities. Hitler did not want to conquer the world. He knew that he could not achieve that. The world was too large for one nation to control. That — and not only his half-baked respect for British imperialism — was the main reason for the grand design of his offer for a settlement: America for the Americans, Europe dominated by the Third Reich, the British Empire largely untouched. He wanted to make his German Reich more powerful, prestigious, vital and healthy than ever; after the war (as he often said to his intimate circle) he would retire to peaceful occupations. He was interested in building, not razing; but if building required razing, razing it must be — with no exceptions and no mercy. Here was the categorical nature of the ideas and the merciless nature of the mind of this man. Hitler was less interested in accretions to his power than in compliance with it. Within Germany, he did not care whether men such as Papen or Weizsäcker joined the Nazi Party or not; he wanted them to serve his purposes. Beyond Germany, he was less interested in territory than in vassalage. The record shows this. What he wanted in 1938 in Austria was a Nazi, pro-German government; it was only when he was carried away by popular enthusiasm in the city of his youth that he decided to proclaim the union of Austria with Germany, then and there in Linz. In 1939 he did not entirely incorporate Czechoslovakia into the German Reich; he made Bohemia and Moravia into a German "protectorate" and permitted an "independent" Slovak state, as long as it was wholly subservient to Germany. Regarding Poland, his main purpose was not the reconquest of Danzig; it was the drastic reduction of Polish independence. In 1940 and thereafter the question was not how much or how little of France would be annexed to or occupied by Germany; his main interest was that the Pétain government should never become independent enough to reduce its subservience to Germany.

I am writing this because in 1940 for England, too, that was the crux of the matter. The crux of the matter was not Hitler's supposed peace terms — for example, which of the former German colonies or other British possessions a peacemaking British government might transfer to the Third Reich. The crux of the matter was the character of British government. Hitler would perhaps make peace with Britain, leaving its imperial possessions largely untouched (though he might have some trouble with Mussolini in that regard); but then that British government must be something less than neutral: it must be indifferent to the German domination of Europe, and cultivate its relations with Germany rather than with the United States. (It must also restrict opponents of Hitler within Britain — for example, Socialists, Liberals, Churchillian Conservatives, Jews, the anti-German press — in sum, the British government must identify, isolate and suppress these, largely in compliance with Hitler's wishes.) The inclination to demand compliance with one's ideas is a more extreme and aggressive trait than the brutal demand to somebody to relinquish some of his possessions. That aggressiveness is at least in part the outcome of insecurity, eventually leading to hatred, is a common wisdom. In July 1940 Hitler was stunned by the British unwillingness to listen to him. Thereafter his former respect for the British began to vanish. He would not only attempt to subdue them by force; he would punish them for waging war against him — a reaction somewhat similar to his treatment of the Poles, whom he brutalized after September 1939 for having dared to oppose him, going to war. In the summer of 1940 Hitler still said on occasion that he would deplore the dissolution of the British Empire to the profit of the United States, Japan or others. Four years later he talked with relish about the shrinking of the Empire and the reduction of Britain to a shivering and starving island. In July 1940 he was still reluctant to order the bombing of Britain. Four years later he would order the destruction of London with his monstrous rockets.

What did his opponent want? There was an aggressive strain in Churchill's character, too; but it was not dominant. Hitler wrote in *Mein Kampf* that he was a nationalist and definitely not a patriot; Churchill was a patriot rather than a nationalist; and patriotism, unlike nationalism, is not aggressive. Churchill's patriotism was defensive. He believed in the Empire and, as he said later in the war, he would not preside over its liquidation; but he would give up much of it rather than comply with Hitler's peace terms. The reason for this was neither stubbornness nor hatred. Churchill knew what compliance with Hitler's wishes would mean: a giant German empire in Europe, able to force a remnant England into all kinds of eventual concessions because of the armaments, port cities, naval shipyards and factories at Germany's disposal; but even before that, an England necessarily not only adjusting its status to German power but complying with many of Hitler's ideas, at the cost of her traditional liberties, her conscience and her self-esteem. Churchill admired many things about Napoleon, whereas he was fierce about Hitler. Hitler was no Napoleon. Even a breathing space, such as the Peace of Amiens that a British government in 1802 had concluded with Napoleon (and which a year later Napoleon chose to cancel), was not possible with Hitler. It was not only that in 1940, unlike in 1802, there was no peace party in England of the caliber of Lord and Lady Holland and Charles James Fox. It was that the Peace of Amiens was an honorable armistice; and an honorable armistice, meaning that either party has agreed to respect not only the other's fighting abilities but its remaining independence, was impossible with Hitler. Churchill knew that — which is why he became the savior of England and of Europe, too — even at the cost of transferring many of the Empire's possessions and much of its imperial role to the United States, if need be.

AT THE end of June the realization of a change in Hitler's mind activated some people at high levels of the German command. The eagerest among them were in the Luftwaffe, where a paper detailing plans for a landing in England was prepared on 25 June. (Hitler was wont to say that he had a conservative army, a reactionary navy and a National Socialist Luftwaffe.) It was then decided not to present the plan to the Führer, who had not yet contemplated crossing the Channel. But on the last day of June Jodl sat down to prepare a long memorandum. Jodl's chief was away that day, motoring (and presumably enjoying the drive) through Alsace. More than presumably, Jodl had taken to his desk with Hitler's approval. Throughout the entire war no one understood Hitler's mind better than Jodl. This is one of the reasons why his memorandum of 30 June is important. It is a forerunner of Hitler's directive, issued seventeen days later, ordering the preparation for the invasion of England. The strategic conceptions and even some of the language of the Jodl memorandum and the Hitler directive are almost identical.

"Continuation of the War Against England" was Jodl's title. It began: "If political means do not bring results, the English will to resist must be broken by force." It went on: "The final German victory . . . is now only a matter of time. Enemy attacks of importance are no longer possible. So Germany can choose a method of warfare [*Kampfverfahren*] that preserves its own forces and avoids risks. *At the beginning stands the fight against the English air force* [Jodl's italics]. . . . Any landing prepared only as a last resource. Since England fights or can fight no longer for victory but only for the preservation of its situation, everything indicates that it will incline to peace, once it learns that it still may reach that aim relatively cheaply." That Jodl was suffused with the importance of his task appears, too, from the circumstance that, contrary to his customary habit and professional competence, he devoted considerable space in his memorandum to political speculations involving other world powers. The next day

Jodl presented his paper to Hitler. Hitler seemed wholly to agree with it, except for one thing. One of the military means Jodl mentioned was "terror-attacks [*Terror-Angriffe*] against English population centers." Hitler was not yet ready for that. He would order the Luftwaffe to aim at the destruction of the Royal Air Force, "but before everything the inflicting of great damages on the civil population must be avoided."

Hitler was more reluctant than his generals: but he thought that the first step from waiting to action, from political to military expectations, must now be made. Sometime on 1 July he gave Jodl his permission to instruct all three armed forces, the army, the navy and the Luftwaffe, to begin drafting plans for a landing in England, with certain conditions in mind, of which the most important was achieving command of the air over southern England. These were the first definite orders for an invasion plan. The instructions went out on 2 July. Yet during his short and idyllic stay at his new headquarters, Hitler also said that the time had come to "make a peace proposal on a great and generous scale." He hoped that the English people would respond, and put pressure on their warmonger government. (It is interesting to note that Hitler now spoke of the English people, no longer of those Conservatives who did not like Churchill.) Goebbels had come to see Hitler in "Tannenberg." He found Hitler in a splendid mood, "glowing." They talked about England. Goebbels brought news that morale in London was down and the English were divided. On 3 July Goebbels wrote in his diary: "Churchill was clearly a madman [*ein reiner Narr*]. Opposition against him increasing. England may be defeated in four weeks. . . . But the Führer does not want to destroy the Empire." Hitler would make his "last offer." On Saturday Hitler would return to Berlin, and on Monday make a great speech to the Reichstag, the main theme of which would be "generosity [*Grosszügigkeit*]." On Friday instructions went out to the German press: it was still the aim of German propaganda to separate the people of England from their government. "Certain political mediations [*Zwischenspiel*] are still being awaited."

At three o'clock on the afternoon of 6 July Hitler's train pulled into the Anhalter station. After a week of overcast skies the sun had come out; it was a brilliant afternoon; large crowds cheered Hitler as he drove slowly to the splendid new Reich Chancellery. He had not been in Berlin in more than eight weeks. Nearly two months before, he had left Berlin at night, secretly, his great train taking him to the

first of his three headquarters, to preside over the German conquest
of Western Europe. Now he returned openly, in triumph. Göring and
the entire government waited for him in the Anhalter station. It was a
wonderful day, full of military celebrations and popular jubilation.
Goebbels had helped to arrange it. Yet he was a bit fretful. "I admire
the Führer's patience" (he actually wrote "*Engelsgeduld,*" angelic patience). Ciano, who saw Hitler the following day, was again impressed with his reserve. In reality, Hitler's patience and reserve were
the garments of his hesitation — well-fitting garments, but garments
nonetheless. He had already chosen to wait a little longer. He would
speak not on Monday but five days later, on the thirteenth. Goebbels
issued new instructions: the press and radio must attack Churchill
"but not the English people as such." In his diary he wrote that "opposition to Churchill grows in the country and probably also in Parliament. We keep attacking him, but we spare the English people on
psychological grounds." Then Hitler changed his mind again. He
would go to his mountain house, the Berghof, on the Obersalzberg
above Berchtesgaden, where his mind was at its clearest, ready to
contemplate great decisions. Goebbels was not happy about this.
"Despite everything the Führer still has a very positive attitude toward England. He is not yet ready for the final strike. He will go to
the Obersalzberg and think over his speech there, in quiet." Hitler
wanted quiet; but he was also restless. He now postponed his speech
again, to the nineteenth.

BY 1 JULY a fortnight had passed since the French collapse, and a
month since Dunkirk. Now the specter of a German invasion of England rose. But there was a lull. Still during the next two weeks
Churchill's energy was relentless. In the first days of July the spirit of
this physically soft and aging man would harden into a resolve that
was more than aggressive: it contained an element of ruthlessness,
and even of cruelty. We have seen that on 1 July he contemplated the
drenching of the beaches of England with gas, to suffocate those
Germans who would set their feet on them. By that time he had already decided on another brutal tack. He would seize or destroy the
battleships of his former allies the French, to make certain that Hitler
should not be able to lay his hands on them.

He convinced the War Cabinet of the rightness of that decision as
early as 27 June. The final terms of the armistice that Hitler had im-

posed on the French had been made public five days before. Hitler knew that if he demanded the French fleet he would not get it; those modern and impressive warships — a fleet larger than the German one at that moment — would sail away to the west and the south, out of his reach. Pétain's government had been relieved to learn that the Germans had not demanded a wholesale surrender of the fleet. That would have made the negotiation (if that was what it was) for the armistice difficult, to say the least. What had happened was a kind of tradeoff: the French fleet would not sail away, and Hitler would leave a portion of France unoccupied, allowing Pétain's people to function — in circumscribed conditions, of course. The naval clause of the armistice required the French fleet to remain in French ports, manned by their own crews, under German and Italian supervision on land. (The exact word in the armistice text was *contrôle,* wherein resided a nuance of misunderstanding: the English naturally translated *contrôle* into "control," whereas in French the exact meaning is "verification.") But this did not matter much. What truly mattered was that Churchill did not trust Hitler. Nor did he think that he could afford to trust the resolution of the French.

The most modern French battleships, the *Dunkerque,* the *Strasbourg,* the *Richelieu* and the *Jean Bart,* were beyond Hitler's reach. The first two, the most modern battle cruisers, together with an array of other ships, were at the naval base of Mers-el-Kébir in French Algeria, three miles west of Oran. Churchill's Operation Catapult aimed at them. He had another plan, too, Operation Susan, a British landing in French Morocco. His naval and military advisers persuaded him to drop that plan, since it would have required an unnecessary dispersal of British forces at the time of the home island's greatest need. As so often, Churchill fretted against their cautionary advice but then he gave in. (That was all to the good: a British landing in Morocco, even if successful — and that was questionable — might have activated Hitler — and Franco — to go after them, with the probable result of conquering Gibraltar and closing the Mediterranean to the British.) Operation Catapult itself was a bit reminiscent of Nelson's cruel and unexpected destruction of the neutral Danish fleet at Copenhagen in 1801. There was, however, a difference. Nelson attacked a potential enemy of Britain. Churchill would attack the ships of Britain's recent ally, ships and sailors who had no inclination to side with Germany.

What happened at Oran (or Mers-el-Kébir) on 3 July had the elements of a Greek tragedy. Admiral M.-B. Gensoul, the French com-

mander, was an honorable man. Aboard his ship he heard the terms
of British Vice-Admiral Sir James Somerville, communicated by Captain Cedric Holland, an intelligent, sympathetic and Francophile officer. The British ultimatum gave Gensoul three main choices: sail to
British ports (wherefrom the crews would be sent back to France, if
they so wished); sail to American waters; or sink the ships themselves.
If he refused, his ships would be attacked by the British warships outside the entrance to the bay. Admiral Gensoul refused. A few minutes
before six Captain Holland's launch passed out of the boom of the
harbor. He was returning to the British flagship with a heavy heart.
Before the first fading of the sun on that hot Mediterranean afternoon the British opened fire. It lasted nine minutes. The *Dunkerque*
and another old French battleship ran aground. Another one blew
up. The *Strasbourg* drove out of the harbor. Twelve hundred fifty
French sailors were dead. On the same day the British navy used force
to take over some of the smaller French craft still in British ports. At
Alexandria in Egypt an agreement was made whereby the French
warships were to be immobilized, under conditions not dissimilar to
what Hitler had achieved in his supervision and immobilization of
French ships in European ports.

Oran was not a complete naval success. The *Strasbourg* escaped;
the *Richelieu,* attacked by the British a few days later at Dakar, was
only partly damaged. But it was a political success for Churchill, in
more than one way. We shall come to its repercussions in Britain in a
moment. Even more important were its repercussions throughout the
world. It was a symbol of the British willingness to fight, of Churchill's resolution to thrust and parry in his duel with Hitler. Across
the ocean many Americans, among them their naval-minded President, were impressed. He told the British ambassador that he agreed
with what Churchill had done. In Italy Ciano wrote in his diary: the
British action "proves that the fighting spirit of His Majesty's fleet is
quite alive, and still has the aggressive ruthlessness of the captains and
pirates of the seventeenth century" — phrases very different from
what Ciano's father-in-law, Mussolini, had said not so long before,
that the British were no longer what they had been in the past, they
were now governed by tired old men. In Madrid the Spanish press
screamed invectives against the British, but most people, including
Franco, were startled and impressed.

Oran was a psychological turning point of sorts. But — this must
be said in his favor — Churchill was not gloating. "Nothing succeeds

like success" — that was typical of Hitler's mind, not of Churchill's. He told Colville that night that what happened at Oran was "heartbreaking for me." This was not a rueful reaction after a cruel deed. Five days before Oran Churchill had told the War Cabinet: we must convince the French people "that we were being cruel in order to be kind." The night before the tragic day he sent Vice-Admiral Somerville this message: "You are charged with one of the most disagreeable and difficult tasks that a British Admiral has ever been faced with . . ." ("but we have complete confidence in you and rely on you to carry it out relentlessly"). In this duality of sentiments — if that is what it was — Churchill was in accord with the British people. All of the evidence and reports of public opinion show that the people of Britain harbored little resentment for the French at the time of their collapse; on the contrary, many people expressed sincere sympathy for them. That was one side. The other side — seemingly contradictory, but perhaps only seemingly — was their undivided approval of what Churchill had ordered at Oran. There was a sudden rise of Churchill's domestic and political support on the morrow. The morning after Oran Churchill reported to the House of Commons. It was a long speech. The enthusiasm was tremendous. Churchill was deeply affected, with tears streaming down his face. It was "unique in my experience," Churchill remembered. "Up till this moment the Conservative Party had treated me with some reserve." This scene in the House was very significant in itself. Many observers, including foreign diplomats, had noticed in May and June how many of the Conservative members, former Chamberlainites, showed their restraint about Churchill. Around 1 July one of Churchill's admirers (incidentally, a German refugee journalist) brought this to Chamberlain's attention, who then told his friend the Conservative Whip to speak to some of the members about that: there must be no impression that Churchill's support was not strong enough, suggesting a division of minds. Together with Churchill's announcement of the aggressive British action at Oran, its result was the extraordinary cheering that he received on 4 July.

There was another, connected matter that Churchill brought to the attention of the House that day. It again concerned national morale. The home secretary, Sir John Anderson, had told the Cabinet the day before that public opinion was somewhat "jumpy." Churchill was still worried about defeatist talk. He drafted an Admonition, which he first read to the Cabinet and which was then sent out to all leading officials. "The Prime Minister expects all His Majesty's servants in high places to set an example of steadiness and resolution. They should check and rebuke the expression of loose and ill-digested opinions in their circles, or by their subordinates. They should not hesitate to report, or if necessary remove, any persons, officers, or officials who are found to be consciously exercising a disturbing or depressing influence, and whose talk is calculated to spread alarm and despondency." He read the entire message to Parliament.

On 1 July Kennedy saw Chamberlain and told him that "everyone in the U.S.A. thinks [England] will be beaten before the end of the month." This was an exaggeration. There was, at the same time, an evacuation of English children to Canada and the United States. At the end of June Chips Channon packed up his son Paul for America. "At the station there was a queue of Rolls-Royces and liveried servants and mountains of trunks." Churchill did not like this. On 1 July he said to the War Cabinet that the sending of British children across the Atlantic "encouraged a defeatist spirit." Eighteen days later: "I entirely deprecate any stampede from this country at the present time." (Hitler knew what was going on: in his speech he would make a reference to Canada, "where the money and the children of those principally interested in continuing the war have already been sent.") On 10 July Halifax again suggested to Churchill that it might be worthwhile to ascertain something about Hitler's terms. But this suggestion was different from those of late May when Halifax had been challenging Churchill's leadership and chosen course. Now their purposes were the same: to gain time for Britain. Churchill understood that — which is why, in all probability, he did not discourage a few careful and confidential attempts to throw some bait to German agents — more precisely, to pretend to listen to them. But on the larger and public level the impression of an unbreakable British resolve to fight had to be maintained.

By this time — two months after his assumption of premiership — Churchill was the virtual dictator of England. He ruled the government, the chiefs of the armed services and Parliament. Harold Nicolson wrote in July that "Winston's dominance over the House is something which even Lloyd George [during the First World War] never attained to." He was a "dictator" in the ancient, original Roman meaning of the word: a man entrusted with very great powers at a time of a great national emergency. He could dismiss or elevate virtually anyone from or to almost any position. He took responsibility for almost everything. He insisted on the written evidence of any decision or plan; consequently there are few of those decisions whose origins cannot be traced to him. What vexed him — sometimes rightly, sometimes wrongly and unfairly — was the caution and inefficiency of the governmental and the military bureaucracies and of some of their commanders. The working conditions of his opponent were very different. Hitler could rely on the efficient, pedantic administration of the great German state. (There *was* a handicap: added to the government and the armed services, the National Socialist Party and the security organization developed parallel bureaucracies and secret services of their own, at times contravening one another; but in July 1940 these internecine conflicts did not yet matter much.) Most of Hitler's subordinates and the commanders of his armed services were eager, some of them even fanatic, more confident than Hitler himself. The sources of some of his decisions were (and still are) difficult to trace, in part because of his secretiveness, and also because of his uninterest in the written, that is, documentary, record. Throughout the war the origins of some very important, and some very ominous, acts of the German political, police and military hierarchies, amply documented by their leadership and their bureaucracies, could be traced no further than to the admittedly categorical information communicated to subordinates: "It is the Führer's wish . . ."

In July 1940 Hitler's mind was restless and hesitant; Churchill's mind was unhesitant as well as restless, but in a different sense of the latter adjective. On the weekend of 13 July he told Colville that human beings do not require rest, "what they require is change, or else they become bloody-minded." He drank much that weekend but Colville noted that he was hale and exuberant. He had come to like weekends at Chequers, which, as Colville wrote, "has an air of calm and happiness about it. The surrounding country is exquisite." But Chequers did not mean to Churchill anything comparable with what the Berghof, his mountaintop house on the Obersalzberg, meant to Hitler.

HITLER HAD come up to the Obersalzberg during the twenties. He was impressed by the setting and the grandiose views it offered. Later he rented what was once a small pension, Haus Wachenfeld. In 1934 he bought it; in 1936 he had it rebuilt, much enlarged, into the Berghof. The Bavarian peasant furniture became dwarfed by other, more monumental pieces (the large marble paneling of the fireplace was a gift from Mussolini). The Berghof became the center of a compound of buildings for the staff and the guards, including a small tea house a short walk away. Hitler paid great attention to the furnishings, including the design for the china and the selection of flowers for the tables. The largest dining table would seat twenty-four. The food served at his meals was simple, in accord with his vegetarian preferences; but Hitler, as always, was careful to make a good impression on his guests; they would be served meat dishes that resembled Hitler's vegetarian cutlets. The atmosphere was very different from that of Chequers or Chartwell. (Churchill drank some champagne every day; Hitler disliked champagne; on one occasion he screwed up his face: how could people like that "vinegary water.") But the view was magnificent. Often he sat at the large plate-glass window, especially in the late afternoons, looking at the incomparable sight of the Bavarian Alps at dusk.

On 10 July Hitler arrived at the Berghof at night. He had spent the day in Munich, conferring with Ciano and the Hungarian prime and foreign ministers, warning the latter not to think of a Hungarian war against Rumania. He needed peace in the Balkans. He needed no disturbance now. On his mountaintop he would ponder his most important decisions, undisturbed by foreign visitors. Yet during the next few days he chose not to be alone. The masters of his armed forces came day after day. There was now little of the solitude and quiet that the Berghof could offer him. There were military conferences every day, starting at noon, with some of the high chiefs of his armed forces (for example, Admiral Raeder) remaining in attendance for more than a day. There was another difference. He was also working on a speech, dictating, rereading, drafting and redrafting it day after day. He felt the necessity to discuss it with some of these people. That was quite unusual for him. Restlessness now prevailed over the former calm of the Berghof, a restlessness that was not only the result of the comings and goings of many important people, but also a restlessness within Hitler's mind. An agonizing decision developed there during the next six days.

On 11 July came the commander in chief of the German navy. Admiral Raeder was a stiff and humorless North German, incarnating some of the less agreeable qualities of an older generation of Anglophobe German sea dogs, while at the same time an unquestioning loyal follower of Hitler. Because of his knowledge of the sea and naval power, Raeder was skeptical and cautious about the risks of crossing the Channel. He laid forth what he saw as the inescapable conditions that must precede a German landing in England; these prerequisites were often at variance with what the Luftwaffe and the army command were saying. However, there was one essential condition on which all three armed services, as well as Hitler, agreed: before anything else, complete air superiority over southern England must be achieved. The "concentrated bombing" of the island must begin forthwith, Raeder said. But that day Raeder's ideas and ambitions reached further (as had Jodl's on 30 June). His memorandum to Hitler dealt with world strategy on the grandest scale. The British, Raeder said, must accept Germany's domination of Europe. At the same time he foresaw a British-American maritime alliance. Because of this, Raeder said, the time would soon come to transform the relatively secondary role of the German fleet: the building of a great navy, including large battleships, must begin.

Hitler did not contradict him; but he told Raeder that the invasion of England should be undertaken only as a "last resort" — the phrase that kept recurring during that first fortnight in July. Since Raeder and the navy were especially aware of the difficulties of crossing the Channel, it is hard to tell whether this disconcerted or surprised Raeder. What was surprising was Hitler's unusual request. He asked Raeder to listen to passages of his speech in which he would proffer peace to England (again, as a last resort). What did Raeder think? Did he like it? The admiral said yes.

Then Hitler went back to work on his speech. Next day it was the army's turn. General Jodl had brought up another paper, a further elaboration of his 30 June memorandum. This was entitled "First Considerations Concerning a Landing in England." Jodl wanted to move the preparations one more important notch. He was aware of Hitler's hesitation. He knew that Hitler's peace speech was coming. But at the same time he understood that Hitler's mind was changing, that the decision to prepare the invasion of England was maturing. Operational planning had become urgent. Jodl's paper gave the code name of the operation: "Lion." His paper also stated (not because of sycophancy; Jodl was not only unreservedly loyal to Hitler but genuinely respectful of his genius) that the entire operation must be directed by Hitler.

Jodl had already arranged the larger conference that would take place next day. On Saturday, 13 July, General Brauchitsch, commander in chief of the army, General Halder, the chief of staff, Admiral Raeder and Jodl assembled in the main room of the Berghof. This was an unusually short meeting. It began with Jodl's summary of the situation over the last twenty-four hours. Preparation of the military directives for the eventual invasion may begin forthwith, Hitler said. He also said, significantly, that the planned reduction of the army (agreed upon six weeks before) must be limited to fifteen divisions, not the thirty-five previously planned. "Hesitant" is no longer accurate to describe Hitler's attitude that day. The proper word is "preoccupied." As General Halder wrote in his diary: "The Führer is very strongly preoccupied by the question why England is still unwilling to choose the way to peace." But Hitler's uncertainty no longer acted as a brake against the military decision.

On Sunday the fourteenth Hitler left the Berghof for another day trip, to Wels and Linz in upper Austria, towns dear to him from his youth. This was the fifth of such side trips in two months, a recent practice, another symptom of his restlessness. Either that night or next noon he had reports of Churchill's speech of the previous day. He was insulted by it. The unbending nature of Churchill's rhetoric angered him. He went through his own speech again and again. (As Ciano noted a week before: "he wants to weigh every word.") He kept discussing England during the fifteenth, talking about Mosley, the duke of Windsor and the duchess's relations to American "high finance" circles. Hitler's adjutant, Major Engel, wrote in his diary: "My impression is that Hitler is still undecided and he does not know what and how he must do." The German radio began to cast doubts on the capacity of England to defend itself. ("The idea of Fortress England was made up by Churchill personally.") Next day — 16 July 1940, a Tuesday — Hitler was ready. He read and signed his Directive No. 16: "About the Preparation of a Landing Operation Against England."

The die was cast. Or was it? The phrasing of Directive No. 16 reflected accurately Hitler's mind. (Perhaps so had its title, changed from "Operation Lion" to "Sea Lion" — "Seelöwe" in German — not a fierce beast.) The directive began: "Since England, in spite of her hopeless military situation, shows no signs of being ready to come to an understanding, I have decided to prepare a landing operation against England and, if necessary, to carry it out." *If necessary:* he still hoped that it would not have to come to that. "The purpose of this operation is to eliminate the English mother island from continuing the war against Germany and, if that becomes necessary, to occupy it in its entirety." There followed the directives of the entire operation (the main one "a surprise crossing on a wide front from about Ramsgate to west of the Isle of Wight"). "The preparations for the operation must be completed by the middle of August." Directive No. 16 contained almost no rhetoric. The four-page text was full of technical military details. Seven copies were made and distributed to the highest commands of the army, navy and Luftwaffe.

That die was cast. The other one was ready to roll. Hitler completed his speech. Once more, on the eighteenth, he talked about it with the visiting Franz von Papen, a "Konservative," the chancellor of Germany in 1932. Before he left the Berghof Hitler ordered the collection of *all* information from England, "about its moral and economic power of resistance, the relationship of the government to the people, and circumstances within the English Government." After the midday meal Hitler's car sped down the serpentine highway from the Obersalzberg to Munich, where he boarded his special train early in the evening. Supper was served as the train moved through Bavaria. The train steamed north through the night at moderate speed; Hitler's late-rising habit called for its arrival in Berlin not earlier than half past eleven next morning. From the station Hitler was driven to the Reich Chancellery, ready for his historic speech to the Reichstag, to the German people, to the world at seven o'clock that evening.

FIVE DAYS before, on 14 July, Sunday night at nine, Churchill broadcast a speech to the people of England, almost a month after his "finest hour" speech. In many ways this speech was more revealing of Churchill than his earlier, more famous one. He said moving words about the French on the day of their national holiday. ("I proclaim my faith that some of us will live to see a fourteenth of July when a liberated France will once again rejoice in her greatness and her glory.") There was a touch of magnanimity in his phrases about what had happened at Oran. ("When you have a friend and comrade . . . smitten down by a stunning blow, it may be necessary to make sure that the weapon that has fallen from his hand shall not be added to the resources of your common enemy. But you need not bear malice because of your friend's cries of delirium and gestures of agony.") He exhorted the British people. (If the invader came, there would be "no placid lying down of the people in submission before him, as we have seen, alas, in other countries.") There would be fighting in London itself, till the end. (Fighting "street by street could easily devour an entire hostile army; and we would rather see London laid in ruins and ashes than it should be tamely and abjectly enslaved.") In that speech, often using the words "the British race," Churchill's phrases encompassed a more universal vision. (Britain was fighting "*by* ourselves alone, but not *for* ourselves alone." London was "this strong City of Refuge which enshrines the title-deeds of human progress and is of deep consequence to Christian civilization.") He shared with the people his uncertainty about the invasion, together with the unchanging character of his resolution. ("Perhaps it will come tonight. Perhaps it will come next week. Perhaps it will never come. We must show ourselves equally capable of meeting a sudden violent shock or — what is perhaps a harder test — a prolonged vigil. But be the ordeal sharp or long, or both, we shall seek no terms, we shall tolerate no parley; we may show mercy — we shall ask for none.") There was nothing in the speech that could give Hitler even a glimmer of satisfaction. It was another contribution to British unity. In 1940 Audience Research of the BBC was still in a somewhat rudimentary form, but it provided some basic figures "for the estimated size of [Churchill's] audience, expressed as a percentage of the total adult population of the United Kingdom." Fifty-one percent of that population had listened to Churchill's first broadcast as prime minister on 19 May; 52.1 percent on 17 June (his two-minute statement about France); 59.8 percent on 18 June (the "finest hour" speech); and now, on 14 July, it was 64.4 percent — a constant increase.

Churchill meant what he said about London. Twelve days earlier he had sent a minute to General Ismay: "What is the position about London? I have a very clear view that we should fight every inch of it, and that it would *devour* [his italics] quite a large invading army." Ten days later at Chequers there was a discussion about what the people should do if the Germans came. Churchill insisted that to "stay put" (the wording of a government pamphlet) did not mean that they ought to stay in their homes. "W. is sufficiently ruthless to point out that in war quarter is given, not on grounds of compassion but in order to discourage the enemy from fighting to the bitter end. But here we want every citizen to fight desperately and they will do so the more if they know that the alternative is massacre ... even women must, if they wish, be enrolled as combatants. . . . The outlook is not gloomy." That day Churchill dictated another suggestion about the rousing effects on civilian morale of "even small parade marches" and military bands.

His mind coursed ceaselessly, in many directions. Principally he was preoccupied with the prospect of a German invasion; but he was annealed, too, to his purpose of not only withstanding the Germans' blows but striking at them where and when that might be possible. That explains his insistence on setting up an enormous fourteen-inch gun at Dover, capable of firing across the Channel. It was a cumbersome and only occasionally effective piece of ordnance that some (rightly) called Churchill's "caprice," a "stunt." More important was his decision of 16 July. After a War Cabinet meeting that day he called in a handful of close advisers, including the head of the British secret service. The Special Operations Executive was set up then. It would be "a new instrument of war," coordinating sabotage and clandestine activities against the Germans throughout the Continent, headed by Hugh Dalton, to whom Churchill said: "Set Europe ablaze."

That was on the very day, perhaps in the same hour, when Hitler signed Directive No. 16 for the invasion of England. Here is another of those "spiritual puns," a telling coincidence that is perhaps the peak of the Duel: Hitler readying to set out from Europe to invade England; Churchill making his first plans to liberate Europe from England.

For London was more than the capital city of Britain and the British Empire by then. It was, as Churchill said on the fourteenth, a City of Refuge; a Bastion City of a free Europe. Its streets were enlivened by the various unaccustomed uniforms of Polish officers and soldiers; Norwegian and Belgian military; Free French sailors with their red pompoms. On 10 July the queen told Harold Nicolson that she received instruction every morning in the garden of Buckingham Palace on how to fire a revolver. "I expressed surprise. 'Yes,' she said, 'I shall not go down like the others.'" The others: four times in May and June the king and queen had come to Victoria or Waterloo station to welcome foreign heads of state in exile — the queen of Holland, the king of Norway, the grand duchess of Luxembourg, the president of Poland. In the buildings housing the embassies and legations of European states (including, in some instances, the representatives of governments that were officially neutral or compelled to align themselves with the Third Reich) lived men and women whose minds had made common cause with England, knowing that England's survival meant the survival of civilization as they themselves knew it. What had remained of the elegance of London inspired some people; and George Orwell was probably wrong when he wrote around that time that the sight of a lady in a Rolls-Royce was more damaging for morale than a German bomb. In the summer of 1940 London was something different from William Cobbett's enormous "wen," from Gustave Doré's den of dark miseries, from George Gissing's smoke-laden swelling, from Hippolyte Taine's funereal Sunday emptiness. It did not, of course, revert to Canaletto's golden river-city; but it had become something else again. From London the broadcasts of the BBC, in many European languages, had become staple events in the daily lives of many people on the Continent, important not only for their morale; the BBC's reputation was high because of the reliable nature of its news information, rather than because of its propaganda value.

We must keep in mind that on 10 July the first phase of what later would be called the Battle of Britain had already begun. Göring had ordered the intensification of air warfare against the Royal Air Force and British ship convoys. That would last for a month, until 13 August, "Eagle Day," when the primary air battles for the destruction of the RAF began; another month later, on 7 September, that turned into the Blitz, the incessant bombing of London. But we are running ahead of our main story, which is that of Churchill and London, his mind and that of the people. Air Marshal Hugh Dowding told Churchill that he was worried about civilian morale when the serious bombing would begin. Churchill was less concerned. (He was exercised about excessive plans for food rationing. He opposed the rationing of tea, beloved by the working classes: "the way to lose the war is to try to force the British public into a diet of milk, oatmeal, potatoes, etc., washed down on gala occasions with a little lime juice.") On 16 July Orwell noted that many intellectuals of the London Left were "completely defeatist," ready to give up, while ordinary middle-class people were not. He had disagreed with Cyril Connolly; he did not think that the people would panic when the bombs began to fall.

On 17 July, Wednesday, when Hitler was still on the mountaintop fretting over his speech, Churchill drove to inspect coastal defenses. General Alan Brooke thought that Churchill was "in wonderful spirits, and full of offensive plans for next summer." Others, including his close friend Brendan Bracken, also noted that Churchill was in top form. On 18 July he reworked a paper for the Cabinet, drafted some days earlier, in which he spelled out the reasons for his confidence that a large-scale German invasion was not, or at least not yet, in the making. He was still fretting about problems of morale. In the House of Commons that day he excoriated "alarmist and depressing rumours" connected with the practice of sending children across the Atlantic; "a large-scale exodus" was "most undesirable." At that very hour Hitler was on his way to Berlin.

Whatever problems *he* was fretting about, German morale was not among them. He had no reason to doubt that the German people were behind him. As a matter of fact, German popular sentiment had begun to move ahead of him. While he was not impatient to start up the invasion of England, his people were. A year before, and when he started the war, the German people showed none of the frenzied enthusiasm with which they had gone to war in 1914; in 1939 they were disciplined and silent. Even to his nearly fantastic successes in France, the people reacted with incredulous surprise rather than with loud bursts of enthusiasm. When Paris fell there was little or none of the national frenzy that had accompanied German triumphs on the western front during the First World War. But now the people's resentment against the English rose to the surface of their minds. The English were to be blamed for keeping the war going. They deserved to be beaten. The evidence of this change in German popular sentiment exists in reports of the secret police. Unlike Hitler, many — if not most — Germans were eager to let go. One of the reports of 20 June, for example: "People wish, sometimes openly, that Churchill would not give up because then, instead of saving their skins by capitulating, the British will really get it in the neck!" A week later: "Overwhelming is the hope that the Führer attack England immediately." Another week passed: "What are we waiting for? [*Wann geht es los?*]" On the day of Hitler's victory parade in Berlin, 6 July, the German radio played for the first time the popular war song of 1940, "*Denn wir fahren gegen Engelland,*" "We're Going Against England." (A year later some Germans, among themselves of course, gave that song an untranslatable pun: the "Niegelungenlied," "The Song of No Success.") In mid-July there was "a widespread desire . . . for the total destruction of Britain. For the first and almost only time in the Second World War, there was what can fairly be described as a generally prevailing popular 'war mood,' disdaining any premature and presumed over-generous peace with Britain, and even somewhat disappointed with Hitler's new and 'final' peace offer . . . aimed at assuaging world opinion." According to one report, "people could hardly wait for the attack to start, and everybody wanted to be present at Britain's impending defeat . . . in this case 'the entire population took the view that England should at all costs be destroyed.' "

This last report was culled from the expressions of people in Bavaria (*not* one of the most Nazified German lands). It was less typical of Berlin. The Hitler regime had not entirely liquidated the sophistication of that modern metropolis. Foreign observers as well as some of the diaries of that period recorded the considerable skepticism among the aristocracy and some of the upper middle classes regarding Hitler and Nazi propaganda. Among other classes of the population of Berlin, too, there was an odd mix of exasperation together with a remnant of respect for the English. This duality may have been reflected in the text under two photographs in the *Berliner Illustrierte* on 18 July. One showed the bewigged royal herald in the City of London as he read the proclamation of the war blockade against Italy. The caption read: "As antiquated as are the methods with which England hopes to save herself from the windstorm of a new era." The other photograph showed Anthony Eden: "Elegant as always, he steps across the wire barricade."

In any event, on 19 July, Friday, there was an air of somber expectation among the people of the great city of Berlin, still unharmed by bombs. The light summer evening of northern Europe lay over the dark shadows of its massive Wilhelmian apartment houses. The pale rays of a sinking sun painted the wide avenues through which Hitler's cortege drove to the Kroll Opera House for the great Reichstag session. Around the entrance was a multitude of fanioned automobiles, a commotion of uniforms, a sense of self-conscious importance. "Tonight," Goebbels said excitedly, "the fate of England will be decided."

HITLER BEGAN to speak a minute or so after seven — a long speech, about twelve thousand words, lasting two hours and seventeen minutes. His voice was less shrill than usual. He began with a direct statement of his purpose. "In the middle of the tremendous struggle for the freedom and for the future of the German Nation I have called you together to this session." He was doing this for three reasons: to give his people the historical account of what had happened; to thank the armed forces for what they had done; "and to direct a last appeal to universal reason." Two thirds of the speech was Hitler's summation of the past ten months, his story of the war. Then came his list announcing the promotion of commanders of the triumphant campaign, with a special emphasis on Göring, whom Hitler praised at great length and named Marshal of the Reich. Hitler went on to describe the extraordinarily advantageous situation of Germany, regarding its armaments, its material situation and its relations with other powers. Then he stopped for a moment: that was one of the two carefully planned rhetorical pauses during his speech. There was only about five minutes left. As he had expected, there was a hush. His listeners knew that the climax was coming: the Führer's great pronouncement on war and peace. And now his tone and his voice changed. He had mentioned Churchill's name contemptuously, referring to him as "Mister Churchill" two or three times before; but now his actual subject was Churchill. "My stomach turns when I see such unscrupulous destroyers of entire peoples and states. My purpose was not to wage wars but to build a new social state of high culture. Each year of this war robs me of this work. And the sources of this are ridiculous nonentities. . . . Mister Churchill has only now again declared that he wants war." (He now accused Churchill of having begun the bombing of civilian targets six weeks before.)

I have not really responded to that until now. But that does not mean that this is or will remain my only answer.

I am clearly aware that our coming answer might bring nameless suffering and misfortune to people. Naturally not to Herr Churchill, because he will then surely be sitting in Canada. . . . This time Herr Churchill should make an exception and believe me when, like a prophet, I say the following: Because of that, a great world empire will be destroyed. A world empire, whose destruction or even whose harming has never been my aim. I alone know clearly that the continuation of this struggle can end only with the entire destruction of one of the two opponents. Herr Churchill may think that this will be Germany. I know that it will be England.

I feel obliged, in this hour, by my conscience to direct once more an appeal of reason to England. I believe I can do this not as someone who has been defeated, but as a victor speaking reason. I see no compelling ground for the continuation of this war. . . .

Herr Churchill may dismiss this declaration of mine, screaming that it is the result of my fears and of my doubts about our final victory. In that case I have freed my conscience about what is to come.

The speech ended with the customary *"Deutschland Sieg Heil!"*

There were several remarkable matters — and omissions — in this speech. In his lengthy summary of the war Hitler made no mention of the battle in Flanders, including Dunkirk, except for an unusually inaccurate phrase about "the annihilation of the entire British expeditionary force." He spoke not a single word about the United States. Repeatedly he expressed his satisfaction with Russia. "German-Russian relations are firmly fixed forever." He spoke at some length about that, referring three times to the "hopes" (on one occasion, "childish hopes") of English statesmen about a conflict of interests between Germany and Russia. It was obvious that here, too, Hitler's statements were directed at the outside world.

At the same time the Great Speech reflected Hitler's mind clearly. More than ever before — or after — he saw the fate of the entire world and of the war hinge on his duel with Churchill. In this Hitler the statesman may have made a mistake. Had he said most of the above *without* mentioning Churchill, his offer of peace to Britain might have evoked a different echo. In speaking as he spoke — and that was, rather obviously, an outcome of that powerful inner drive of his psyche, his hatred for his opponents — he achieved nothing of his main aim, which was the separation of Churchill from the English people. To this we may add the crude intemperateness of his language. That was perhaps less frequent in this speech than in many of his other orations: but there it was nonetheless, in his habitual phrases of "blood-stained Jewish-capitalist warmongers," "the international Jewish poisoning of peoples," in his references to Poland ("a puffed-up scarecrow," "a swollen cyst") and, last but not least, in his references to Churchill: "that practised liar" (twice), "an inciter and agitator," "a blood-covered dilettante," and so on. More than thirty years later a respectable German scholar and historian of German-British relations of that period wrote that in this speech Hitler had employed "a restrained [*zurückhaltendes*] vocabulary." Restrained, perhaps, to German ears.

Mussolini thought that the speech was much too clever. Ciano, who was in Berlin, wrote in his diary that the Reichstag ceremony was solemn and stagy. "Hitler speaks simply, and, I should say also, in an unusually human tone. I believe that his desire for peace is sincere. In fact, late in the evening, when the first cold English reactions to the speech arrive, a sense of ill-concealed disappointment spreads among the Germans." He saw Hitler next day. Hitler said that the

English response meant that the German air attack on Britain would begin in a few days, and that British resistance would collapse after a few hard blows.

Much of that was meant for Italian ears. That night Hitler saw Goebbels, who wrote in his diary: "The Führer does not yet want to regard England's answer [or lack of answer] as genuine. He thinks of waiting a little longer. After all his appeal was to the English people, not to Churchill." Next day Hitler met with the commanders of the three armed services again. He said that Britain's situation was hopeless. A reversal of the fortunes of the war was totally impossible. The reason why England was holding out lay in its hopes in the United States and Russia. A landing in England was a risky matter. "This is not just a river crossing." It should be undertaken only if there were no other ways to force the English to make peace. Before that, England must be crippled by air warfare and submarine attacks. Generals Halder and Rundstedt noted that Hitler was still hoping for political results. There was, in these days, feverish activity in Berlin, collecting every political rumor from London and elsewhere about a possible crisis in London: reports mentioning the duke of Windsor, Lloyd George, even Chamberlain and Halifax. Goebbels claimed to detect a subtle change in the tone of the London press. "Certain signs of reason . . . so one must wait to see whether the people of England give us a sign. . . . The Führer will not rush into a decision headlong. He has gone to the Berghof for a few days." Yes: Hitler had already left Berlin for another three-day spell: but not to the Berghof.

He now sought relief — and inspiration — for his mind not from the high mountain air. He would seek inspiration — and relief — by immersing himself into the depths of Wagner's music. At three o'clock on the sunlit afternoon of 23 July, Tuesday, a performance of *Götterdämmerung* began at the festival of Bayreuth. Upon his arrival Hitler was surrounded by the social, intellectual and artistic elite of Nazidom: stout women in large flowery dresses, servants in white jackets, men in uniform: one of the few grand social events of the Reich during the war. A Wehrmacht troupe sounded the fanfare from "Siegfried." Then he stepped into his box. He was alone.

What moved through his mind during those long four hours we do not know. What we know is what Wagner meant to him throughout his life. Among other sources, his friend from his youth, Kubizek, the musician, told us about that. They together had listened to "Rienzi" on a summer evening in Linz, in 1903, when Hitler was fourteen years old. After the performance ("Rienzi" was Wagner's first music drama; its topic is the rise and fall of a tribune of the people) they walked the streets into the dawn hours. The young Hitler was deeply agitated. He began to speak to Kubizek about something that his close friend had not expected at all. He had a vision. He said that his destiny was to help raise the German people to the greatest heights. Thirty-five years later, in August 1939 at Bayreuth, he encountered Kubizek again, and said: "In that hour it had begun." And now, on 23 July 1940, he saw Kubizek in Bayreuth again. The Twilight of the Gods was over. Kubizek thought that Hitler looked very good. They talked for a few minutes. Hitler told his friend how he rued the war. There was so much to do, so many things to be built, so much to be done for the German people; and the war kept him from achieving those things. Once more, when his car drove slowly from the festival grounds through the cheering crowds of Bayreuth, he had the car halt and shook Kubizek's hand. Neither of them could know that Hitler had listened to a Wagner music drama for the last time in his life.

There is no reason to doubt Kubizek's reminiscences of Hitler. Kubizek thought (so had others) that listening to Wagner filled Hitler with a sense of deep calm. But next day, after Goebbels saw Hitler in Berlin (where he returned for a day before going to the Berghof), Goebbels wrote that Hitler was "full of fury against London." Two days earlier Halifax had rejected his peace proposal. "He speaks with contempt against Halifax's speech; he is sarcastic about their stupid propaganda methods. He will answer them first with massive air attacks. These will begin very soon. Then the English will live to learn something. The way in which they imagine a modern war is absurd." The previous day Goebbels wrote in his diary: "German public opinion is boiling hot. Everyone had feared that England would grasp the Führer's offer of peace. Now everything is clear. . . . The war against England will be a relief. That is what the German people want. The nation is aflame." Goebbels's information came, among other sources, from the confidential public opinion reports of the German Security Service. A week before, the Berlin *Nachtausgabe* wrote: "The whole of England is trembling on the brink of a decision." On 24 July the headline of the *Völkischer Beobachter* proclaimed: ENGLAND HAS CHOSEN WAR.

AT SIX in the evening on 19 July (there was an hour of difference then between German and English time) the teletype began to clatter in London: the text of Hitler's speech was coming in piecemeal; sections of it were being translated and transmitted to the prime minister's office every five minutes or so. At the Ministry of Information Harold Nicolson listened to it. That night he wrote in his diary: "Considering everything Hitler is really rather modest and temperate and he only starts screaming when he thinks of W. C." Next day he wrote: "The reaction to Hitler's speech yesterday is a good reaction." He was right about that. Churchill refused to reply to Hitler. He said to Colville: "I do not propose to say anything in reply to Hitler's speech, not being on speaking terms with him." (For some time he liked to refer to Hitler as That Man.) Yet Churchill was pressed to do so. He first thought of a solemn, formal debate in Parliament; but the War Cabinet thought that "this would be making too much of the matter, upon which we were all of one mind." Churchill then decided that Halifax would state the British answer. On Sunday Halifax came to Chequers to draft it — a somewhat unusual procedure. Halifax's statement was to be a brief rejection. On 20 July R. R. Stokes, a Labour member with a solid reputation of rectitude, had sent Churchill a telegram, asking that he eschew a contemptuous dismissal of Hitler's proposals; he followed this up by a thoughtful letter that was signed by a number of other members. Churchill read it carefully and replied to Stokes a few days later. "To embark upon a new discussion of generalities about the kind of Europe and world we wish to see is futile till the immediate and grievous dangers by which we are faced have been surmounted. Such a discussion would be in fact detrimental to National Defence at a most grave moment. Even the steps which you have thought it right to take, if they become generally known, will be a powerful stimulus to Fifth Column activities." On 25 July Orwell wrote in his diary: "There are now rumours that Lloyd George is the potential Pétain of England."

Such rumors, including some very insubstantial ones, were eagerly recorded in Berlin. The Germans were engaged in a continuous diplomatic (if that is the word) activity. During the last ten days of July (as also during the last week of May and also of June) there were all kinds of flurries about peace negotiations. The most important of these came from Washington. Even before Hitler began his speech on 19 July the German chargé, Hans Thomsen, approached Lord Lothian, the British ambassador, through an American Quaker intermediary. (It is difficult to believe that Thomsen would do that without Hitler's, or at least Ribbentrop's, permission. Probably this had something to do, too, with Hitler's decision not to make any mention of the United States in his speech.) Churchill instructed Lothian not to respond. Lothian (who had been a pacifist and a spokesman for British-German understanding in the thirties; he was one of those Englishmen who had met Hitler and were impressed with him) persisted for a few days: German terms were available, they should be ascertained. On 22 July Halifax's statement put an end to that. That day the German minister to Ireland cabled from Dublin that the Irish foreign minister thought there might be divisions in London. A Dutch businessman, Albert Plesman, volunteered to mediate between Berlin and London; he had Göring's approval. On 26 July Cadogan noted in his diary: "I should judge Hitler doesn't like the look of invasion and is trying to tempt us to parley." There was another attempt by the pope, through his secretary of state, Cardinal Maglione, to suggest that perhaps the British government ought to come forth with a response to peace proposals. Maglione's letter went to Archbishop Godfrey, the papal nuncio in London, who was to discuss this with the cardinal of Westminster; but Cardinal Hinsley was steadfast, insisting that such a move could be wrongly interpreted, associating the Holy See "with an invitation to surrender."

One of the more interesting of these "parleys" actually happened in Switzerland — interesting because it is at least possible that Churchill had very confidentially trusted the British minister at Bern, Sir David Kelly, to go ahead. The day before Hitler's speech Kelly asked Prince Hohenlohe to meet him at a dinner in the house of Barcenas, the Spanish minister in Bern. Carl Burckhardt and the Swiss minister to Britain had been working to bring them together. The atmosphere was good. In a private room of the Spaniard's residence Hohenlohe and Kelly talked after dinner. Hohenlohe said that Kelly "must surely be aware what an unserious man Churchill was, and how often he is under the influence of alcohol. I could not believe that this man represents the English people." Kelly listened without saying much. Hohenlohe recognized that Kelly conducted their conversation "openly, and with the wish to weave this thread further." But Hohenlohe was clever enough to report that he did not respond to that, "since the suspicion, that [they] wish to gain time with these parleys, is probable."

Hohenlohe's report reached Ribbentrop and Hitler on the twenty-third. Around that time the business of the Windsors reached a somewhat critical stage. This had gone on now for three weeks. Readers will recall that Churchill had requested the duke to return to

England, that the duke then spent a long ten days in Madrid and that on 3 July he arrived in Lisbon. The idea — a very unusual one — to appoint him as governor and commander in chief of the Bahamas was Churchill's. The king agreed. It was not only that they wanted the Windsors out of Europe. They now preferred to keep them out of England. To hurry this along, the appointment was made public on 10 July. But there were difficulties. The duke wanted to have his manservants, Britishers of military age, exempted from their military duties. There was the more serious problem of the wish of the ducal couple to visit New York before going on to Nassau. Churchill and the Foreign Office were against that. The duke (and in this matter especially the duchess) turned recalcitrant. Underneath all of this were their political inclinations, of which Churchill was much aware. As early as 4 July he sent a telegram to the prime ministers of the Dominions, which he drafted and redrafted himself. (In the first draft he wrote that the duke's inclinations "are well-known to be pro-Nazi and he may become a centre of intrigue." Then he changed this — after Windsor had reluctantly accepted the Bahama posting: "Although his loyalties are unimpeachable, there is always a backwash of Nazi intrigue which seeks to make trouble about him.") In Lisbon all kinds of German (and Spanish) agents pullulated around the Windsors. They were especially active after 19 July, Hitler's speech day. The German idea was to keep the duke in Europe as long as possible, and convince him to move from Lisbon to Madrid. On 23 July the German ambassador in Madrid reported on conversations between Windsor and a Spanish friend, "toying with the idea of disassociating himself from the present tendency of British policy and breaking with his brother." That was perhaps an exaggeration, though not entirely devoid of substance. To another Spanish acquaintance the duke had "paid tribute to the Führer's desire for peace . . . he was convinced that if he had been king it would not have come to war." The duke now asked for a week's delay before sailing. It was a tug of war: the Germans trying to pull him back to Madrid, Churchill trying to push him across the Atlantic. After more difficulties about arranging for the sailing (on an American ship) Churchill had his way. His former friendship with the duke may have been instrumental in that. On 27 July he sent a last, important letter to the duke with a close friend of both of them. It was a masterly combination of firmness, tact and the persuasive expressions of a convinced royalist, ending with the phrase: "I thought your Royal Highness would not mind these words

of caution from / Your faithful and devoted servant." On 2 August
the duke and duchess sailed away.

HITLER KNEW about the tendencies of the duke of Windsor. He
also knew that Windsor was a weak man. He did not expect much
from him. In any event, when he came back to the Berghof on the
twenty-sixth (he had spent only one day in Berlin, back from Bayreuth) he knew that his peace speech had been largely in vain. Yet this
did not mean that his mind now switched from the political to the
military track. Operation Sea Lion was being prepared by his commanders but they, as well as he, were aware of its difficulties. On
many details the navy and the army did not seem to agree. There was,
however, overall agreement about one thing. The Luftwaffe must
come in first and pound the English into a state of fatal weakness, if
not submission.

It is significant that — unlike during the planning and the achievement of the Western European campaign — Hitler did not assert his
command, meaning that he demonstrated little active interest in the
actual details of the coming operations (even though, as we have
seen, Jodl's first draft of 30 June asserted Hitler's command of the
entire enterprise). Hitler saw Admiral Raeder in Berlin on the twenty-
fifth, and listened to shipping and transport plans. Raeder said that
the crossing of the Channel might not be possible before May of next
year. Hitler did not say much. During the next four days at the
Berghof he did not devote much attention to military matters. He
chose to deal with political matters in southeastern Europe: he received Rumanian and Bulgarian ministers and the head of the Slovak
state. He also talked with Papen, then his ambassador to Turkey,
whom he had asked to the Berghof before Papen's return to Ankara.
Hitler trusted Papen's diplomatic abilities. Just as in 1933, when
Papen had been his most serviceable connection with the German
Konservatives (indeed, Papen was instrumental in convincing Hindenburg to appoint Hitler to the chancellorship, with results that are
well known and which were very different from what Papen had then
intended), often during the war Hitler thought that Papen was a useful adviser, and perhaps even contact, in matters of diplomacy. In
Berlin Goebbels was impatient. On 26 July: "Our military chances are
as good as ever. Only the decision to begin the great attack on England comes difficult [*fällt schwer*]. General Bodenschatz again shows

me the preparations of the Luftwaffe. They are grand. England will have nothing to laugh about. But the Führer still broods over that." On 29 July: "We wait and wait. When will the Führer let go against England?" The following day Goebbels speculated about America. He saw the movie *Gone With the Wind.* He loved it. "A great American achievement. One must see it more than once." (He had it shown again the next year, on the night before Germany invaded Russia.)

On 1 August Goebbels wrote about the previous day: "Our feelers to England [are] without results . . . the Führer now too sees no other possibility but war."

It was not as simple as that. Goebbels admired and loved Hitler, but in 1940 he was not one of Hitler's closest confidants. His diary entries reveal this. Certain important decisions reached Goebbels secondhand, though from the top of the Nazi hierarchy of course. Hitler's political mind was more subtle than Goebbels's. For instance, Goebbels was not aware of Hitler's increasing preoccupation with America and Russia. At the end of June Jodl's basic memorandum referred to Russia as one of the world powers that could be employed in the German world strategy against the British Empire, a potential beneficiary of the defeat of the latter. In his great speech on 19 July Hitler went out of his way to express his satisfaction with Russia. His purpose was to tell the world that everything was in order there, and that the British need not entertain any hope of an eventual friction, not to speak of a conflict, between Germany and Russia. Yet this was not how he talked to his close military collaborators. He spoke to them at the end of May about an eventual conflict with Russia. On 3 and 4 July General Halder wrote in his diary — note the contradiction with Jodl's memorandum — that military planning against Russia might become necessary. At the large command conference at the Berghof on 13 July Hitler said that the English had some hopes about Russia; he also said that he was worried about the Russian moves in the Baltic and about the — suspected — increase in the number of Russian troops in eastern Poland. At the next top command conference, on 21 July, Hitler said something to the commander in chief of the army, Brauchitsch (it seems after the others had left), that Halder wrote down in his diary next day: the Führer wished to go ahead with the military preparations against England as quickly as possible; the English kept on with the war because they were expecting some kind of decisive turn in America; they also had hopes about Russia. This was significant, yet it did not mean that

Hitler was already determined to attack Russia. (In the same Halder diary entry there is another sentence: "If England wishes to go on waging war, political attempts will be made to encircle her entirely. Spain, Italy, Russia.") Brauchitsch told Halder to start thinking about military plans in the east; he knew Hitler was thinking about that, even though Hitler had not made a direct request for such plans. During the next ten days — whether in Bayreuth, Berlin or on the Berghof — Hitler's thoughts about Russia matured further. While his expectations about a political settlement with Britain diminished, his prospective ideas about Russia increased apace.

On 30 July, after the Balkan supplicants had left, Hitler was alone. He read a long memorandum addressed to him by the German ambassador in Washington. Hans Dieckhoff made a survey of Roosevelt's foreign policy of the last few years, concluding that what Roosevelt now wanted was to assume the leadership of the "democratic" forces against Germany. On the last day of July Hitler saw Admiral Raeder again. Somewhat cautiously — Raeder was not a man who would risk a quarrel with the Führer — Raeder repeated what he had said before: the German navy could not responsibly guarantee a wide coastal landing in England before next year, save for a landing at a smaller stretch in September, after the maiming of England's air defenses had been achieved. Hitler heard him out. Then he dismissed Raeder; his conference with the leading generals, Brauchitsch, Halder and Jodl, was to begin.

THROUGHOUT JULY the consideration of American help was at the back of Churchill's mind. His main preoccupation, of course, was to prepare for what the Germans would do. That Britain could not win, or perhaps even survive, without the Americans' help Churchill knew; but during the six weeks after the fall of France his efforts to enlist their support were not as intense as they had been before. There were two other reasons for his relative reticence. One was his understanding of the American political situation: too much British pleading and propaganda would be undignified as well as counterproductive. The other was his knowledge that slowly, gradually, the President was coming around — especially as Roosevelt and other American leaders were becoming assured of the British willingness and ability to fight on. The ruthless naval action at Oran made an impact on Washington. Churchill did not need confirmation to know that. At the same time he chose not to write to Roosevelt directly. That was not because of anxieties about the detection of such messages by hostile intelligence. It was a question of timing. Too many of those direct messages would reduce their import and effect. It is remarkable, in retrospect, that during the six or seven weeks of greatest danger, from 15 June to 31 July, the crucial phase of his duel with Hitler, Churchill did not write to Roosevelt at all, except for one occasion: on 9 July he sent a brief note to inform him of the decision to send the duke of Windsor to the Bahamas. (Most of the text of that letter simply repeated his earlier message to the prime ministers of the Dominions.) Before that, on 5 July, he had drafted a message to Roosevelt that he then decided to cancel. It was an urgent plea for the destroyers. He also wished to inform Roosevelt about Ireland. He accused De Valera and his party; Ireland was unprepared: "It may be necessary for us to forestall German action by a descent on certain ports." It did not come to that; Churchill's fears in that regard were greatly exaggerated; he also misread De Valera's intentions. But then the cable was not sent. Still, the draft at least suggests his awareness of the Irish element in American politics, including the presence of Irish-American isolationists in Roosevelt's Democratic Party. On 19 July Roosevelt received his nomination for a third term. It was the day of Hitler's great speech (in which, as we have seen, he carefully refrained from mentioning the United States at all).

In the meantime a trickle of American arms and munitions moved across the ocean, arriving safely in British ports. During the month of July it was no more than a trickle; but its direction and its gradual broadening were encouraging signs. More important were the political developments. Around the middle of the month Roosevelt decided to send two confidential missions to London. His confidant, Colonel William J. Donovan (an Irish-American advocate conversant with international affairs, whose inclinations were the opposite of those of the isolationists), left New York on 14 July (the day of Churchill's defiant speech). Two weeks later three senior officers of the American armed services arrived in Britain, officially designated as the Standardization of Arms Committee. In reality, the purpose of both missions was the same: to ascertain the British capacity to continue the war.

Churchill knew what this meant. Consequently, on 30 July he drafted a message to Roosevelt. He said to Halifax: "I am sure that this is the moment to plug it in, and it may well be that we were wise to hold back the previous draft. But pray let this go now." Its essence was there in its first two sentences: "It is some time since I ventured to cable personally to you, and many things both good and bad have happened in between. It has now become most urgent for you to let us have the destroyers, motor boats and flying-boats for which we have asked." Later: "Mr. President, with great respect I must tell you that in the long history of the world, this is a thing to do now. . . . I know you will do all in your power but I feel entitled and bound to put the gravity and urgency of the position before you." Churchill was aware, too, of Kennedy's inclinations. (So were the Germans: Hans Thomsen, in Washington, reported later that Kennedy "perseveres consistently in his opinion that the defeat of England is unavoidable.") Kennedy was especially angered in July for having been bypassed by Donovan in his ambassadorial functions; he kept telling Donovan that England was a lost cause. Churchill thought it best to cosset Kennedy's vanity; he even suggested to the Cabinet and the Foreign Office that his messages to Roosevelt should now be sent through Kennedy. They thought that this would not be desirable. However, Churchill chose to send this latest message to Roosevelt "through Kennedy, who is a grand help to us and the common cause." That concluding sentence was obviously meant for Kennedy's eyes, rather than for Roosevelt's.

The cable was sent on the afternoon of 31 July, a Wednesday. On the same day Kennedy wired Roosevelt: "Don't let anybody make any mistake: this war, from Great Britain's point of view, is being conducted from now on with their eyes only on one place and that is the United States. Unless there is a miracle, they realize that they haven't a chance in the long run."

WE ARE now in the middle of a story the end of which is known to every reader. Hitler did not invade England. But that is not all. The actuality of history (as indeed the actual life of a man) must be considered together with its potentialities. What happened in July 1940 was not identical with what could have happened; but the actualities and the potentialities are not separable. Had Hitler invaded England successfully he would have won the war. And that was within the Germans' capacity to do. Churchill knew that. But he thought that it would not happen. To a remarkable extent he understood Hitler's mind. What he did not know was whether an actual German invasion would succeed or not. As Pascal said: "We understand more than we know" — a deep human truth, contradicting quantitative or scientific "logic."

The Germans could have invaded England before, during or immediately after Dunkirk. Parachutists could have secured landing grounds into which German troops could have been poured, even without the ferrying across of soldiers by the small German navy. This would have been possible because of the unorganized, unequipped, mangled and weak state of the British army at that time, together with the stunned state of the minds of many Englishmen and Englishwomen, who were not yet aware of the immediacy of the supreme dangers they faced, nor yet roused to their new role by Churchill. By early July the state of their defenses — the defensive structures on the southern coasts, the reassembling and organization of the army, the readiness of the navy, the increasing number of their aircraft — was much better, improving by the day. Yet a German landing was still possible. About the French, in Napoleon's time, Lord St. Vincent had said: "I do not say they cannot come. I only say they cannot come by sea." But now there was the air. This is not a military study or a military history of the summer of 1940. We must only keep in mind that the crucial matter was that of the landings. If the Germans had secured a landing area, they would have conquered England.

Churchill did not see it that way. Yet in the fifty years that have passed since 1940 something of a military consensus may have emerged in Britain, something more than a minority opinion: the Germans might have tried, and succeeded. Some English authors have been sufficiently fascinated by the potentialities of July 1940 to write hypothetical historical reconstructions of a German invasion, beginning in the second week of July and ending with the Germans arriving in London about three weeks later. In one of these, *Invasion: The German Invasion of England, July 1940,* by Major Kenneth Macksey (1980), Churchill and the royal family leave for the north and Canada; it ends with a lonely and bitter General J. F. C. Fuller (a former Mosleyite and pro-German sympathizer) waiting for the German commissioner to arrive in Downing Street. *If Britain Had Fallen,* by Norman Longmate (1972), ends with Churchill shouldering a rifle and then being killed by the advancing Germans at a barricade near Downing Street. Perhaps something may be said for such "If " histories, an entertaining genre in which English amateur historians have excelled in the past. But for this historian the most telling of such books is not a military history, and it does not deal with 1940 or Hitler. It is *When William Came,* a relatively unknown book, written in 1913 by the witty and profound (a rare combination) Edwardian English writer H. H. Munro, "Saki." *When William Came* describes life in London after a sudden and successful German invasion of England. That life is marked by the adjustment of all kinds of people to the new conditions, in all kinds of different ways, ranging from collaboration with the occupier to the first flickers of resistance. It is an uncanny, a precise rendering of what would be going on in the minds and lives of certain well-bred people in European capitals under a rather different German occupation — and of what could have happened in London — in 1940. The plot of *When William Came* is weak, the chapters are a series of morality episodes, but on the level of character description it is more profound than Waugh, whose World War II trilogy consists also of superb character sketches. While each of Waugh's characters incarnates one particular set of ideas, Munro not only gives a brilliant series of sketches of opportunists; he writes of a split England, where the main divisions exist not so much between different Englishmen and Englishwomen as they exist within their own minds; most of them are patriotic and unpatriotic, collaborationists and resisters, at the same time.

Collaboration and resistance: these human inclinations would have been incarnated by Englishmen and Englishwomen in ways different from elsewhere. But there can be little doubt that they would have existed in England too. In July Clement Attlee said about the term "fifth columnists": "I don't like it. I prefer the old-fashioned word 'traitors.' I don't think there are many active traitors in this country." But, as Philip Bell adds, "the soundness of this opinion was never put to the acid test of invasion or occupation."

All this being said, there was a decisive difference. Nineteen forty was not 1912 or 1914. There is no hero, no national leader in *When William Came.* In 1940 there was Churchill. In early June he said to General Ismay: "In three months we may all be dead." He would die in battle, if must. Did he expect the same from a mass of Englishmen and Englishwomen? He probably did, at least to a considerable extent: for we tend to think about others as we tend to think ourselves, especially when those others are close to us by blood.

And he represented more than England. Fifty years later we are accustomed to seeing the duel between him and Hitler as one between

Good and Evil. There is an element of truth in that view. But it is not the whole truth. And many, if not most, people in 1940 did not see it in that way. I am not only thinking of the British and the German peoples. For the former, Churchill has plainly been their savior in 1940. To the latter — including the great majority of Germans who have lived to reject Hitler with embarrassment or even shame — Churchill represents not the antithesis of Hitler but a determined British opponent of Great-German ambitions. But here we must, if necessarily in a summary way, contemplate the reactions of Europe's peoples to their duel — if for no other reason than the fact that their duel was about Europe. Hitler wanted to persuade and/or force Britain to accept his domination of Europe; and it was against this that Churchill fought.

There were, of course, people in every country of Europe who understood that then. But they were a minority. And we must, no matter how briefly, consider the majority — its composition, its gradations, its development and its gradual dissolution. It consisted of the inhabitants of the Continent who in July 1940 thought that Germany was winning the war, or that it had already won it, by and large. They had many reasons to think that. Among this inchoate majority was a distinct minority who believed that the Germans deserved to win — in other words, those who rejoiced or at least took satisfaction in Hitler's continental triumphs. These people were a minority in every country. They were, of course, the majority in Germany and Austria and among some of the peoples allied with Germany in 1940. There is no need at this point, in this book, to describe the many variants of non-German National Socialists — Hitler himself paid little attention to them. Nor is there any need to describe the scattered Communists, whose ranks had been thinned after Hitler's pact with Stalin and who, at any rate in the summer of 1940, formed ineffective, insignificant and rudderless conventicles in most European countries.

It is the nature of most people, and especially of governments, to adjust their ideas to circumstances, instead of trying to adjust circumstances to their ideas. This was well-nigh inevitable for those governments — the remnants of independent national administrations — that continued to function under German occupation: in Denmark or Belgium, for example. They believed — again, not without reason — that they had to collaborate with the Germans for the principal purposes of securing the survival and protecting the identity of their nations. The governments of those countries that had not been occupied by Germany had to change their course, too. In order to protect their countries, they had to realize the relative character of their independence, indeed, of their neutrality; they had to accommodate certain German demands in a suddenly new Europe. Such accommodations varied from cautious calculation in some cases (as, for example, in Sweden) to enthusiastic opportunism in others (as, for example, in Rumania). Again, this is not the place to describe the variants, except to note that they differed from country to country because of different geographical, historical, political and social conditions. But within almost every one of these governments there was a latent division between those who were (or who had become) convinced pro-Germans and those who did not wish Hitler well — which meant that their minds and hearts inclined to the British side, though they were often compelled to conceal that (with indifferent success, since their opponents, and the Germans, were suspicious and perceptive).

In the summer of 1940 there was more than that. Many (if not most) members of the Danish and Norwegian parliaments were ready to collaborate with the German occupiers. The legal and democratic Danish government — which in 1940 the Germans had chosen to keep in place — issued a statement in July: "The great German victories, which have caused astonishment and admiration all over the world, have brought about a new era in Europe, which will result in a new order in a political and economic sense, under the leadership of Germany." At the end of May there occurred a break between the king and the government of Belgium, since the first decided to seek an armistice from Hitler, while the latter retreated to France, refusing to capitulate; but a month later, after the collapse of France, that government seriously contemplated ceasing its resistance and rejoining Leopold III in Belgium. (Eventually most of its members made their separate way to London, forming a government-in-exile, but not until October.) In July a number of Dutch refugee political figures returned to Holland, attempting to form a conservative movement of national union. These tendencies of accommodation were more than merely governmental. They corresponded, at least for a while, with the sentiments of their peoples. In Belgium, for example, people were pleasantly surprised by the largely correct behavior of the German army. To some extent that was true in France, too. In the summer of 1940 (and for at least two more years) the great majority of Frenchmen were loyal to Marshal Pétain, in whom they saw something like the redeemer of France. They were not pro-German; they did not wish the Germans to win; but they thought that their former government — its ideology, its system, including the alliance with England — had been tainted, corrupt and wrong. There was more to such ideas than opportunism (though opportunism played a significant part in the thoughts and actions of some).

Beyond and beneath such appearances of popular sentiment there was, thus, a widespread current that meant more than accommodation with the impressive semblance of German power. Many people in the world saw in what had happened an evidence and a justification of their own ideas about the corrupt and inefficient, the hypocritical and antiquated nature of parliamentary government, of bourgeois democracy, of liberal capitalism — institutions and causes of which, after the collapse of France, Britain seemed to be the only remaining representative in Europe. This current surfaced across the globe. On the day of France's capitulation Gandhi wrote in the Indian newspaper *Harijan,* on 22 June: "Germans of future generations will honour Herr Hitler as a genius, as a brave man, a matchless organizer and much more." Gandhi and the Aga Khan were very different men; but the latter told Hohenlohe in Switzerland on 25 July that he and the khedive of Egypt "will both drink a bottle of champagne when the Führer sleeps in Windsor Castle. Churchill was paid by Jews." In her Balkan Trilogy the English writer Olivia Manning described how in July 1940 the British colony in Bucharest suddenly found themselves shunned and deserted and even subjects of mistreatment.

More significant, perhaps, was the fact that some of the best minds of Europe sympathized with National Socialism because of their contempt, and in some cases their hatred, for the old order that Churchill's Britain now represented alone. "The artist is the antennae of the race," Ezra Pound wrote twenty-eight years earlier; and we know what he thought and where he stood in 1940. Here is a list of European thinkers and artists who in 1940 welcomed what they saw as a cleansing wave of the present and future: the great Dutch musician and conductor Willem Mengelberg, the French writer Henry de Montherlant, the Rumanian philosopher Mircea Eliade, the Belgian political thinker Henri de Man, Giovanni Papini and Giovanni Gentile in Italy, the greatest of Scandinavian writers, Knut Hamsun, who was an enthusiastic supporter of Hitler's. This list is not, of course, complete, and it does not mean that all of these people were convinced Hitlerites. In France, for example, it included such diverse people as the extreme radical Louis-Ferdinand Céline, the intellectual brawler Robert Brasillach, the elegant and once very Anglophile Paul Morand, the bourgeois antibourgeois Pierre Drieu la Rochelle and the later celebrated Jesuit scientist-philosopher Teilhard de Chardin. ("How," asked Drieu, "can you believe that the winner of this war would be an empire of which every part is an anachronism? Someone who today believes in the victory of England is like someone who in 1900 had prophesied the victory of China, with its mandarins with pigtails and jade buttons, over the European empires with their motors and cannons. . . . In face of Hitler, Mussolini and Stalin, don't you see that Churchill and Roosevelt are grotesquely antiquated?" Teilhard, in a letter from Peking: "Personally, I stick to my idea that we are watching the birth, more than the death, of a World. . . . Peace cannot mean anything but a HIGHER PROCESS OF CONQUEST. . . . The world is bound to belong to its most active elements. . . . Just now, the Germans deserve to win because, however bad or mixed is their spirit, they have more spirit than the rest of the world.")

In his Argentinian exile José Ortega y Gasset, the writer and prophet of *The Revolt of the Masses,* refused to say anything about Hitler. On 7 July André Gide wrote about Hitler in his diary: "perfidious, cynical if you wish, but here again he acted with a sort of genius . . . his great cynical strength consisted in not deigning to take account of any token values, but only of realities." Ortega and Gide were not among those others who in 1940 proved that they hated democracy more than they loved liberty. Nor were the kings of Belgium and Sweden. Yet these monarchs, together with many very different people, thought that an accommodation with a new Europe was something more than a response to dire necessities. On 25 June the president of Switzerland in a national broadcast admonished his people to adjust to a new order in Europe. Throughout June and July the Vatican expected Hitler to invade Britain and succeed. By "the Vatican" I mean Pope Pius XII and most of the cardinals of the Curia. In June the French cardinal Tisserant felt almost alone among them. Most of these cardinals were not in favor of Hitler. They wished, however, to mediate some kind of peace. Important religious personages in Europe (including Monsignor Orsenigo, the papal nuncio in Berlin, and Monsignor Tiso, the head of the Slovak state) sympathized with the German cause; many more (including the three most important state secretaries of the pope, Maglione, Tardini and Montini) did not. The Vatican was traditionally and studiously neutral. Yet it did not prefer the nominally still Catholic Hitler, the leader of a partially Catholic nation, over Protestant Britain, governed by Churchill, about whose religious beliefs the Holy See knew nothing. In 1940 the majority of the peoples of Europe had long ceased to be assiduous churchgoers and unquestioning believers. The Duel was a contest between an ex-Catholic and — perhaps — an ex-Protestant. While the ex-Catholic Hitler did not represent Catholic Europe (his most radical and vicious followers were often ex-Catholics, too), Churchill did not represent the Protestant world either; yet to use Tertullian's phrase, both in his thoughts and acts Churchill was more of an *anima naturaliter christiana* than Hitler.

There were Slovak (and Spanish and other) newspapers that in 1940 wrote that National Socialism was a form of Catholic Christianity. These were radical voices, the opposites of someone like the reactionary Spanish cardinal, Segura, who angered Franco when he said that Hitlerism was as bad as Communism, and probably worse. When the Germans entered Paris on 14 June they were received much better in the working-class districts and suburbs than in the bourgeois *quartiers*. On 5 July the Belgian socialist thinker Henri de Man published a manifesto to the working classes of Belgium: "Don't think that you must resist the occupying power; accept the fact of its victory and try, rather, to reap the lessons therefrom for the building of a new social order. The war led to the collapse of the parliamentary regime and of the capitalist plutocracy of the so-called democracies. For the working classes this collapse of a decrepit order, far from being a disaster, is a liberation." There *was* a radical, proletarian and National Socialist potential among the lower middle classes and the industrial working classes of Europe to whom Hitler could have appealed in 1940, with considerable success. He neglected to do that (and admitted later, in his last conversations in 1945, that he should have done so). He also had little interest in the designs cobbled together by some of his functionaries in Berlin about the creation of a Greater European economic community — under German leadership, of course — to which many of the industrialists of Europe would have responded.

At the end of June the majority of the peoples of Europe thought that the Germans had either won or were definitely winning the war.

But a month later that belief was no longer definite. In some places this meant more than a gradual mutation of sentiments. On 25 July, exactly one month after their cautious president, Marcel Pilet-Golaz, told the Swiss to adjust themselves to a new European order, General Henri Guisan, the commander of the Swiss army, called his officers to assemble on the historic plateau of the Rütli. He instructed them to hold themselves in utmost readiness to defend the independence and liberty of their country. There survives a photograph of that event: the officers in a circle, leaning forward in their long greatcoats, listening earnestly to the general of their democratic citizen-army, who spoke to them without notes and without a microphone, in a quiet tone of determination, on that grassy cliff above a silent lake on a cool and gray day. Elsewhere, too, people were beginning to see that Hitler had not yet won his war. Slowly the wave of belief in the virtue, and perhaps even in the necessity, of cooperating with a new German-ruled Europe was beginning to ebb, especially among the peoples in the western half of the Continent, for two reasons. One was the Germans' indifference to their physical and political needs and wishes. The other was the increasing evidence that the British were holding their own, that they would fight on. There was a phrase current in those days: *L'Angleterre tient.* That was all to the good; but the Battle of Britain was about to begin.

VI

THE SECOND
COINCIDENCE

The 31st of July

IN THE gloomy year 1948 Churchill wrote about 1940. The war
had been won but the peace was lost. He was seventy-four years old
and not in the best of health. He wrote that his book was "only a
contribution to the history of the Second World War." It is more than
that. Especially *Their Finest Hour* is vintage Churchill; and that vintage is 1940. The same kind of insight that was his inestimable asset
during his duel with Hitler in 1940 was his asset in the reconstruc-
tion of it eight years later. He and his writing can no more be sepa-
rated than can mind from memory. In 1948, with all of the undoubtedly great and valuable facilities around him, including the devoted
and assiduous assistance of his researchers and friends, Churchill had
only a portion of the recovered German documents at his disposal.
Yet he read Hitler's mind well. "Duel" is my choice of a word, not
his. But in 1948, in the last paragraph of the first part of his book,
ending with July 1940, before the Battle of Britain was to begin, he
concluded it in terms of a duel:

> . . . our many anxieties and self-questionings led to a steady increase
> in the confidence with which from the beginning we had viewed the
> invasion project. On the other hand, the more the German High
> Command and the Fuehrer looked at the venture, the less they
> liked it. We could not, of course, know each other's moods and val-
> uations; but with every week from the middle of July to the middle
> of September, the unknown identity of views upon the problem be-

tween the German and British Admiralties, between the German Supreme Command and the British Chiefs of Staff, *and also between the Fuehrer and the author of this book* [my italics] became more definitely pronounced. If we could have agreed equally well about other matters, there need have been no war.

At the end of July there was another reason for Churchill's confidence. That was his knowledge of the American situation: that Roosevelt was coming close to the decision to transfer the destroyers to Britain, the first definite American departure from neutrality that would impress the world.

Had Churchill known what Hitler revealed to his generals on 31 July he would have had yet another reason to be confident: for on that day Hitler said that he would invade Russia probably before England.

At the cool and cloudy Berghof Hitler declared his decision — on the same day, 31 July — when on a muggy summer day in the White House Roosevelt made his decision to tack and beat out of the harbor of American neutrality, skirting the barrier reefs of constitutional and congressional opposition. If the tenth of May was the First Coincidence, then the thirty-first of July was the Second.

HITLER'S DECISION about Russia crystallized during the last ten days of July. It was a consequence of his realization that the British would not respond to his peace proposal. Ten days elapsed between his important conference with his generals in Berlin on the twenty-first to their conference at the Berghof on the thirty-first. He wanted to convince the generals and, perhaps, himself.

He *was* vexed by Stalin: by the brutal abruptness with which Stalin had moved his rooks into the Baltic states during the days when France was falling. There were other instances of Soviet malfeasance that had come to Hitler's notice. Yet less than a year before, the Baltic states had been allotted to Stalin by Hitler himself. And the Soviet government not only went out of its way to congratulate the Third Reich on its successes; it was fulfilling its material and economic commitments to Germany with extraordinary reliability. More important: Stalin was bending over backwards to impress Hitler with his friendship. He was evidently unwilling even to listen to the British. On 13 July Stalin himself sent an accurate account to the German embassy in Moscow of his talk on 1 July with the then newly arrived

Stafford Cripps, carefully emphasizing his indifferent responses to the latter. During the month of July Cripps's expectations of an improvement in British relations with Russia largely evaporated. Stalin's minion Molotov refused to see him. On 1 August Molotov delivered an ugly speech, complimenting Germany, dismissing Britain. The previous day Cripps had cabled Halifax that under such conditions he ought perhaps to be withdrawn from Moscow. (On 2 August Halifax told him to stay on.)

Twice in June and July Hitler dropped hints to some of his generals about his potentially difficult task of explaining to the German people a future confrontation with Russia before — or after — the victory over England. First, he thought, he had to convince his generals. He knew how his German-Russian pact with Stalin had impressed them. They had welcomed it. He also knew their respect for the Bismarckian tradition, to the effect that Germany must never be involved in a two-front war. Thus his collection of worrisome Russian portents was meant for his military advisers. It was to be the first, the introductory, phase of his argument. After the routine situation report at noon on 29 July he asked Jodl to stay. He wanted to say something to him privately. (Field Marshal Keitel was on leave.) He told Jodl that he was worried: the Russians might change their course. There were too many Russian troops on the other side of the German-Russian border. "In the East we have as much as nothing." (Why? He no longer needed all those divisions in the west.) The Russians might break into Rumania and seize the oil wells there. "Then the war would be lost for us." (An exaggeration, to say the least.) He asked Jodl: what were the chances of deploying the army in the east and, if necessary, attacking and defeating Russia in the autumn? That would be impossible, Jodl said. Such preparations would take four months at least. Hitler told him that in any case this must be handled in absolute confidence, known only to a minimum of staff officers. Jodl now descended from the Berghof to the station in Reichenhall, where a military staff, including General Walter Warlimont, was lodged in a special train. They were told to address themselves to the study of this eastern deployment, under the code name "Aufbau Ost."

There are contradictions between Jodl's and Warlimont's accounts of these events, in their testimonies at Nuremberg as well as in Warlimont's later recollections. Warlimont said that he and his staff were stunned, if not shocked, by Hitler's idea. Jodl denied this. Jodl also said that 29 July was the first time the Führer had spoken thus about

Russia. (Jodl's Nuremberg paper bore the title "First Thoughts of the Fuehrer About Russia's Inimical Attitude Against Us.") At Nuremberg Jodl — who remained the most steadfast and loyal servant of Hitler till the end — wished at least to suggest that Hitler's decision to attack Russia crystallized relatively late, and that Hitler saw it as an unavoidable defensive measure. Yet when Hitler had dropped remarks to them about Russia before, the generals had nodded. On 13 July, for example, Halder, after noting that the Führer was preoccupied about the English unwillingness to give in, wrote: "He sees the answer to the question, *just like ourselves,* that England has some hopes about Russia." Next day Halder added: "The collapse of Russia should convince England to give up the struggle." Hitler need not have worried about his generals. Their assertions after the war that Hitler's decision to prepare an invasion of Russia had filled them with astonishment and foreboding are not convincing. None of them contradicted Hitler. None of them counseled caution. (The same thing was true of their thoughts and words eleven months later, when the war against Russia was about to begin. They were even more confident than was Hitler then.)

When Hitler summoned them on the thirty-first he drew the larger picture of the war. Having spoken to Jodl about it two days before, he now hardly said anything of his anxieties about Stalin. He spoke about England. He said he might have found a way to win the war without having to invade England. (We have seen that Admiral Raeder was excluded from this conference.) He told Jodl, Halder and Brauchitsch that the air attack against England was now beginning; but "if results of the air war are not satisfactory, [invasion] preparations will be halted." Then he went on, according to Halder's original typescript:

> *England's hope is Russia and America. If hope on Russia is eliminated, America is also eliminated,* because enormous increase in the influence of Japan in the Far East will result from the elimination of Russia.
> *Russia is the factor on which England is mainly betting. Something has happened in London!* The English were already quite "down" [this word is in English in the typescript], now they are a bit up again [*aufgerichtet*]. We have tapped their telephone conversations. . . . *However: should Russia be smashed, then England's last hope is extinguished. . . .*
> *Decision: In the course of this contest Russia must be disposed of. Spring '41. The quicker we smash Russia the better. Operation only*

makes sense if we smash the state with one hard blow. Winning a
certain amount of territory does not suffice. A standstill during the
winter hazardous. Therefore better to wait, but decision definite to
dispose of Russia. . . . Aim: Annihilation of Russia's living force
[*Lebenskraft*].

The italicized passages were underlined by Halder. He was obviously
impressed with Hitler's reasoning. We are less inclined to that. But
only for one reason. We know what happened to the German army in
Russia; we know that, after having invaded Russia, Hitler lost the
war. Yet in Russia, in 1941, he came very close to winning it. And
what would have happened then? There was more to his reasoning
than megalomania. Nor was it a return to the main objective of his
life that he had set forth in *Mein Kampf,* the winning of the European east for the German people and their Reich. That may have been
his main objective once. But not in 1940. *Lebensraum* would be the
secondary, perhaps the long-range, benefit, to be organized after the
conquest of Russia. His primary aim was to win his war against England: to eliminate Russia, in order to eliminate Churchill. There was
more than geopolitical calculation in that. Churchill, as Hitler
thought, had two hopes: America and Russia. Against America he
could do nothing. But with Russian power destroyed, his continental
power would be unbeatable. Then Churchill, and Roosevelt, could
do nothing to defeat him. There would be people in Britain — and, as
he thought, many in America — who would then take some comfort
from the defeat of Communist Russia. The British and the American
people would then realize the futility of Churchill's and Roosevelt's
policy of persisting with a protracted and unwinnable war.

That this was Hitler's primary purpose is ascertainable from many
sources. (Here is yet another entry from Halder's war diary, as late as
14 June 1941, that is, eight days before the invasion of Russia: "After
lunch an all-inclusive speech by the Fuehrer [giving] the basis of his
reasons for the attack on Russia and the evolution of his calculation
that the collapse of Russia would induce England to give up the
struggle." And as late as 22 August 1941, with his armies at Lenin-
grad, storming toward Kiev and Moscow, Hitler said his aim was "to
finally eliminate Russia as England's allied power on the continent
and thereby deprive England of any hope of a change in her fortunes
with the help of that last existing Great Power.") Yet most historians
even now assert that Hitler's ideological desire to conquer European
Russia was his principal aim throughout the war. Andreas Hillgruber,
the leading German historian of Hitler's war strategy, argued

throughout his career that Hitler had a "Stufenplan," a war plan in stages: after the war against England, the war against Russia, his primary goal. This is the main thesis of Hillgruber's massive *Hitlers Strategie 1940–1941* (1965); in a debate with another German historian, Bernd Stegemann, in 1982, Hillgruber again insisted that after July 1940 the war against England was of secondary (*"zweitrangig"*) importance to Hitler. That this argument is not tenable has been asserted by a few historians, including myself. But the purpose of this book is not a historiographical quarrel.

Hitler said later that he had needed "great spiritual strength" for his decision to turn against Russia. Yet revealing that to the generals and ordering the first preparations on 31 July gave him a sense of relief. He had faced the difficult question whether the English would or would not give up the struggle against his conquest of Europe. He still faced the consequent question whether to risk an invasion of England or not. Now there was an answer to these questions, and a third alternative. Once he destroyed Russia's power, Churchill (and behind him, Roosevelt) would have to give up. Meanwhile, as behooves a statesman and war leader, he had yet another instrument: the air war against England. He was not certain about its ultimate success; but even if that instrument did not bring the English to their knees, he now had a great alternative, a grand contingency plan.

Churchill did not know what took place at the Berghof on 31 July. But he had suspected something like that for some time. As early as 27 June he wrote to Smuts: "If Hitler fails to beat us here he will probably recoil eastward. Indeed he may do this even without trying invasion." On 8 July he said the same thing to Beaverbrook.

THUS AT the end of July 1940 Hitler, after some hesitation, made his decision to prepare the invasion of Russia at the very moment when Roosevelt, after some hesitation of his own, decided to definitely commit the United States on the British side. There was yet another chronological coincidence: as in the case of Hitler, it was during the last ten days of July that Roosevelt's decision about the destroyers began to crystallize.

Roosevelt and Hitler were of course very different men. Both were secretive, but in different ways. Hitler kept some of his most important beliefs to himself, while he was a master at convincing people to believe what he wanted them to believe. Roosevelt's ideas were less complicated than Hitler's; but it was his custom to prepare his decisions surreptitiously, denying them in the face of truth, if need be; he was a master of dissimulation. His acts and words were always dependent on his calculations of domestic politics — that is, of his potential internal opposition. He was, of course, not a dictator but the President of a constitutional democracy; but the quality of his leadership was sometimes compromised by his habit of politic calculation. To this we may adduce his habit of procrastination, which increased later in the war, probably apace with the waning of his physical strength toward the end. In 1940, however, calculation rather than procrastination marked the evolution of the destroyer deal. As late as 22 July he still thought that he might not be able to proceed with it. By 1 August he had made up his mind to go ahead in the politically most feasible way.

Four factors helped make up his mind. There was the message from Churchill that he received in the late afternoon of 31 July — as we have seen, the first important message from Churchill for more than six weeks. There were the reports from his confidential envoy in London, Colonel Donovan, telling Roosevelt what he had hoped to hear: that the British were holding out in earnest and that they were therefore worth supporting. Before Donovan would return to Washington, he agreed with the conclusions of the Anglophile general Raymond E. Lee: "Donovan gives odds of 60–40 that the British would beat off the German attack." (Lee thought that the odds were better than that: 2 to 1. Kennedy was much vexed by the Donovan mission; but Donovan told Kennedy before he left that "the American policy was to help in every way we can and it doesn't help these people any to keep telling them that they haven't got a chance.") The third fortifying factor was the gradual change in the evaluations by the highest American military and naval authorities, including General George C. Marshall and Admiral Harold R. Stark: they no longer believed that the British were a losing cause. The fourth factor was the informal, confidential but highly instrumental activity of a group of influential Americans who represented the opposite of what the so-called isolationists stood for. Most of these people were members of the Committee to Defend America by Aiding the Allies, the central core of which was the Century Group — the antithesis of the gathering group of America Firsters. In 1940, unlike fifty years later, most of the respectable members of the eastern American social, financial, cultural, intellectual and publishing elite were men and women of

Anglo-Saxon (and Anglo-Celtic) ancestry. Many of them were committing themselves to the British cause. Their private and public influence was considerable. There were both Republicans and Democrats among them: all in all, an elite whose character, intelligence and composition — as well as their management of a more or less enlightened public opinion — were very different from those which prevail in the United States fifty years later.

On 19 July Franklin Roosevelt was nominated for a third term by the Democratic Party convention in Chicago. He had not gone to Chicago. He stayed in the White House, where he broadcast his acceptance speech (in the very hour when Hitler made his great speech in Berlin). Immediately afterward Roosevelt met with his closest foreign policy advisers, the secretaries of war, of the navy, of the treasury (Stimson, Knox, Morgenthau) and Undersecretary of State Sumner Welles. That same day Benjamin Cohen, a presidential assistant, spurred by an influential member of the Century Group, gave the President a long legal memorandum, arguing that it was within the latter's constitutional prerogative to sell or transfer the destroyers without the approval of Congress. As often during that summer, that Friday night Roosevelt sailed off on the *Potomac,* the presidential yacht, for a weekend fishing cruise. Back in Washington on the twenty-second he wrote a note to Knox: he doubted the validity of Cohen's argument. Three days later the Century Group prepared another memorandum about the vital British need for one hundred — not fifty — destroyers, detailing the various ways in which the President could bring that about. The British ambassador was aware of the gist of that paper; presumably so was Churchill. There is reason to believe that it contributed to his decision to "plug in" his message to Roosevelt then and there. Probably because of the unbearable heat wave in Washington the President had decided to take a day off. He left on the *Potomac* Sunday afternoon; he returned to the White House Tuesday morning, the thirtieth. Next day, the thirty-first, may have been the crucial one. Churchill's cable was coming in in three installments that afternoon. The President read it that evening. He had already decided to receive three members of the Century Group the following day, a Thursday filled with appointments (including a fifteen-minute visit by Noël Coward). Yet on the thirty-first he was alone — mostly, but not quite. There are two manuscript records of Roosevelt's appointments. One is a typed appointment book that is at times not complete (and for 31 July 1940 it misdates the day of the week, probably by accident). The other is the handwritten log of the

President's usher. The first does not mention that the President saw William C. Bullitt for an hour on the morning of the thirty-first; the second does. Bullitt had just returned from Europe, full of energy, wholly convinced that the United States must commit itself on the side of Britain. (Eighteen days later he would make a very strong interventionist speech at Independence Hall in Philadelphia, the draft of which he would discuss with Roosevelt at Hyde Park.) No record of their conversation in the White House on 31 July exists. It is safe to presume that they talked about the destroyers.

On 1 August the three members of the Century Group presented their memorandum to the President. They were not altogether encouraged by him. They thought that he had not yet made up his mind, and that he was very cautious, perhaps especially in view of the coming election. The second of these considerations was probably true, the first not. Roosevelt seems to have made up his mind before their meeting, but he wanted to sound them out about political matters. The thing to do, they said (and Roosevelt agreed), was to work on Willkie, to get the Republican presidential candidate to endorse the destroyer deal and influence the Republican leaders in Congress to that effect. That night Lord Lothian called the secretary of the navy during the latter's dinner. It was urgent that they meet, he said. They talked about and agreed on the idea of selling the destroyers in exchange for the British transfer of some of their western Atlantic and Caribbean bases to the United States. Next day — Friday, 2 August — Roosevelt met with his Cabinet after lunch. The session began with Knox reporting on his talk with Lothian the night before. Roosevelt said nothing about his meeting with the three men of the Century Group, nor about the message from Churchill. He did not need to; he was pleased to see that agreement in the Cabinet was unanimous. He was aware of the importance of that Cabinet meeting. Well after the members left, indeed after dinner, Roosevelt returned to his desk and wrote out their conclusions in a memorandum, a very unusual practice for him. It began:

> At Cabinet meeting, in afternoon, long discussion in regard to devising ways and means to sell directly or indirectly fifty or sixty World War I old destroyers to Great Britain. It was the general opinion, without any dissenting voice, that the survival of the British isles under German attack might very possibly depend on their getting these destroyers.
>
> It was agreed that legislation to accomplish this is necessary.

It was agreed that such legislation, if asked for by me without any preliminaries, would meet with defeat or interminable delay in reaching a vote.

The rest of the memorandum dealt with two matters. Most of it concerned an approach to Willkie, to use his influence to avoid a virtually unanimous opposition by the Republicans in Congress to a destroyer deal. The other matter was the conditions of the deal with the British: the demand that they give "positive assurance . . . that the British Navy, in the event of German success in Great Britain, would not under any conceivable circumstances fall into the hands of the Germans"; nor would it, in such an event, sink itself but sail to North America instead. We shall see in a moment that neither of these matters worked out in quite that way. Nevertheless the destroyer deal was on its way to a conclusion; and thus the neutrality of the United States in the war between Germany and Great Britain became a thing of the past.

HITLER'S DECISION to begin planning the invasion of Russia did not amount to the salvation of Britain. He may not have had his heart in invading England. But he had a very hard heart. It is wrong to pay too much attention to his statements of admiration for the British race. Nor was he ready yet to attack Stalin's empire. He would see first whether his air force could destroy the capacity and then the will of the English to defend themselves. We have seen that on 31 July when he spoke to his generals about the matter of grand strategy, he had first talked to the chief of his navy, whom he excluded from the conference with the generals. To Admiral Raeder he said that at least eight days of intensive air attacks against England were about to begin; after that he would make his decision about the projected landing; if the Luftwaffe had not destroyed the British air force, the landing would have to be put off until May. The next day Hitler issued Directive No. 17: "I have decided to carry on and intensify air and naval warfare against England in order to bring about her final defeat." The principal goal was the elimination of the Royal Air Force. He added at the end: "Terror bombing as reprisals is a matter to be decided by me." (He underlined this sentence in the directive.) It should be noticed that this directive no longer mentioned or suggested the purpose of making England consider peace (even though on 2 August German bombers dropped leaflets over southern England with excerpts from Hitler's speech printed on them). The solution now was the military one. The Luftwaffe understood it that way. Its first and most important objective was to destroy as many British airstrips and fighters as possible, sweeping them from the sky over southern England. The air offensive was to begin on the fifth; because of unfavorable weather, it was postponed first to the eighth and then to the thirteenth.

Before the Battle of Britain began Churchill was still concerned with political undercurrents. A few of his Conservative enemies were muttering against him again. On 1 August Sir John Simon, a former arch-appeaser, wrote to the former Germanophile and pacifist Philip Noel-Buxton that Hitler might become more reasonable in time. What Churchill knew was that on 1 August the king of Sweden made a proposal of mediation — indeed, of an international conference. Churchill's rejection was stern and indignant. He commented on the Foreign Office's draft answer two days later. "The ideas set forth in paragraph 5 of the Foreign Office memorandum appear to me to err in trying to be too clever, and to enter into refinements of policy unsuited to the tragic simplicity and grandeur of the times and the issues at stake. At this moment when we have had no sort of success, the slightest opening will be misjudged. Indeed, a firm reply of the kind I have outlined is the only chance of extorting from Germany any offers that are not fantastic." *Extorting any offers that are not fantastic:* it is at least interesting to note that on 3 August 1940 Churchill still saw that undoubtedly very remote possibility. Any such offer would have to amount to more than a general statement by Hitler about a suspension of hostilities with the English — that is, their reciprocal recognition of the status quo. That status quo meant the British willingness to accept German rule over the Continent; and that was unacceptable to Churchill. On the other hand, if the still generally accepted idea is true — that Hitler's principal aim was to conquer Russia — then one may question why his peace offer included not a word about Europe, suggesting at least a partial restitution of the independence of Western European states, in order to achieve some kind of agreement with the British, after which he could devote himself to his main task in the east. But all that seems never to have entered Hitler's mind. He was convinced that his offer to leave the British Empire alone was sufficiently generous and reasonable.

While Churchill, as we have seen, suspected that Hitler was reluctant to attempt invasion, he was nonetheless aware of the terrible danger that would arise if the presence of the Royal Air Force on the ground and in the air over southern England should diminish dangerously. What neither he nor Hitler foresaw were the actual effects of severe bombing of the cities. We know that the English people withstood the later Blitz; indeed, we know that the effects of such bombardments during the entire war, with very few exceptions, did not fulfill their planners' expectations. Yet no one knew that in August 1940. Nor must we think that Hitler's express order at that time to refrain from bombing population centers was an outcome of his prevalent respect for the English race. That respect had begun to vanish fast. The bombing of the cities, and especially of London, would come, if must. At the same time it seems that Churchill was more confident than was Hitler of the capacity of the British people to stand up to air bombardment, "the effect of which in these days was greatly exaggerated." The Germans "wondered . . . whether [the British people] would crumple and force His Majesty's government to capitulate. About this Reichsmarshal Goering had high hopes, and we had no fears." This may have been an exaggeration; but not much.

Göring's hopes were higher than Hitler's. Hitler was reluctant to risk the invasion because — he repeated this to his commanders on several occasions — a failure would mean a great triumph for England's prestige. As early as 14 August — that is, only one day after Göring's air offensive had begun — Hitler already sensed that it would not be decisive. That intuition corresponded with his realization that his navy was far from being ready to cross the Channel. He said that invasion preparations must be continued, even if the invasion should not occur in that year, for the purpose of keeping up the threat ("Bedrohung") before the English.

This is not the place to recapitulate the story of the Battle of Britain, of which excellent and detailed accounts exist. The sum of the story is the successful resistance — resistance rather than complete victory — of the Royal Air Force above southern England; Hitler's decision (his response to the first, and very ineffective, British bombing raids on Berlin) to switch on 7 September to the bombing of London; and his decision, ten days later, to cancel the invasion project for that year.

Thus the duel between Hitler and Churchill became the battle above Britain, splintered into many dozens of duels each day between

British and German pilots. It may even be said that the daring German pilots were more inspired by Hitler's ideas of German greatness than were the brave British pilots by Churchill's rhetoric; but that did not matter much. What mattered was the willingness of the British people to trust Churchill's leadership; and by August 1940 there was more to that than the inspiration of his rhetoric.

ON 2 AUGUST, after dinner and before returning to his desk to write that unusual memorandum about his Cabinet's conclusions that afternoon, Roosevelt made a telephone call to William Allen White, who was a well-known journalist and editor, a liberal Republican, an important member of the Century Group and a friend of Wendell Willkie's. White and Willkie were vacationing in Colorado. Roosevelt asked White whether the Republican presidential candidate could influence his party's leaders in Congress to dampen down the Republican isolationists' opposition to a destroyer deal. That horse would not run. Willkie, as both Roosevelt and White knew, was no isolationist; but he was both ambitious and a weak reed. He was not opposed to the destroyer deal, but he was loath to endanger his position in the Republican Party. The destroyers were no longer a secret: on 5 August "Destroyers for Britain" was the title of an eloquent editorial in the internationalist Republican newspaper, the *New York Herald Tribune;* also General John J. Pershing, of World War I fame, delivered a speech in favor of assisting Britain. (It was written for him by Joseph Alsop.) Yet Roosevelt still thought that he could not circumvent the Congress, and that it was within the power of Republicans to obstruct indefinitely the passage of a bill about the destroyers, not to speak of the deleterious effects of such debates on Roosevelt's own reelection prospects. He now thought to sweeten the deal (his words were: giving molasses to Congress) by announcing two British offers in return, in order to convince Congress and the American people that the destroyer deal was, in reality, a hard bargain and a good one. The old destroyers would be sold to Britain in exchange for naval and air bases on British possessions in the Western Hemisphere, ranging from Newfoundland to Trinidad. The other condition was a declaration by the British government that in the event of a British defeat in the home islands the fleet would come over.

Churchill did not want that. After two discussions in the War Cabinet his reaction was summarized in his memorandum to Halifax:

> We have no intention of surrendering the British fleet or sinking it voluntarily. Indeed such a fate is more likely to overtake the German fleet or what is left of it. The nation would not tolerate such a discussion of what we should do if our island were overrun. Such a discussion, perhaps on the eve of an invasion, would be injurious to public morale, now so high. Moreover we must never get into a position when the United States Government may say "We think the time has come for you to send your fleet across the Atlantic in accordance with our understanding of the agreement when we gave you the destroyers." We must refuse any declaration such as is suggested and confine the deal solely to the Colonial bases.

A few days later this deadlock was broken. Roosevelt made up his mind (on 13 August, the day Göring's air offensive began) to proceed without an act of Congress. He was strengthened by a letter published by four prominent American lawyers, which stated that the President was empowered to proceed without congressional action. (Willkie had also told White that he would not personally oppose a destroyer deal.) At the same time Roosevelt agreed not to require a public declaration by the British government about the fleet; he also agreed to the British request that the granting of the bases to the United States would be in the form of ninety-nine-year leases. There were further difficulties, including serious bureaucratic errors and legal tergiversations, and a multitude of drafts being cabled back and forth between Washington and London. (There was Kennedy, in London, complaining that he was being treated like a "dummy"; Roosevelt felt that he could not alienate him further; on 28 August he wrote Kennedy a carefully conciliatory letter: "There is no thought of embarrassing you and only a practical necessity for personal conversations makes it easier to handle details here. . . . Don't forget that you are not only not a dummy but are essential to all of us both in the Government and in the Nation.") Finally on 2 September the instruments were solemnly signed by the British ambassador to the United States and the American secretary of state. The President was on his way to a short vacation in West Virginia. He gathered reporters at his train. He read for them his message to the Congress. (To the text he added, in his own handwriting, that the British grant of American bases in Newfoundland and Bermuda was "generously given and gladly received. The other bases mentioned have been acquired in exchange for fifty of our over-age destroyers.") He said to the reporters that this was probably the most important thing that had come to American defense since the Louisiana Purchase. (It did not seem to occur to him that the Louisiana Purchase was a purchase, not a lease, and that it had little to do with American defense; it was a giant accretion to American territory, the first step toward the creation of the American continental empire.)

The destroyer deal *was* a hard bargain. The fifty old ships — as Roosevelt himself explained to one of the isolationist Democratic senators — had been appraised at a scrap value of between $4,000 and $5,000 each. In sum, the United States received a string of western Atlantic and Caribbean bases for the total value of something like $250,000. The old vessels also needed more repairs than it had been thought at first. By the end of the year only nine of them had reached Britain. But by that time it did not matter: Roosevelt was about to take another large step ahead with the announcement of Lend-Lease, "The Arsenal of Democracy."

What Churchill thought about the destroyers is difficult to tell. We have seen that the first appearance of the idea had come from Bullitt early in May. (As a matter of fact, the American minister to Norway, Mrs. Florence ["Daisy"] Harriman, had suggested as early as 1939 that the United States sell a few over-age destroyers to Norway.) Of course from the very beginning Churchill knew the great political significance of such an American commitment; but it is too simplistic to conclude that he had no real interest in their material contribution to the sea defense of Britain. After all, he wrote Roosevelt in June that the ships were "a matter of life or death." (Reading this, Roosevelt's confidant Henry Morgenthau Jr. wrote in a memorandum to the President on 18 June: "unless we do something to give the English additional destroyers, it seems to me it is absolutely hopeless to expect them to keep going.") On 26 June King George VI wrote a personal letter to Roosevelt about the destroyers, surely at Churchill's suggestion. However, it is fairly ascertainable from the War Cabinet records that throughout August the importance of the naval factor gradually paled while the political element grew apace in Churchill's mind, as also in his colleagues'. By 23 August he said that, if necessary, "we could do without the destroyers." What now mattered was hardly the eventual transatlantic passage of these aged ships. It was the great political importance of the definite departure of the United States from its once avowed neutrality, beginning the commingling of British-American efforts in the war.

The Anglo-American alliance had begun to function. When the destroyer-bases agreement was signed in Washington at seven in the evening on 2 September, in Europe it was already the third. That was exactly a year after Great Britain and France had declared war on Germany, when the Second World War had begun. During that first year it was a European war. Now it had broadened into a world war. We have seen that the decisions leading to that had been taken, on the Obersalzberg and in Washington, on 31 July or thereabouts. Churchill did not know what Hitler said about Russia to his generals that day. Neither did Roosevelt or Stalin. Nor did they know that orders had already gone out from the Berghof and Berlin, contravening the earlier plans for a partial reduction of the German army: that formidable army was to be increased again. (The first plans drafted by General Erich Marcks, for a Russian campaign, were ready by 8 August — the day when the German air war against Britain had been scheduled to start.)

In the German language a duel is a *Zweikampf,* a struggle of two men. Hitler and Churchill would remain fierce opponents, principal personages of the Second World War for years to come. The eighty days of their duel had been decisive, not only for the eventual outcome of the Second World War but for the next fifty years in the history of the world. But it was no longer their *Zweikampf.*

VII

AFTER FIFTY YEARS

ON 17 SEPTEMBER 1940 Hitler, after various postponements, ordered the indefinite adjournment of Operation Sea Lion. Churchill did not know that, but he had many reasons to suspect it. That day he and his wife had moved to the Annexe, at Storey's Gate. Shielded by steel shutters during air raids, they would spend their weeknights there during most of the war, even though he preferred to stay at 10 Downing Street as long as he could. (By that time the War Cabinet met in the underground War Room too.)

Both Churchill and Hitler were settling down for a long war. That war Hitler could not win in the end. But that end was far off. There had been one man in Hitler's way of winning the kind of war he had intended; and that man was no longer alone. In a way their duel went on, but its conditions and circumstances were no longer the same. In Scandinavia, and then in Western Europe, Hitler had won: 2–0. Then Churchill parried his thrust: 2–1. In the spring of 1941, in the Balkans and Greece and Crete, Hitler would win again: 3–1. But then Russia came into the war, and America, and Russia held out. The score on Pearl Harbor day was 3–3. But such scorekeeping does not reflect the reality, which is that after December 1941 Hitler could no longer win — not against the combined powers of America, Russia and Britain. (He knew that even before Pearl Harbor; on 18 November 1941 he dropped such a remark to Halder; he talked of a possible draw.) After 1941 he hoped to split his enemies. To achieve that, he would need a decisive victory over one of them. Otherwise they would not negotiate. One year later he, his armies and his people started down their rocky, rather than slippery, slope. The slope was long, their foothold was firm, they kept fighting while fire rained down on them, holding together till the end.

Many dramatic episodes during the war still had characteristics of a duel between Hitler and Churchill. One was the *Bismarck* episode, which I mention only because its story reflected the course of the entire war. In May 1941 that largest German battleship sank the *Hood,* the largest British battle cruiser, in a few minutes with one well-aimed shot. A fleet of British warships drove out for the *Bismarck.* It took four days until she was hunted down and sunk. The fantastically successful German bull's-eye shot; the British incapacity to hit back in time; their maddeningly slow comeback; Churchill insisting and insisting that the *Bismarck* be tracked down, come hell or high water; "Various Parties Converging on the Sea"; the assembly of overwhelming force; surrounded and pounded from every side, the burning and rudderless German ship still floats and floats; she sinks in the end.

On a larger and more protracted scale the duel between Hitler and Churchill went on in the air. Both overestimated the efficacy of bombing. Hitler had learned that in September 1940. As early as July 1940 Churchill thought that eventually the massive bombing of German factories and cities would have to bring about Hitler's defeat, that it was "one sure path" to victory. "We have no continental army which can defeat the German military power," he told Beaverbrook on 8 July. As the war went on, Churchill's respect for the fighting qualities of the German army grew and grew. He also learned that the saturation bombing of German cities was at best a secondary instrument for winning the war, not the decisive one. Still, he went along with that mass destruction till the end, for the main reason of sparing the British and American armies from huge losses on the ground. He succeeded postponing the Anglo-American invasion of Western Europe until June 1944, to a time when their superiority was overwhelming. But he was still worried about the possibility of a great bloodletting campaign in the fields of Western Europe, recalling the frightful, slogging, slaughtering battles of World War I. In turn, Hitler began to launch Wernher von Braun's rockets on London a few days after D-day. It should be recalled that the *V* in V-1s and V-2s was the German abbreviation of *Vergeltungswaffen,* "revenge weapons." By that time Hitler's erstwhile appreciation of the qualities of the British nation was gone. His rockets were instruments of German revenge and, perhaps, his instruments to make a war-weary enemy rethink the war one last time. It did not work for him. Perhaps that was the last episode of their duel.

Late in 1940 Churchill spoke to the American people. "Give us the tools and we will finish the job." Did he mean it? If the job meant to keep Hitler from conquering Britain, yes. If the job meant to conquer Hitler, no. Before his third-term election Roosevelt spoke in Boston to an audience of Irish-American Democrats, most of them isolationists, whose support he thought he needed badly. Joseph Kennedy stood at his side. Roosevelt said: "I have said this before, but I shall say it again and again and again. Your boys are not going to be sent into any foreign wars!" Did he mean it? Probably not. At the latest by the spring of 1941 Roosevelt, and Churchill, knew that American armaments and the undeclared American warfare against the German navy and its submarines halfway across the Atlantic were not enough, that the United States had to enter the war in full force. And even that would not be enough. After Pearl Harbor Churchill began to recognize the awful reality: the American and British empires together, with their enormous resources, would not be able to conquer the will and the wherewithal of the German armed power that Hitler had wrought. They would not be able to reconquer Europe without the Russians.

Churchill began to sense this as early as August 1940; Roosevelt not until about two years later. Before that, there was the Hess episode. On 10 May, one year to the day since Churchill had come to power, London had its worst night, with nearly fifteen hundred people killed. (Some observers thought that the morale of the people was brittle.) That night a solitary German plane crossed the east coast of Scotland. The pilot let the plane crash; he bailed out. He was no less a personage than Hitler's deputy, Rudolf Hess. He had taken it upon himself to embark on a lonely and desperate mission to England for the sake of making peace before Hitler's invasion of Russia was to begin. Hess flew off from Germany without Hitler's knowledge; yet he was convinced that his aim was in accord with what Hitler wanted. This was so. Hess told his British interrogators that there was one unalterable German condition: Churchill and his "clique" must go. That was the essence of Hitler's wishes. Churchill decided that British propaganda should not make too much of the Hess mission, otherwise a boon to British prestige. He was concerned with the possible effects of a German peace initiative on British morale. May 1941 was, in a way, another round of the Duel: Hess, the *Bismarck* episode, the German victory over the British in Crete. But all of that would pale before the coming German invasion of Russia, on which, as we now know, the outcome of the war would depend.

Exactly one year passed from the British declaration of war on Germany, on 3 September 1939, to the American declaration of the destroyer deal. Exactly one year passed, too, from the signing of the French capitulation to Hitler, on 22 June 1940, to the day of his invasion of Russia. There was a drama latent in a triangle of elective affinities. Hitler wanted an agreement with England. He did not get it. Stalin wanted friendship with Hitler. He did not get it. Churchill wanted an agreement with Stalin. He did not get it — until Hitler invaded Russia.

Of course Hitler's decision of 31 July to prepare that invasion was not unalterable. He did not issue his definite directive (No. 18, "Operation Barbarossa") until 18 December, the target date then being fixed for 15 May 1941; it would be postponed by another five weeks. However, these delays were due to military and materiel contingencies, not — as when he had been confronting England — due to Hitler's hesitations. He did not let himself be influenced by the Russian government's attempts to please him, attempts that became more and more extraordinary as signs of the German invasion increased.

The night before that fatal 22 June 1941 Hitler had two flashes of intuition. To Goebbels he said that he still had "a high estimate of the peace party in England. Otherwise they would not have kept so systematically silent [*totschweigen*] about the Hess case." More striking was Hitler's intuition of uncertainty and darkness. One of Ribbentrop's adjutants who had been in Russia spoke of it as "a big bubble." The generals were, without exception, confident. Hitler suddenly became thoughtful; he said that Russia was rather like the ship in *The Flying Dutchman*. "The beginning of every war is like opening the door into a dark room. One never knows what is hidden in the darkness."

THE PRINCIPAL, and most detailed, history of the planning of Operation Sea Lion is that by the German Karl Klee, who wrote in the introduction of his two massive volumes: "The tragedy of what was to come is that the British, who concentrated only on the struggle against their immediate opponent, were ready to accept any partner — that means, also the Soviet Union — in that war. [The British] did not foresee that their policy would only lead to the replacement of a strong Germany by the overwhelming power of Russia." This argument — amounting, in essence, to a kind of selective indignation — appeals to some people even now, and not only in Germany. I am compelled to correct it here. It was not only that without that "partner" the British could not expect to win. That "partner" was forced into an alliance with Britain by Hitler himself. It is also that Churchill saw the choice clearly: either all of Europe dominated by Germany, or — at worst — the eastern half of Europe dominated by Russia; and half of Europe was better than none.

This was common sense, and not — as many people even now are inclined to see it — the reaction of a war leader half blinded by his hatred for Hitler. It is true that as early as August 1940 one may detect the inclination in British foreign policy to welcome certain Russian assertions of their presence in Eastern Europe, and that after 1941 Churchill would praise Stalin, at times extravagantly. But — unlike Roosevelt — he saw clearly where Stalin's ambitions lay. He saw Stalin as a statesman, not as a revolutionary. "If Hitler invaded Hell I would make at least a favourable reference to the Devil in the House of Commons," he said to Colville the night before the German attack. At nine P.M. next night he spoke to the British people and the world. It was a great speech, on which he had worked through the entire day. He said that he did not take back anything he had said against Communism in the past, but that now the issue was not Communism but Russia and Hitler's invasion of it. During the next four years the tide of pro-Russian sentiment among the British people ran ahead of Churchill. As early as September 1941 he instructed his close friend Brendan Bracken at the Ministry of Information "to consider what action was required to counter the present tendency of the British people to forget the dangers of Communism in their enthusiasm over the resistance of Russia."

Unlike Roosevelt, Churchill had few illusions about Stalin's war aims, his occasional praise of Stalin notwithstanding. As the war neared its end Churchill tried, in vain, to commit the Americans to a joint policy that would limit the extent and the conditions of Russian expansion in central Europe. This is not the place to discuss, or even to sum up, the complicated story of the Churchill-Roosevelt-Stalin relationship at that time, except to draw attention to the comment Churchill made to General de Gaulle in November 1944. It was recorded not by Churchill but by de Gaulle in his war memoirs. In answer to the latter's anxious query Churchill said yes, the Americans were rather thoughtless in not considering seriously the dangers of Russian expansion in Europe; yes, Russia now was a hungry wolf in the midst of sheep. "But after the meal comes the digestion period." Russia would not be able to digest the peoples and their states in Eastern Europe. Churchill would live to see the first evidence of those digestive troubles twelve years later, when he was very old and out of power. In 1990 it is only too obvious how right he was in 1944.

Still, as the war came to an end his mind was beset with the fear that the German danger would be replaced by the Soviet one. There was not much of a sense of triumph in his speech to the British people on the tenth of May in 1945, five years after the stunning day when he had come to power. "There were few whose hearts were more heavily burdened with anxiety than mine. . . . I struck a sombre note. . . . 'I must warn you . . . that you must be prepared for further efforts of mind and body and further sacrifices to great causes.' " But the British people were, understandably, tired. Less excusably, Churchill had little support about Europe and Russia from the Americans, especially not from General Eisenhower. Churchill played down these differences in his memoirs — because of political calculation, but also out of his habit almost never to berate people by telling them "I told you so." But the title of the last volume of his war memoirs, written in 1952 and 1953, was *Triumph and Tragedy*.

THE NIGHT before his war against Russia was to begin Hitler issued a peremptory order to German naval forces in the Atlantic. They were rigorously forbidden to fire at American craft, even in self-defense. Hitler knew what Roosevelt wanted: an incident in the Atlantic that would enable him to go to Congress with a message of war. He would not give Roosevelt that opportunity. There were incidents between American vessels and German submarines, hardly avoidable ones, especially in the dark Atlantic nights, but not enough to enable Roosevelt to go to war with a largely undivided people and Congress behind him.

All that would change with Pearl Harbor. That — and the reversal of the German advance before Moscow twenty-four hours before, half the world away — was *the* turning point of the Second World War. People have argued that it was Hitler's megalomaniac underestimation of America that made him declare war on the United States three days after Pearl Harbor. In reality, he hardly had another choice. He could not plainly betray his Japanese allies by welshing on the alliance that he himself had offered them (a day or so after he had canceled Operation Sea Lion in September 1940). He also knew that American naval and air warfare in the Atlantic would intensify against him: in sum, that the actual difference between a declared and undeclared war would diminish even without a definite proclamation of war. When his foreign minister called in the American chargé in Berlin, Ribbentrop declared, scowling: "Your President wanted this war." That may have been true; yet that war was but the continuation of the war that Hitler had started more than two years earlier. From that moment Hitler's strategy changed. He knew that he could no longer achieve a complete victory. But he would fight tough — so tough that sooner or later that unnatural alliance between America, Britain and the Soviet Union would break apart. Here, too, he had his predecessor Frederick the Great constantly in mind. One hundred and seventy-five years before, Frederick, battered and encircled by three enemy powers, won by beating one of them, after which another one suddenly withdrew from the war. He, Hitler, would split his enemies too. In that he was both right and wrong. The Anglo-American-Russian alliance did break apart, but too late for him: not until after he was dead, and his Third Reich overrun in its entirety.

What Hitler's ultimate war aims were we do not know. This may be a surprising statement; but so it is. A great and powerful Third German Reich, dominating most of Europe, incorporating most of the European east, yes; but what would its limits be? Hitler made no definite statements about that, deliberately. When it came to frontiers or the government of his conquered nations he dismissed the discussion again and again by saying that those were matters to be decided when the war was over. We may, at the same time, discern something about Hitler's minimal aim (if that adjective is precise, which it is not). That was the union of all German-speaking people in one German state. It is another historical irony that, with the notable exception of Austria, most of this came about as a result of his defeat. Even before his suicide, millions of Germans from Eastern Europe were fleeing into Germany (with his tacit consent). After these refugees came more millions of Germans, expelled from Eastern European lands where some of their ancestors had settled centuries before. By 1950 there were hardly any Germans left east of the Oder River, a novel condition after eight hundred years. That was the greatest change in the national and political geography of Europe consequent to the Second World War.

Meanwhile, like the result of Luther, that other fiery German nationalist more than four hundred years before him, the result of Hitler was the division of Germany itself, now between the Oder and the Rhine. Forty-five years later, as these words are written, that chapter of the two Germanies, East and West, is over. Had Churchill had his way, the division of a defeated Reich would have taken other, more traditional forms, into four or five of its traditional component states: Bavaria, Prussia, Württemberg, the Rhineland, Saxony, perhaps. Such a division might have been more lasting than the unnatural division into an East German Communist and a West German democratic state. We cannot tell.*

CHURCHILL WAS at Chequers on Sunday evening, 7 December, when the news of Pearl Harbor came over the radio. Eight years later he remembered: "No American will think it wrong of me if I proclaim that to have the United States at our side was to me the greatest joy. . . . Many disasters, immeasurable cost and tribulation lay ahead, but there was no more doubt about the end . . . after seventeen months of lonely fighting and nineteen months of my responsibility in dire stress, we had won the war. England would live; Britain would live; the Commonwealth of Nations and the Empire would live." All this came true, except the last. A few months after Pearl Harbor Churchill pronounced the phrase that would haunt his reputation: "I did not become the Prime Minister to preside over the liquidation of the British Empire." Yet the liquidation — if that is the word — of the Empire was closely connected with the British alliance with the United States. Churchill himself had more than one glimpse of that, even during the negotiations of the destroyer deal. It is not correct to ascribe (as some of his critics have done) that liquidation to Chur-

---

* In Zurich in 1946, Churchill proposed a final reconciliation of Germans and French, leading to a European unity. Many Germans even now see Churchill as the most relentless and unforgiving adversary of their nation — a sentiment of which I found echoes in the otherwise respectful articles in their newspapers in 1965, at the event of Churchill's death and funeral. They are wrong. He extended his magnanimity to the German people as soon as the war ended in 1945. "My hate had died with their surrender; and I was much moved by their demonstrations, and also by their haggard looks and threadbare clothes," he wrote of his visit to the ruins of Berlin. Nor was there anything racist in his view of the German-speaking peoples. He always regretted the breaking up of the Second Germanic Empire, of the Habsburg state of Austria-Hungary.

chill's unrelenting enmity toward Germany, together with his unrelenting advocacy of the American alliance. Long before the war the
British people themselves had grown uncertain, and perhaps unwilling, to carry on with some of their imperial tasks. The hard Victorian
carapace (and discipline) of their imperialist convictions had cracked
after the First World War.

Neither the Duel nor the Second World War had much to do with
the British Empire. They had everything to do with the survival of
Britain, and of Europe. It is in this respect that the British dependence on the United States — more precisely, the gradual evolution of
an alliance of equals to the increasing dependence of the former on
the latter — is a melancholy tale. Had Churchill had his way, at the
end of the war the British and American presence and the general
cause of liberty and democracy in Europe would have been more advantageous than what actually came about. A division of Europe with
Stalin's Russia could not have been avoided; but that division —
geographically and perhaps even politically — would have been
formed along lines surely less unsatisfactory, and perhaps less worrisome, than the unnatural division along a brutal iron curtain.
Churchill did not have his way, mostly because neither Roosevelt nor
the American military and political establishments supported his
views at that time. We have to carry this story a little further. In
Triumph and Tragedy Churchill went out of his way to underempha-
size his disagreements with the Americans, including General Eisenhower, in 1944 and 1945, because of the latter's ascent in the American political firmament.* Then Eisenhower became President of the
United States at the same moment when Stalin died and when a weary
Churchill was prime minister of Great Britain again. Churchill saw
the opportunity of a new and unsure Russian leadership, inclined to
renegotiate the division of Europe and perhaps put an end to the so-
called cold war. His attempts — feebler than before, because of Britain's declining strength and his own — were thoughtlessly and even
contemptuously rejected by the same Eisenhower who eight years
before had gone over Churchill's head to please the Russians and

---

* Churchill to Colville on 1 January 1953 — note that he said this *before* Stalin's death
and the change in the Russian leadership: "[Churchill] said that if I lived my normal span I
should assuredly see Eastern Europe free of Communism. . . . Finally he lamented that
owing to Eisenhower winning the presidency he must cut much out of Volume VI of his
War History [*Triumph and Tragedy*] and could not tell the story of how the United States
gave away, to please Russia, vast tracts of Europe they had occupied and how suspicious
they were of his pleas for caution."

who had chosen for his secretary of state John Foster Dulles, who distrusted Churchill, preferred the West Germans and who in 1940, at the time of Britain's greatest peril, had opposed American help to Churchill's Britain. Had Churchill had his way in 1953, it is possible that the cold war might have wound down decades sooner than it did. We cannot tell.

What we can tell is the larger story: the failure of Churchill's grand vision. To Churchill the cause of the British-American alliance in 1940 was more than the necessary instrument for surviving and eventually winning the war. For at least sixty-five years of his long life — from about 1895 to 1960 — the ideal of an eventual confederation of the English-speaking peoples of the world stood in his mind. His four-volume *History of the English-speaking Peoples* was to serve that ideal, too. He thought that, far beyond the necessities of a wartime alliance, an increasing cooperation and evolving political connection of the English-speaking nations of the world would be the greatest instrument for the peace of mankind in the twentieth century and after, something resembling the Age of the Antonines in the history of Rome. This would not happen for many reasons, one of them being Churchill's own overestimation of the extent and influence of Americans who were, by origin or inclination, Anglophiles. It is the failure to translate that vision into reality, rather than his failure in maintaining the Empire, that allows us to contemplate tragedy as well as triumph in the exceptional career of Winston Churchill.

OF COURSE there was more triumph than tragedy in Churchill's life, but not in Hitler's. Near the end of the war Churchill wondered at times what Hitler would do. "At any time in the last few months of the war he could have flown to England and surrendered himself, saying, 'Do what you will with me, but spare my misguided people.'" On 1 May 1945 the news of Hitler's death came over the radio during dinner. Churchill said at the table: "Well, I must say I think he was perfectly right to die like that."

Hitler's ashes were blown away in the wind; what remained of his bones was lost in the rubble of a destroyed Berlin. He did not have a funeral. Churchill survived him by nearly twenty years; his funeral was a great and solemn occasion.

Old age (de Gaulle said this) is a shipwreck. The last ten years of Churchill's life were not heroic. The deterioration was sometimes horrid. His wife destroyed the portrait by the English painter Graham Sutherland, which had been commissioned for Churchill's eightieth birthday. It is perhaps odd that the best portraits of this old-fashioned aristocrat are photographs.

There are still admirers of Hitler; their number does not compare with those who admire Churchill. Even among Hitler's admirers there are few who are inclined to give the Nazi salute, the outstretched arm, or cry "*Sieg Heil!*"; Churchill's wartime gesture of the V-sign, his two outstretched fingers, have become a nearly universal gesture of freedom leading to victory or the reverse. Near the end of the war Hitler said that he was Europe's last chance. A year after the war the French writer Maurice Druon said at a meeting dedicated to the European mind: "I have known two Europes, two Europes that existed. . . . One, the Europe of the night, which began in 1940 for us and for other peoples even earlier, was a Europe in which for a moment the same sun rising in the Caucasus set in the Atlantic. . . . I have known another Europe, a weak Europe being born, having its seat in London, a Europe made up by a few exiles, all Europeans, because they truly belonged to a common struggle, and it is this Europe which, in the end, had won." In 1940 that was largely due to one man, Churchill.

Some years after the war someone asked Churchill which year of his life he would like to relive. He said 1940, "every time, every time."

We began this book with Hitler's great train steaming westward in the night before that fatal tenth of May in 1940. On 2 May 1945 it was blown up by SS troops outside a small station in Austria. When a few days later the first British soldiers drove into Mallnitz, they met its charred wreck.

EPILOGUE

IN JUNE 1940, a few days before Paris fell, Premier Reynaud broadcast to the French people: if Hitler wins this war, "it would be the Middle Ages again, but not illuminated by the mercy of Christ." A few days later, on 18 June, in his "finest hour" speech Churchill evoked the prospect, not of a return to the Middle Ages, but of a lurch into a New Dark Age. If Hitler wins and we fall, he said, "then the whole world, including the United States, including all that we have known and cared for, will sink into the abyss of a New Dark Age, made more sinister, and perhaps more protracted, by the lights of perverted science." That was a more precise statement than Reynaud's — and perhaps more apposite now, fifty years later, when within and without the great conurbations of the Western world many of the signs and symptoms of a New Dark Age are rising.

Hitler was a radical. Churchill was a traditionalist. There is an especial meaning in this now, when the entire so-called Modern Age that began about five hundred years ago is ending. Hitler wished to put an end to it, to destroy what he saw as the weakness of its tired and hypocritical liberalism. Churchill wanted to preserve its values and to ensure as much of its continuation as he could.

Their duel was a duel between a revolutionary and a statesman. Adolf Hitler was the greatest revolutionary of the twentieth century. He was a revolutionary greater than Lenin or Stalin or Mussolini, not only because of his fanatical dedication to his cause and his vision, and not only because his astonishing triumphs could not be undone except by the assembled forces and efforts of the greatest empires of the world, intent on putting an end to him. In one important sense Hitler's vision survived him. Early in his life Hitler realized the failure of materialistic political philosophies. He realized that strength was more important than wealth, that nationality was more important than class, that nationalism was more powerful than internationalism. During the twentieth century the compound of nationalism with socialism has become the nearly universal formula for all states in the world. Hitler was not the founder of National Socialism, not even in Germany; but he recognized the potential marriage of nationalism with socialism, and also the practical — and not merely rhetorical — primacy of nationalism within that marriage. International socialism is a mirage. At the same time every state in the world has become a welfare state of sorts. Whether they call themselves socialist or not does not matter much. Hitler knew that. He also knew that old-fashioned capitalism was gone; that belonged to the nineteenth century. Before he had come to power someone asked him whether he would nationalize the German industries. "Why should I nationalize them?" he said. "I shall nationalize the people." The economic structure of Germany that he had in mind (and achieved) had few of the characteristics of either Marxian or state socialism; but it could not be called capitalist either. Fifty years later it cannot be denied that nationalism remains the most potent force in the world. We are all national socialists now. Of course the proportions of the compound of nationalism and socialism vary from country to country; but the compound is there, and even where social democracy prevails, it is the national feeling of the people that ultimately matters. What was defeated in 1945, together with Hitler, was German National Socialism: a cruel and extreme version of national socialism. Elsewhere nationalism and socialism were brought together, reconciled and then compounded, without violence and hatred and war. But Hitler's nationalism was profoundly different from traditional patriotism, just as his socialism had none of the marks of the traditional philanthropy of the earlier Socialists.

His hatred for his opponents, domestic and foreign, was greater than his love for his own people. His main obsession was with Jews. We do not and will never know the source of that deep obsession. There may be a mysterious meaning in the history of Jews, both before and after the coming of Christ, a significance beyond and beneath the relationship of a religious or racial minority to the majority of the peoples among which that minority lives. Hitler's recognition of the significance of that minority was not only corrupted by his hatred: it *was* the dreadful product of it.

Fifty years later we in the English-speaking world have not yet been able to come to terms with the historical figure of Hitler, who was not a madman. Eighteen years ago I wrote that to ascribe the evil acts of men to "abnormality" does not only obscure our necessary understanding of Hitler, it also obscures and damages our necessary understanding of human nature itself. Besides, there is all of the historical evidence to the contrary. All the stories of the dictator foaming at the mouth, throwing himself at the carpet and chewing it in a mad rage, are false. The contrary, rather, was true. What was frightening in his character was his cold and almost inhuman detachment. Hitler was an unhappy child, an unhappy adolescent, an unhappy man, an unhappy artist, an unhappy statesman. He was spurred by shame and resentment, surely after 1918.

He was a desperate man — while at the same time a visionary of a new, heroic, pagan and scientific world. Churchill was the defender of a traditional and now antiquated world, and of its surviving standards — a defender of Western civilization rather than a champion of progress. Four or five hundred years ago — at the beginning of our present age of historical consciousness — people, distinguishing it, rightly, from the Middle Ages, coined the term Modern Age, believing, wrongly, that this new, "Modern" Age would last forever. It is because of our historical consciousness — a form of thought that hardly existed five hundred years ago — that we pay our respects to Churchill now, as this age is ending. One Englishman who sensed this was George Orwell. His book *1984* is not his best, and much of what he foretold in it more than forty years ago did not come to pass, at least not in the way he had written it. Yet how significant it is that in his book this English Socialist writer gave the name Winston Smith to his hero; that Winston Smith was born in 1945; and that in his first act of revolt against darkness and oppression Winston Smith raises his glass and toasts the Past.

It was, and it remains, inspiring that in their duel, on which the destinies of the world depended, near the middle of the twentieth century, toward the end of the Modern Age, a great statesman prevailed over a great revolutionary; the writer over the orator; a cosmopolitan over a racist; a democratic aristocrat over a populist demagogue; a traditionalist over a radical; a patriot over a nationalist — during the Second World War which was a catastrophe for millions of people but whose outcome spared the world an even worse one.

References

References from diaries refer either to their page numbers or to the dates of the diary entries.

CHAPTER I. THE EIGHTY DAYS' DUEL

Page 2. "Gentlemen": Schroeder, 102. *Page 6.* "Oh, I don't know about that": Gilbert, 306. *Page 7.* Thompson-Churchill: Thompson, 444. *Page 7.* "As I went to bed": GS, 667. *Page 15.* "we need first of all to have a clear conscience": Weil, 227.

CHAPTER II. THE FIRST COINCIDENCE

Page 16. "When, in the year 1918": Speech at Platterhof, 26 May 1944, article by Hans-Heinrich Wilhelm, MgM, 1976 (2). *Page 16.* "If I live": CDG, I, 44. *Page 17n.* "His most beautiful phrase": Goebbels D, 16 June 1926. *Page 22.* Hitler on "Weserübung": AOK/KTB, 1 April 1940. *Page 23.* "we seem to be very near": Manchester, 336 (his reference is unclear). *Page 26.* "The House of Commons": Watt, 593. *Page 26.* "an uncomfortable feeling": Rock, 222. *Page 26.* Chamberlain to Roosevelt, 5 November 1939: Rock, 229. *Page 26.* "He would be willing": Irving, 224. *Pages 27–28.* "weather continues" etc.: Delafield 28, 294. *Page 29.* The British chargé in Moscow: Le Rougetel, FO 371 N 1068/96/38. *Page 30.* "first among equals": GS, 587. *Page 30.* "fluid, friendly, but unfocused circle": GS, 589. *Page 32.* "I certainly bore": Ismay, 116. *Page 32.* "a muddy waddle": GS, 649. *Page 32.* "It was a marvel": GS, 650. *Page 33.* "If I were the first of May": Colville, 115. *Page 33.* Chamberlain on 2 May: CAB 65 (7) 40. *Page 33.* Lloyd George: GS, 660. *Page 34.* "Usually I talk": GS, 663. (He mistakes the date.) *Page 34.* Kennedy: Irving, 262. *Page 34.* "The atmosphere": Nicolson, 7 May. *Page 34.* Nicolson on New Year's Day: Nicolson D (u). *Page 35.* "What makes it worse": Nicolson D (u). *Page 36.* "not pass up any opportunity": Goebbels D, 28 October 1938. *Page 36n.* "I would gladly have met Hitler": GA, 249–250. *Page 37.* "Shaw": Goebbels D, 11 October 1939. *Page 37.* "how to handle Churchill's case": Goebbels D, 20 October 1939. *Pages 38–39.* "It will certainly not fall": WCR, 819–820. *Page 39.* "Hitler of course declared": NARS microfilm, T 120/5540/K 567887, cited by Irving, 16. *Page 40.* "enormous dimension": GCON, 261. *Page 40.* "Those who have met": Strand magazine, November 1935. *Page 40.* "If our country were defeated": Evening Standard, 17 September 1937. *Page 41.* "did not lead him into Communist ranks": GS, 52. *Page 44.* "the fear that he might look ridiculous": Schroeder, 363. *Page 48.* "If his proposal means": Irving, 47. *Page 49.* "We, who had": GS, 649.

CHAPTER III. THE SLIPPERY SLOPE

Page 56. Robert Byron: in AoW, 15. *Page 59.* Taylor: Taylor EH, 475. *Page 59.* Orwell: New English Weekly, 21 March 1940. *Page 59.* "lost their heads": Channon D, 13 May 1940. *Page 60.* Cadogan: CAD-D, 280– 281. *Page 60.* Butler: Colville, 122. *Page 60.* Edwards: Irving, 266. *Page 60.* Hankey: Rock, 290. *Page 60.* Colville: "Fifty-Shilling Tailors": Colville, 129. *Page 61.* "To a large extent": Reynolds article in DIS, 150. *Page 61.* "If one were dependent": Cudlipp, 145. *Page 61.* "What I mind": Nicolson D (u), 14 May 1940. *Pages 61–62.* "Well, Hitler": Toynbee, 61. *Page 62.* "Poor people": Ismay, 116. *Page 62.* Huntziger, Pétain: Vidalenc, 55; LEW, 78. *Page 62.* de Gaulle: CDG, I, 44. *Page 63.* Hitler in 1932: q. by Rauschning in LEW, 241. (Rauschning's authenticity has been questioned since; yet we must note that he recalled this in 1938, before the war began.) *Page 63.* "The idea of the line being broken": FH, 43. *Page 63.* Churchill on the Maginot: New York Herald Tribune (Paris), 16 August 1939. *Page 64.* "incessant, vehement": FH, 42. *Page 65.* "crowned like a volcano": Baudouin, 44. *Page 65.* Churchill to Cabinet: CAB 65 7 (40). *Page 66.* "absolutely reliable," "political and psychological": War Diary of Army Group A, q. by Ansel, 70. *Page 66.* "the Führer was nervous": Halder KTB; also Jodl NARS microfilm, A-235; IMT, 780-PS, 1811-PS. *Page 68.* "with difficulty escaped": FH, 121. *Page 68.* "in the conflict of Fascism and Bolshevism": FH, 121. *Pages 68–69.* Ciano, 2 May: CAB 65 7 (40). *Page 69.* Churchill-Mussolini and response: FH, 122. *Page 71.* Questionable evidence, Hitler about America in 1931: Calic, 60–61. (In an-

other matter and book, Calic's sources turned out to be questionable.)
Page 72. British Chiefs of Staff, October 1939: LEW, 67, note 26. *Page 72.* "gathered unexpected strength": Rock, 230. *Page 73.* Welles, Berle: Leutze article, 481. *Page 73.* Ickes, Roosevelt, Miss Perkins, Mrs. Roosevelt: Leutze article, 480. *Page 74.* Kennedy: Jews. Landis papers, q. by Irving, 446, 636. *Page 74.* Chamberlain-Kennedy: FDRL, Box 8; also Leutze article, 479. *Page 74.* "Make no mistake": Rock, 236. *Page 74.* "ruthless and scheming," "certain strong Jewish": Moffat ms. diary, in Leutze article, 476. *Page 74.* Kennedy to Bullitt, March 1940: Rock, 278. *Pages 74-75.* Vansittart, Halifax on Kennedy: Rock, 276-277. *Page 75.* Churchill to Roosevelt, 15 May: CH/FDR, I, 37. *Page 76.* Bullitt to Roosevelt: CAB 65 7 (40), WM 129 (90). *Page 76.* "we are determined to persevere": CH/FDR, I, 37. *Pages 77-78.* Bullitt to Roosevelt: Irving, 278, 620. *Page 79.* Duff Cooper: CAB 65 7 (40). *Page 79.* Beaton and Calder: Calder, 106. *Page 80.* Nicolson, 20 May: Nicolson D (u). *Pages 80-81.* Hitler on Mosley: Engel D, 56. *Page 80.* Mitford-Byron: AoW, 7. *Pages 80-81.* "beside himself," "The English": Jodl D; also NARS microfilm, A-235; also IMT, 1811-PS, 1760-PS. *Page 82.* "his spirit is indomitable": Colville MV, 216. *Page 83.* "In all the history of war," "depressed," "Poor man": *Colville,* 138. *Page 83.* "must not overestimate": Hillgruber, 62-63. *Page 84.* "regretted that decision": FH, 79. *Page 86.* "The army is England's backbone": Schroeder, 105. *Page 86.* Jeschonnek: Ansel, 85. *Page 86.* Hitler, February 1945: Hitler/Bormann, 90. *Page 87.* Hitler-Göring: Engel D, 23 May. *Pages 88-89.* Churchill, Calais: FH, 81-82. *Page 92.* "We must make peace": Villelume, 353. *Page 92.* Halifax in December 1939: CAB 65/2, WM 107 04-02. *Page 92.* "One firm rock": Reynolds article in DIS, 149, note 10. *Pages 92-94.* Cabinets, 26 May: CAB 65/13 WM (40), 139th Conclusions, Confidential Annex; also CAB 65/13, WM 142, 140th Conclusions, Confidential Annex. *Page 93.* Villelume on Halifax and Churchill: Villelume, 356. *Page 93n.* Wilson-Léger: Horace Wilson papers, CAB 127/158. *Page 94.* Cadogan: CAD-D, 290. *Page 95.* Ismay on Churchill, 26 May, evening: Ismay, 131. *Page 95.* "British Strategy in a Certain Eventuality": WP 140 (168), CAB 66/7, q. by Bell, 49ff. *Pages 95-98.* Cabinet, 27 May: CAB 65-13, WM (40), 142nd Conclusions, Confidential Annex. *Page 96.* Cadogan: CAD-D, 290. *Page 97.* Halifax: Birkenhead, 458; CAD-D, 291. *Pages 97-99.* "there are signs": Colville, 140-141. *Page 98.* Churchill, Westminster Abbey: FH, 99. *Pages 98-99.* Cabinet, 28 May: CAB 65-13, 145th Conclusions, Confidential Annex. *Pages 99-100.* "I have thought carefully": Dalton, 335. *Page 100.* "quite casually": FH, 100. *Page 100.* Cabinet, 28 May, 7 P.M.: CAB 65/13, 146th Conclusions, Confidential Annex. *Page 101.* "there can be no doubt": Bell, 48. *Page 101.* "No countenance": Dalton D, 28 May. *Page 101.* "In these dark days": FH, 91 (according to Gilbert, issued on 29 and not on 28 May). *Page 102.* Lloyd George in June: Addison article, 363. *Page 102.* "The Cardinal is vigorous and tough":

PREM 4/22/3.   *Page 102*. Italian dispatch (Bastianini to Rome): DDI, IX, 4, 522.   *Page 102*. "Bury them in caves and cellars": Gilbert, 449.   *Page 102*. "It looks as if Halifax": Harvey, 372, 377.   *Page 105*. Hitler's remarks: Halder KTB; also cited by Hillgruber, 145.   *Page 105*. "seriously meant": Hillgruber, 144, note 1.

CHAPTER IV. ALONE?

Page 108. "reasonable terms," "The problem": Klee, 189; also Ansel, 107.   *Page 109*. Philippi: Klee, 60, note 181.   *Page 109*. Hess: NARS microfilm, T-175 R-126-N 6751.   *Page 109*. Boetticher: Engel D, 47.   *Page 110*. Teleki: Pesti Hirlap (newspaper), Budapest, 1 June 1940.   *Page 110*. Himmler: IMT, H-174, 1198.   *Page 111*. "At last he rose": Martin, in Action, 140.   *Page 112*. "significant are the frankness and freedom": Bridges, in Action, 122-123.   *Page 112*. "Don't write that down": Schroeder, 357.   *Page 112*. Churchill to Ismay: FH, 141.   *Page 113*. "so that the evacuation of the French could continue": FH, 107.   *Page 113*. "If Germany defeated either": FH, 112.   *Page 113*. Brittany: Churchill papers, 20/13, q. by Gilbert, 453.   *Page 114*. "Many of our soldiers": FH, 115.   *Page 114*. Montgomery: q. by Gates, 482.   *Page 114*. "not daring seriously to molest their departure": Gilbert, 452.   *Page 114*. Churchill to Ismay: Churchill papers, 20/13, q. by Gilbert, 460.   *Page 115*. Churchill to Eden: Gilbert, 477.   *Page 115*. "incapable of action": ibid.   *Page 115*. Orwell: Orwell D, 30 May.   *Page 115*. Churchill to Chamberlain *re* Lloyd George: Churchill papers, 20/11, q. by Gilbert, 474.   *Page 116*. Churchill to newspaper owners: King, 50.   *Page 116*. "could not spare any": PREM 3/486.   *Page 117*. Churchill to Mackenzie King: FH, 145-146.   *Page 117*. "This dastard deed": FO 371 (1940), 24239.   *Page 117*. Interesting to note: Gilbert, 486, note 2.   *Page 117*. Bullitt to Roosevelt: FH, 143, citing Hull.   *Page 118*. Charlottesville speech: Langer-Gleason, II, 516.   *Page 118*. Churchill to Roosevelt, 11 June: CH/FDR, I, 43.   *Page 118*. Churchill to King George VI, Churchill to Baldwin: *Gilbert, 469*.   *Pages 118-119*. "I see only one way through": FH, 146.   *Pages 120-121*. Wiegand interview text: Domarus, 1524-1525.   *Page 121*. "That will be the last declaration of war": Engel D, 82.   *Page 122*. "diabolically clever": FO 371 (1940), C7375/7362/17.   *Page 123*. "Darkness, rather than light": Spears, II, 155.   *Pages 123-124*. "A moment of drama": Eden, 116.   *Page 124*. "he ought also to have been ashamed": FH, 140.   *Page 125*. Beaverbrook: Gilbert, 539.   *Page 125*. Churchill to Cabinet: CAB 65/7, 165th Conclusions.   *Page 125*. Churchill to Roosevelt, 13 June: CH/FDR, I, 47.   *Page 126*. "naval power": CH/FDR, I, 46.   *Page 126*. Churchill to Roosevelt, 15 June: CH/FDR, I, 49-50.   *Page 127*. "I woke up with dread in my heart": Eden, 182.   *Page 127*. "It was not of course possible": FH, 203.   *Page 128*. Cabinet to French: CAB 65/13, 168th Conclusions.   *Page 129*. Churchill, War

Cabinet, 16 June, 3 P.M.: Woodward, I, 279. *Page 129.* Pétain, Ybarnégaray, Mandel: q. by Churchill, FH, 213. *Page 130.* "returned to Downing
Street with a heavy heart": FH, 212. *Page 131.* Ciano-Ribbentrop: Ciano
D, 263. *Page 131n.* Heydrich to Ribbentrop: HH/IfZ. *Page 131n.*
Hitler, "The question is": Engel D, 94–95. *Page 132.* Ciano on Hitler:
Ciano D, 264. *Page 132.* Butler-Prytz: Woodward, I, 205, note 1. (There is
no record of this interview in the Foreign Office archives.) *Page 132.* Fransoni to Rome: DDI, IX, VI, 37. *Page 133.* Halifax to Mallet: FO 371
(1940), N 5848/112/42. *Page 133.* Hewel to Hitler: HH/IfZ. *Page
133.* Hitler "skeptical": Engel D, 82–83. *Page 135.* "I do not regard the
situation": FH, 194. *Page 135.* Churchill to Pétain and Weygand: FH,
216–217. *Page 136.* "What could I have done without his help?": CDG, I,
89. *Page 136.* "Whether [Churchill] was drunk": King, 55; LEW, 97, note
5. *Page 136.* "How I wish Winston": Nicolson, q. in LEW, 98, note 54.
Page 136. "Winston wound up": Channon D, 20 June. *Page 136.* "uneducated people": Orwell D, II, 356. *Pages 136–137.* "Public Opinion in the
Present Crisis": Ministry of Information, INF, 1/264. *Page 137.* Maurois:
cited by Bell, 119. *Page 137.* Orwell, 17 and 21 June: Orwell D, II, 353.
Pages 137–138. Waugh: Waugh, 416. *Page 138.* "not very encouraging":
CAB 65/13, 171st Conclusions. *Page 138.* "the mass of our population":
ibid. *Page 138.* "there was confusion and perplexity": Action, 18. *Page
138.* "a feeling of gloom and apprehension": Bell, 128. *Page 138.* Ministry
of Information reports: ibid. *Page 138.* "rather like a quarrelsome family":
Mosley, 55. *Page 138.* Kennedy to Roosevelt: q. by Irving, 327–328.
Page 138. Kennedy to Lee: Lee, 6. *Page 138.* Lee by the end of the month:
Lee, 7. *Page 139.* Churchill on abandoning Channel Islands: CAB 65/17
(172). *Page 139.* Clementine Churchill's letter: q. by Gilbert, 587–588.
Page 139. Churchill-Halifax-Butler: Gates, 398; FO 800/322, xxxii, 42–
44. *Page 140.* Cabinet, 26 June: CAB 65/7, 171 (40). *Page 140.* Cripps
to Halifax: FO 371/W 8602/8602/49. *Page 140.* "I shall myself never
enter": PREM 4743 B/1. *Page 141.* "I don't think words count for much
now": FH, 228. *Page 142.* "We know President is our best friend": FH,
229. *Page 143.* "very strongly that Hitler's defeat is not vital to us": Patterson, 247. *Page 143.* Taft-Stimson: Patterson, 242. *Page 146.* Churchill
article on Trotsky: GCON, 197–205. *Pages 147–148.* Churchill to Stalin:
FH, 135–136. *Page 149.* "The war in the West is over": Boehme, 79.
Page 149. Luftwaffe High Command: Klee, 61. *Page 149.* Goebbels:
Goebbels D, 24, 25, 26, 27, 28 June. *Page 151.* "killed or maimed to save
the faces of a few politicians": q. by Irving, 357. *Page 152.* Cudahy-Vatican: Chadwick, 138. *Page 152.* "that we do not desire to make any enquiries": FH, 171. *Page 152.* "In these days my principal fear": FH, 167.
Page 152. Bletchley messages: Gilbert, 611. *Page 152.* "the opening of the
Offensive": Gilbert, 617. *Page 153.* "investigate the question of drenching
the beaches": Colville, 182. *Page 153.* "very gay and confident": Wiskemann, 45.

CHAPTER V. GREAT EXPECTATIONS

Page 158. Paper, 25 June: Klee, 61.   *Page 158.* Jodl memorandum, 30 June: IMT, PS-1776; also Klee, 298.   *Page 159.* Hitler at "Tannenberg": Goebbels D, 4 July; also Meissner, 448.   *Page 159.* Goebbels D, 3 July and ff. *Page 160.* Goebbels instructions: Boelcke, 407.   *Page 162.* "proves that the fighting spirit": Ciano D, 273.   *Page 163.* "heartbreaking for me": Colville, 185.   *Page 163.* Churchill to Somerville: FH, 235.   *Page 163.* "unique in my experience": FH, 238.   *Page 164.* "The Prime Minister expects": FH, 237.   *Page 164.* "everyone in the U.S.A.": Macleod, 279.   *Page 164.* "At the station": Channon D, 24 June.   *Page 164.* "I entirely deprecate": FH, 646.   *Page 164.* "Winston's dominance": Nicolson D (u).   *Page 165.* "what they require": Colville, 193.   *Page 165.* Colville on Chequers: Colville, 179.   *Page 167.* Jodl memorandum: IMT, PS-1776.   *Page 167.* Jodl, 12 July: Klee, 72.   *Page 168.* Halder, 13 July: Halder KTB.   *Page 168.* "he wants to weigh every word": Ciano D, 6 July.   *Page 168.* "My impression": Engel D, 15 July.   *Pages 168–169.* Directive No. 16: IMT, PS-442; also Klee, 75ff.   *Page 169.* "about its moral and economic power of resistance": HH/IfZ.   *Page 170.* "estimated size of [Churchill's] audience": BBC Audience Research, letter to the author, 29 December 1989, from BBC/WAC.   *Page 170.* Churchill to Ismay, 2 July: FH, 266.   *Pages 170–171.* "W. is sufficiently ruthless": Colville, 192.   *Page 171.* "even small parade marches": FH, 644.   *Page 171.* "caprice," "stunt": Gilbert, 658. *Page 171.* "Set Europe ablaze": Dalton, 367.   *Page 171.* The queen to Nicolson: Nicolson D, 100.   *Page 172.* Churchill on rationing: q. by Gilbert, 663.   *Page 172.* Orwell, 16 July: Orwell D, II, 362.   *Page 172.* "in wonderful spirits": Bryant, 195.   *Page 173.* "What are we waiting for?": MA 441/2/2057.   *Pages 173–174.* "a widespread desire": Kershaw, 156, note 22.   *Page 174.* "people could hardly wait": ibid.   *Page 174.* "Tonight the fate of England": Boelcke, 430.   *Pages 174–176.* Full text of Hitler's speech: GFK, 47–81.   *Page 176.* "a restrained vocabulary": Martin, 306. *Page 176.* "Hitler speaks simply": Ciano D, 277.   *Page 177.* "The Führer does not yet": Goebbels D, 20 July.   *Page 177.* "This is not just a river crossing": Klee, 190–191.   *Page 177.* "Certain signs of reason": Goebbels D, 22 July.   *Pages 177–178.* Hitler at Bayreuth; also "In that hour": Kubizek, 343.   *Page 178.* "full of fury": Goebbels D, 25 July.   *Page 178.* "German public opinion is boiling hot": Goebbels D, 29 July.   *Page 179.* "Considering everything": Nicolson D (u), 19 July.   *Page 179.* "The reaction to Hitler's speech": Nicolson D, II, 103.   *Page 179.* "I do not propose to say anything": Colville, 200.   *Page 179.* "this would be making too much of the matter": FH, 260.   *Page 179.* Churchill to Stokes: PREM 100/2 ("Peace Feelers").   *Page 180.* "I should judge": CAD-D, 317.   *Page 180.* Cardinal Hinsley: ADSS, I, 471, 474.   *Page 180.* Hohenlohe-Kelly: HH/IfZ.   *Page 181.* Churchill telegram, 4 July: Churchill papers, 20/9 and 20/4, q. by Gilbert, 700.   *Page 181.* "toying with the idea":

Gilbert, 706. *Page 181.* "paid tribute to the Führer's desire for peace":
GD, D, X, 398; DDI, IX, V, 311. *Pages 181-182.* "I thought your Royal
Highness": Gilbert, 705. *Page 182.* Raeder to Hitler, 25 July: Klee, 95.
Pages 182-183. Goebbels on invasion plans: Goebbels D, 26, 29 July, 1
August. *Page 184.* "If England wishes": Halder KTB, 22 July. *Page 185.*
Churchill to Roosevelt, 5 July (not sent): CH/FDR, I, 54. *Pages 185-186.*
"I am sure": PREM 3/462/2/3. *Page 186.* "It is some time": CH/FDR,
I, 56-57. *Page 186.* Thomsen on Kennedy: Whalen, 321. *Page 186.*
"Don't let anybody": Langer-Gleason, II, 712. *Page 188.* "I don't like it":
Bell, 131. *Page 190.* "The great German victories": q. by Longmate,
256. *Page 191.* Gandhi on 22 June: Chaudhuri, 536. *Page 310.* Aga
Khan: HH/IfZ. *Page 191.* Drieu la Rochelle, Teilhard de Chardin: q. in
LEW, 515. *Page 192.* Gide: Gide D, II, 256. *Page 193.* de Man: q. in
LEW, 513, note 174.

CHAPTER VI. THE SECOND COINCIDENCE

Page 195. "only a contribution": GA, v. *Pages 195-196.* "Our many anxieties": FH, 315-316. *Page 197.* Hitler-Jodl, 29 July: Jodl ms. IfZ (December 1945); also IMT, NOKW-065. *Page 197.* Warlimont: IMT, 3032-
PS, NOKW-165; also Klee, 193, note 523. *Page 198.* "He sees the
answer": Halder KTB. *Pages 198-199.* Hitler, 31 July: ibid.; also GD, D,
X, 37-44. *Page 199.* Halder, 14 June 1941: Halder KTB, q. by Schuster-
eit, 109. *Page 200.* Stegemann: article in GWU, 1982. *Page 200.* Hillgruber on war against England: ibid. *Page 200.* "If Hitler fails to beat us
here": FH, 228. *Pages 201-204.* Donovan-Lee: Lee, 27-28. *Page 201.*
Donovan-Kennedy: Lee, 28. *Pages 203-204.* Roosevelt memorandum, 2
August: FDR/L, II, 1050-1051; also FRUS, 1940, III, 58-59. *Page 205.*
Simon to Noel-Buxton: Addison article, 382. *Page 205.* "The ideas set
forth": PREM, 100/3. *Page 206.* "the effect of which": FH, 315-316.
Page 206. Hitler, 14 August: SKL, Klee, I, 106. *Page 208.* "We have no in-
tention": Woodward, I, 366. *Page 208.* Roosevelt to Kennedy, 28 August:
in FDR Library, Navy File, "Destroyers." *Page 209.* Morgenthau, 18 June:
Morgenthau, Presidential Diaries ms., FDR Library. *Page 209.* "we could
do without the destroyers": Woodward, I, 376.

CHAPTER VII. AFTER FIFTY YEARS

Page 214. Hitler to Goebbels, 21 June 1941: Goebbels D, 22 June. *Page
214.* "big bubble," "The beginning of every war": Zoller, 142-143; also
Schroeder, 183 and note 220. *Page 214.* "The tragedy": Klee, Introduction, I, 25. *Page 215.* "If Hitler invaded Hell": GA, 370. *Page 215.*
Churchill to Brendan Bracken: Balfour, 220. *Page 216.* Churchill to de

Gaulle, November 1944: CDG, III, 60.   *Page 216.* "There were few whose hearts": TT, 549.   *Page 218.* "No American will think": GA, 607–608. *Page 218n.* "My hate had died": TT, 630.   *Page 220.* "At any time": TT, 673.   *Page 220.* "Well, I must say": Colville, 596.   *Page 221.* "I have known two Europes": Druon, 206.   *Page 221.* "every time, every time": Gilbert, VIII, 391.

Abbreviations of References

AA   Auswärtiges Amt, Bonn (Politisches Archiv).
Action   Action This Day: Working with Churchill. Memoirs by
              Lord Normanbrook, John Colville, Sir John Martin, Sir
              Ian Jacob, Lord Bridges, Sir Leslie Rowen. Wheeler-Ben-
              nett, J., ed. (London, 1969).
ADAP   Akten zur deutschen auswärtigen Politik, 1918–1945,
              Serie D, vols. X and XI (Frankfurt/Bonn, 1961–1965).
Addison   Addison, P. "Lloyd George and Compromise Peace in the
              Second World War," in Taylor, A. J. P., ed., Lloyd George:
              Twelve Essays (London, 1971).
ADSS   Actes et documents du Saint-Siège relatifs à la deuxième
              guerre mondiale, vol. I (Vatican City, 1965–81).
Amery   Amery, L. My Political Life, vol. 3 (1929–1940) (London,
              1955).
Ansel   Ansel, W. Hitler Confronts England (Durham, N.C.,
              1960).
AOK/KTB   Armeeoberkommando/Kriegstagebuch des Oberkom-
              mandos der Wehrmacht. Schramm, P., ed. (Frankfurt,
              1961–1965).
AoW   Articles of War: The Spectator Book of World War II.
              Glass, F., and P. Marsden-Smedley, eds. (London, 1989).
Balfour   Balfour, M. Propaganda in War, 1939–1945 (London,
              1979).
Baudouin   The Private Diaries of Paul Baudouin (London, 1951).
BBC/WAC   British Broadcasting Corporation, Written Archives Cen-
              tre, Caversham Park, Reading.

Bell   Bell, P. M. H. A Certain Eventuality: Britain and the Fall of France (London, 1974).

Below   Below, N. v. Als Hitlers Adjutant 1937–45 (Mainz, 1980).

Birkenhead   Birkenhead, Life of Lord Halifax (London, 1965).

Boehme   Boehme, H. Entstehung und Grundlagen des Waffenstill-standes von 1940 (Stuttgart, 1966).

Boelcke   Boelcke, W. Kriegspropaganda, 1939–1941: Geheime Ministerkonferenzen im Reichspropagandaministerium (Stuttgart, 1966).

Bryant   Bryant, A. The Turn of the Tide, 1939–1943 (London, 1957).

CAB   Cabinet Office papers, in PRO.

CAD-D   The Diaries of Sir Alexander Cadogan. Dilks, D., ed. (London, 1971).

Calder   Calder, A. The People's War: Britain 1939–45 (London, 1969).

Calic   Calic, E. Unmasked: Two Confidential Interviews with Hitler, 1931 (London, 1971).

CDG   The War Memoirs of Charles de Gaulle (New York, 1960).

Chadwick   Chadwick, O. Britain and the Vatican During the Second World War (Cambridge, 1986).

Channon D   Chips: The Diaries of Sir Henry Channon. James, R. R., ed. (London, 1970).

Chaudhuri   Chaudhuri, N. C. Thy Hand, Great Anarch! (London, 1987).

CH/FDR   Churchill and Roosevelt: The Complete Correspondence, vol. I. Kimball, W., ed. (Princeton, 1984).

Ciano D   The Ciano Diaries (New York, 1946).

Colville   Colville, J. The Fringes of Power: Downing Street Diaries, 1939–1955 (London, 1985).

Colville MV   Colville, J. Man of Valour (London, 1972).

Cudlipp   Cudlipp, H. Publish and Be Damned (London, 1953).

Dalton   Dalton, H. The Fateful Years: Memoirs 1939–45 (London, 1957).

Delafield   Delafield, E. M. The Provincial Lady in Wartime (London, 1940).

Dilks   Dilks, D. "The Twilight War and the Fall of France: Chamberlain and Churchill in 1940." TRHS, vol. 28 (1978).

DIS   Diplomacy and Intelligence in the Second World War. Langhorne, ed. (Cambridge, 1985).

DDI   Documenti diplomatici italiani, Serie IX (Rome, 1952–).

Domarus   Domarus, M., ed. Hitler: Reden und Proklamationen 1932–1945 (Würzburg, 1962–1963).

Druon   Druon, M. L'esprit européen (Geneva, 1946).

Engel D	Engel, D. Heeresadjutant bei Hitler, 1938–1943 (Stuttgart, 1974).
Eden	The Earl of Avon (Anthony Eden). The Reckoning (London, 1964).
FDR/L	Franklin D. Roosevelt: His Personal Letters, vol. II (New York, 1948).
FDR Library	Franklin D. Roosevelt Library, Hyde Park, New York.
Feiling	Feiling, K. The Life of Neville Chamberlain (London, 1946).
FH	Churchill, W. The Second World War, vol. II: Their Finest Hour (Boston, 1949).
Fleming	Fleming, P. Invasion 1940 (London, 1957).
FO	Foreign Office papers, PRO.
FRUS	Foreign Relations of the United States, 1940, vol. III (Washington, D.C., 1952).
GA	Churchill, W. The Second World War, vol. III: The Grand Alliance (Boston, 1950).
Gates	Gates, E. H. End of the Affair: The Collapse of the Anglo-French Alliance, 1939–40 (Berkeley, Calif., 1981).
GCON	Churchill, W. Great Contemporaries (London, 1937).
GD	Documents on German Foreign Policy, 1918–1945, Series D (Washington, D.C., 1948–).
GFK	Der grossdeutsche Freiheitskampf. Reden Adolf Hitlers, vol. II (München, 1941).
Gilbert	Gilbert, M. Winston S. Churchill, vol. VI: Finest Hour, 1939–1941 (London, 1983).
Goebbels D	Die Tagebücher von Joseph Goebbels. Sämtliche Fragmente, vols. 1–4. Fröhlich, E., ed. (München, 1987).
GS	Churchill, W. The Second World War, vol. I: The Gathering Storm (Boston, 1948).
GWU	Geschichte in Wissenschaft und Unterricht.
Halder KTB	Halder, F. Kriegstagebuch: Tägliche Aufzeichnungen des Chefs des Generalstabes des Heeres, 1939–1942, vols. I–III. Jacobsen, H.-A., ed. (Stuttgart, 1962–1964).
Harvey	The Diplomatic Diaries of Oliver Harvey, 1937–1940 (London, 1970).
Havighurst	Havighurst, A. F. Modern England, 1901–1984, 2nd ed. (Cambridge, 1987).
HH/IfZ	Hewel Handakten, in IfZ.
Hillgruber	Hillgruber, A. Hitlers Strategie: Politik und Kriegsführung, 1940–1941 (Düsseldorf, 1965).
Hitler/Bormann	The Testament of Adolf Hitler: The Hitler-Bormann Documents, February–April 1945 (London, 1959).
Hull	The Memoirs of Cordell Hull (Boston, 1948).
IfZ	Institut für Zeitgeschichte (Munich).

238 ABBREVIATIONS OF REFERENCES

IMT	International Military Tribunal, Nuremberg.
INF	Ministry of Information papers, PRO.
Irving	Irving, D. Churchill's War, vol. I (Bullsbrook, Western Australia, 1987).
Ismay	The Memoirs of the General Lord Ismay (London, 1960).
Jodl D	Jodl Ms. in IfZ; also partially reprinted by Hubatsch, W., in WaG, 1952 and 1953; also IMT, PS-1809.
Kershaw	Kershaw, I. The Hitler Myth: Image and Reality in the Thrrd Reich (Oxford, 1987).
Klee	Klee, K. Dokumente zum Unternehmen "Seelöwe," I–II (Göttingen, 1959).
King	King, C. With Malice Toward None: A War Diary (London, 1970).
Kubizek	Kubizek, A. Adolf Hitler, mein Jugendfreund (Graz, 1953).
Langer-Gleason	Langer, W. L., and E. L. Gleason. The Challenge to Isolation, vol. II (New York, 1952).
Lee	The London Journal of General Raymond E. Lee, 1940–1941. Leutze, J., ed. (Boston, 1971).
Leutze	Leutze, J. "The Secret of the Churchill-Roosevelt Correspondence: September 1939–May 1940," in Journal of Contemporary History (10), 1975.
LEW	Lukacs, J. The Last European War, 1939–1941 (New York, 1976; London 1977).
Longmate	Longmate, N. If Britain Had Fallen (London, 1972).
Macksey	Macksey, K. Invasion: The German Invasion of England, July 1940 (London, 1980).
Macleod	Macleod, I. Neville Chamberlain (London, 1961).
Manchester	Manchester, W. The Last Lion (New York, 1987).
Martin	Martin, B. Friedensinitiativen und Machtpolitik im Zweiten Weltkrieg (Düsseldorf, 1972).
Meissner	Meissner, O. Staatssekretär unter Ebert, Hindenburg, Hitler (Hamburg, 1950).
Meldungen/MA	Meldungen aus dem Reich. RSHA (Reich Security Service) microfilm file in IfZ. (A good selection of these in Boberach, H., ed., Meldungen aus dem Reich [München, 1968].)
MgM	Militärgeschichtliche Mitteilungen.
Moloney	Moloney, T. Westminster, Whitehall and the Vatican: The Role of Cardinal Hinsley, 1935–1943 (London, 1980).
Mosley	Mosley, O. On Borrowed Time (New York, 1969).
NARS	National Archives, Washington.
Nicolson	Nicolson, H. Diaries and Letters, vol. II: The War Years, 1939–1945. Nicolson, N., ed. (London, 1967).
Nicolson D (u)	Nicolson diary MSS., Balliol Library, Oxford.

Orwell D	Orwell's 1940 diaries, in The Collected Essays, Journalism and Letters of George Orwell, vol. II: My Country Right and Left, 1940–1943. Orwell, S., and I. Angus, eds. (London, 1968).
Patterson	Patterson, J. Mr. Republican: A Biography of Robert A. Taft (Boston, 1972).
PREM	Prime Minister's Office papers, PRO.
PRO	Public Records Office, Kew Gardens, London.
Reynolds	Reynolds, D. Article in DIS.
Reynolds/FDR	Reynolds, D. "FDR's Foreign Policy and the British Royal Visit to the USA in 1939," in The Historian (1983).
Rock	Rock, W. R. Chamberlain and Roosevelt: British Foreign Policy and the United States, 1937–1940 (Columbus, Ohio, 1988).
Schroeder	Schroeder, C. Er war mein Chef: Aus dem Nachlass der Sekretärin von Adolf Hitler. Joachimsthaler, A., ed. (München, 1985).
Schustereit	Schustereit, H. Vabanque: Hitlers Angriff auf die Sowjetunion 1941 als Versuch, durch den Sieg im Osten den Westen zu bezwingen (Herford/Bonn, 1988).
Spears	Spears, E. L. Assignment to Catastrophe (London, 1954).
Taylor EH	Taylor, A. J. P. English History, 1914–1945 (New York, 1965).
Templewood	Templewood (Sir Samuel Hoare). Nine Troubled Years (London, 1954).
Thompson	Thompson, W. H. Sixty Minutes with Winston Churchill (London, 1953).
Toynbee	Toynbee, A. An Historian's Conscience: Correspondence of Arnold J. Toynbee and Columba Cary-Elwes, Monk of Ampleforth (Boston, 1985).
TRHS	Transactions of the Royal Historical Society.
TT	Churchill, W. The Second World War, vol. VI: Triumph and Tragedy (Boston, 1953).
Velasco/Petit	Velasco, A. A. Memorías de un agente segreto (Barcelona, 1979); Petit, D. P. Espías españoles (Barcelona, 1979).
VfZ	Vierteljahrshefte für Zeitgeschichte.
Vidalenc	Vidalenc, J. L'exode de mai–juin 1940 (Paris, 1957).
Villelume	Villelume, P. Journal d'une défaite (Paris, 1976).
WaG	Die Welt als Geschichte.
Watt	Watt, D. C. How War Came (New York, 1989).
Waugh	Waugh, E. Put Out More Flags (London, 1942).
WCR	Churchill, W. The World Crisis, 1911–1918 (London, 1931).
Weil	Weil, S. Formative Writings, 1929–1941. McFarland, D. T., and W. Van Ness, eds. (Amherst, Mass., 1987).

Whalen   Whalen, R. The Founding Father: The Story of Joseph P. Kennedy (New York, 1964).

Wiskemann   Wiskemann, E. The Europe I Saw (London, 1966).

Woodward   Woodward, L. British Foreign Policy in the Second World War, vol. I (London, 1970).

Zoller   Zoller, A. Hitler privat (Düsseldorf, 1949).

Short Bibliographical Essay

Suggestions for Further Research

THE AMOUNT of material relating to the Second World War is enormous — evidence of the need to rethink some of the very canons of historical research (an argument that I set forth in the Bibliographical Remarks of *LEW*, pages 529ff., more than fourteen years ago, in vain). So far as *The Duel* goes, the problem of the survey of materials is simpler. The scope of this work is only eighty days, and it deals — mainly, though of course not exclusively — with the reciprocal perceptions of two antagonists. What follows, therefore, is a brief survey of existing materials — in addition to the sources and works employed for the research of this book, listed in the previous section and referred to here by their abbreviations — as well as a brief rumination about the evolving tendencies in the historical interpretation of the Churchill-Hitler relationship: about the history of its history, so to speak.

In all of the existing biographies of Hitler (their number is around one hundred at the time of this writing) there is very little about those eighty days, especially in his biographies by English and American historians and writers. (I know only of two short German biographies of Churchill, one by Franz Leunhoff [Köln, 1949], the other by Sebastian Haffner [Hamburg, 1967], in which a few thoughtful pages deal with the years 1940 and 1941.) There is, of course, much more about the eighty days in the English books and articles dealing with Churchill that are listed in the previous section. English works about the invasion prospect of 1940 are concerned mostly with the period after the middle of July. The best work treating Hitler's confrontation with the invasion problem (next to the documentation of *Klee*), perhaps not elegantly written but detailed and thoughtful, is by an American, Rear Admiral *Ansel*. We have, of course, the incomparable tome *FH*, by Churchill himself. The most detailed treatment of the eighty days in Churchill's life is in *Gilbert*'s large and workmanlike volume. Since Gilbert was Churchill's "official" biographer, he had access to Churchill's private papers that are not open to other researchers before 1995. (There exist other British government papers that are closed until 2017.) However, I am inclined to think that the contents of these papers (except perhaps for certain minor details) will not add much to the history I attempted to set forth, for two reasons. One is Churchill's "openness" (about which see pages 111–112). The other is that during this agitated period Churchill devoted less time to his private correspondence than was his custom.

In any event, these papers are deposited in the Churchill Archives Centre, Churchill College, Cambridge, the guide of whose holdings also lists the papers of more than three hundred of Churchill's British contemporaries. The most complete of the bibliographies of English history of the period is *Havighurst*. An excellent running bibliography is in *VfZ*.

The microfiche guide to the *PRO* is of course indispensable for those who wish to study British government records. Here are only a few additional pointers: beyond the well-known CAB 65 and CAB 66 dossiers of the War Cabinet minutes and memoranda, CAB 71, CAB 93, CAB 100, CAB 104 (1) and CAB 127 contain some relevant materials; in the Foreign Office files besides the well-known FO 371 series, FO 438, FO 800, FO 898 and FO 954 may include some materials of interest; besides the PREM 1, 2 and 3 files, this also applies to PREM 4 and PREM 7, also to PREM 100/2. In Germany the extant archives of the government of the Third Reich are in Bonn, Koblenz and Freiburg; the National Socialist Party archives are in Berlin (microfilms of which exist in the National Archives in Washington). To these the extensive holdings of the *IfZ* in Munich must be added.

About the German perception of the Hitler-Churchill subject, involving Hitler's 1940 strategy and the peace feelers of the period, the principal and important works are those by *Hillgruber* and *Martin* (see, however, my criticism of some of the judgments of the former on pages 84, 105 and 199–200; also in *LEW*, especially note 38 on pages 121–122, also on pages 240 and 343). On the American side, a full history of the complex and confidential promotion of the destroyer deal is yet to be written.

Fifty years have now gone by since these momentous events. Their "definite" history, as of any other subject, is a misnomer, as is "revisionism," since history consists of an endless revising of the past. We must be aware of the dangerous temptation of seeing history mainly from the viewpoint of the present, while we must be equally conscious of the condition that what we know at present is an inescapable ingredient of our view of the past. The subject of this book is eighty days in the lives of two men. About those eighty days I find the material almost, but of course not completely, *épuisé,* by which I mean that I doubt that any important piece of material will yet become public that would call for a significant correction of the sequence of events. What will go on and on are the perceptions, interpretations and evaluations of Churchill and Hitler in the minds of future generations, and among historical writers of all kinds. And in this respect I am compelled to say something about these tendencies as they have been evolving.

The historical understanding of Hitler (admittedly a more difficult task than that of Churchill, and not only because of Hitler's earlier-mentioned secretiveness) has often been marred by undue applications of psychoanalytic interpretations; besides, a proper study of Hitler as statesman is still to be written. A proper appreciation of Churchill during this crucial period has been weakened, here and there, by two obvious tendencies: on the one hand by certain uncritical appreciations by his admirers, on the other by the tendency of many professional historians not to take Churchill's own historianship seriously enough. But at the time of this writing we are at (or, more precisely, already beyond) a watershed in the political and intellectual history of the world because of the evident collapse of the reputation and, consequently, of the influence of Marxism as well as of "Leftist" liberalism; and this is bound to lead to all kinds of novel, though not necessarily salutary, tendencies of historical interpretation. That is why I am compelled to direct attention to the tendencies represented by three, otherwise very different, historical writers: Irving, Ponting and Cowling (the last being the only professional historian of the three). The assiduous researches of the British journalist David Irving are such that any serious historian dealing with his subjects must not refrain from looking at them because of the small nuggets of materials that Irving may have unearthed; but two serious caveats are in order here. One is that Irving's extensive gathering of documents must be treated with especial caution: I have found archival numbers in some of his notes erroneous or even nonexistent; in sum, references to his sources must be carefully verified. The more important caveat involves the purposes of Irving's writing. He is an admirer of Hitler's; yet, with all of his drive to be a daringly unconventional historical writer, he does not quite have the courage of his convictions. His method of rehabilitating Hitler is by denigrating Hitler's opponents — in this case, the blackening of Churchill in every possible way. One (and not the worst) example of this is the sentence with which Irving concludes his *Churchill's War*: he sums up Churchill as a man who, because he was adamantly opposed to Hitler, did "drag his country into ruin." Ponting, unlike Irving, has no sympathy for Hitler; but his debunking *1940: Myth and Reality* (London, 1990) argues that the decisive event in 1940 was not Churchill's resistance to Hitler but the bankruptcy of the British Empire. Finally I am obliged to cite a passage from a chapter on Churchill by the Cambridge historian Maurice Cowling:

> . . . *the belief that Churchill had understood Hitler better than anyone else. This was not true,* except so far as he perceived Hitler as a symptom of social decay, like the Labour party in England: it would be truer to say that Churchill picked on Hitler, just as he had picked on Gandhi, and treated the problem in one way because he was out of office [from 1933 to 1940] where, if he had been in office, he might have treated it in another.
> All this is well understood and needs no emphasis.*

It surely needs no emphasis; but well understood it is not.

---

* In Cowling, *Religion and Public Doctrine in Modern England* (Cambridge, 1980), page 311. The italics are mine.

Acknowledgments

I wish to express my gratitude for the important help I received from the Earhart Foundation; from the staff of the Institut für Zeitgeschichte in Munich, especially its archivist, Herr Hermann Weiss; from the staff of the Public Records Office in London; from the archivist of the Churchill Archives Centre in Cambridge; from the librarian of Balliol College, Oxford; from the staff of the Franklin D. Roosevelt Library in Hyde Park, New York, especially its director, William Emerson; from the Lilly Library of Indiana University; and, last but not least, from Dr. Helen Hayes, director of the Logue Library of Chestnut Hill College. Scholars who were kind enough to read parts of the draft manuscript include Professors George F. Kennan, Robert H. Ferrell and, very especially, Philip M. H. Bell. I wish to thank Collins, Ltd., and Nigel Nicolson for their permission to peruse Harold Nicolson's manuscript diaries deposited in Balliol.

"Pickering Close"
Williams' Corner, near Phoenixville,
Pennsylvania
1988–1990

Index